Economic Growth in Twentieth-century Britain

Economic Growth in Twentieth-century Britain

Edited by

DEREK H. ALDCROFT

PETER FEARON

MACMILLAN

Published in 1969 by
MACMILLAN AND CO LTD
Little Essex Street London W C 2
and also at Bombay Calcutta and Madras
Macmillan South Africa (Publishers) Pty Ltd Johannesburg
The Macmillan Company of Australia Pty Ltd Melbourne
The Macmillan Company of Canada Ltd Toronto
Gill and Macmillan Ltd Dublin

Printed in Great Britain by
RICHARD CLAY (THE CHAUCER PRESS) LTD
Bungay, Suffolk

Contents

Preface

THIS volume contains a selection of some of the recent articles written on the growth and development of the British economy in the twentieth century. With one exception the articles appear as published in the original apart from one or two minor revisions and corrections. We should like to thank the authors, and the editors of the journals concerned, for permission to reproduce them here.

D. H. A.

University of Leicester   P. F.

Acknowledgements

THE editors and publishers wish to thank the following for permission to reproduce the articles contained in this volume. They are listed in the order in which they appear.

C. H. Feinstein, 'Production and Productivity 1920–1962', *London and Cambridge Economic Bulletin*, Dec 1963 in *The Times Review of Industry and Technology*.

K. S. Lomax, 'Growth and Productivity in the United Kingdom', *Productivity Measurement Review*, XXXVIII (1964). The Appendix Table to this article is reprinted from *Journal of the Royal Statistical Society*, A122 (1959).

Derek H. Aldcroft, 'Economic Growth in Britain in the Inter-War Years: A Reassessment', *Economic History Review*, XX (1967).

J. A. Dowie, 'Growth in the Inter-War Period: Some More Arithmetic', *Economic History Review*, XXI (1968).

R. C. O. Matthews, 'Some Aspects of Post-War Growth in the British Economy in Relation to Historical Experience', *Transactions of the Manchester Statistical Society* (1964).

John Knapp and Kenneth Lomax, 'Britain's growth Performance: The Enigma of the 1950s', *Lloyds Bank Review* (Oct 1964).

C. W. McMahon and G. D. N. Worswick, 'The Growth of Services in the Economy: I. Their Stabilising Influence', *District Bank Review* (Dec 1960).

C. W. McMahon and G. D. N. Worswick, 'The Growth of Services in the Economy: II. Do They Slow Down Overall Expansion?', *District Bank Review* (Mar 1961).

G. D. N. Worswick and C. G. Fane, 'Goods and Services Once Again', *District Bank Review* (Mar 1967).

F. W. Paish, 'The Management of the British Economy', *Lloyds Bank Review*, (Apr 1965).

T. Wilson, 'Instability and Growth: An International Comparison, 1950–65'. Based on a paper read to the Business Economists' Conference held at Oxford in April 1968.

W. A. Eltis, 'Economic Growth and the British Balance of Payments', *District Bank Review* (Dec 1967).

W. A. H. Godley and J. R. Shepherd, 'Long-Term Growth and Short-Term Policy', *National Institute Economic Review* (Aug 1964).

Introduction

THE study of economic growth and development, both in a theoretical and empirical context, has advanced rapidly in the last two or three decades. In developed and underdeveloped countries alike, planners, government officials and economists have been anxiously seeking ways of raising rates of growth. Interest in growth has not been confined solely to the present however. In fact a by-product of the work in this field has been the collection of new statistical time series on a long-term basis. Thus for Britain and a number of other developed economies continuous statistical series extending well back into the nineteenth century are now available for such aggregates as national income, domestic output, capital formation, industrial production and exports. It is, therefore, much easier to compare the performance of different countries over time. Yet although we now have a much better idea of the long-term dimensions of growth we are still far from clear as to its causes.

This volume offers a selection of the most recently compiled long-term economic indicators together with a number of essays dealing with various aspects of growth and short-term fluctuations in the twentieth century. These studies are primarily empirical in nature and are concerned specifically with the British economy, though in a number of cases comparative data for other countries is used as a means of assessing British performance. Thus the main statistical series are presented in the first two articles and then followed by two dealing specifically with inter-war developments. The fifth and sixth essays put Britain's recent growth performance in historical perspective, while the next three deal with the development, and show the importance, of the service sectors. The remaining essays are devoted largely to short-term problems of economic growth and instability in the post-war period.

Although the general theme of growth is common to all the essays contained in this volume the latter do not necessarily represent a unanimous approach to the problems of Britain's growth in the twentieth century. On some issues there is a certain amount of conflict. From the reader's point of view it would be rather futile simply to summarise the main points of each contribution. Each one should be read in its entirety. On the other hand, it may be helpful, especially to those approaching the subject for the first time, if some of the main trends in the British economy over the past half-century are examined in this introductory essay.

The chief concern in the last decade or so has been that of raising the British rate of growth. Efforts in this direction eventually led to the formulation of long-term plans in the 1960s which laid down target rates of growth to be achieved over a period of five years. The reason for this interest is quite simple. Since the war, or more especially from the early 1950s, Britain's growth record has been poor in comparison with that of most Western countries. This is true whatever standard of measurement one uses[1] and it is one point at least about which most economists are agreed. The British record is fairly well known and only a brief résumé need be given here. In 1962 the Organisation for Economic Co-operation and Development published a study showing that in the 1950s Britain came bottom of a growth league ranking all member countries, and that the U.K.'s rate of growth of gross national product was only half that achieved by the six countries of the European Economic Community.[2] Similarly, a recent study by Denison into the causes of differences in growth between countries found that Britain's growth of national income and income *per capita* was very much lower than that of most west European countries over the period 1950–64, and only the United States had a lower rate of growth of national income *per capita*.[3] Britain's relative position has not changed very much in recent years. Given the magnitude of the lag it would be impossible to explain away the poor British performance by alternative criteria or methods of assessment.[4]

But what of the long-term record? How does the recent performance compare with past trends? It is important to put the problem in perspective since there is reason to believe that Britain's overall rate of growth has never been very high. In fact the post-war record compares very favourably with the long-term trend. In the fifteen years or so from 1950 the British economy grew faster and more steadily than at any time in the last hundred years, with the possible exception of the third quarter of the nineteenth century. The long-term growth of income has been very modest indeed; between 1870 and 1913 real income per head rose by 1·6 per cent per annum

[1] The main standard of measurement used here is national income.
[2] O.E.C.D., *Economic Survey of the United Kingdom* (1962).
[3] E. F. Denison, *Why Growth Rates Differ* (1968) p. 18.
[4] See W. Beckerman, *The British Economy in 1975* (1965) p. 19.

while over the somewhat longer period 1870–1964 it was as low as
1·2 per cent per annum. This may be compared with a rate of 2·2
per cent during the years 1950–64.

Moreover, in comparison with other major industrial countries
Britain's long-term performance does not show up at all badly. The
fastest growing countries in the post-war period have been Germany,
Italy and France in that order; yet over the period 1870–1937 they
recorded rates of growth of real income per head of 1·4, 0·9 and 0·8
per cent per annum respectively, as against a rate of 1·2 per cent for
Britain. Even taking the post-war years into consideration the
difference between Britain and these countries is not altered
appreciably. Between 1870 and 1964 the U.K. rate remained at 1·2
per cent while those of Germany, Italy and France were raised to
1·7, 1·4 and 1·5 respectively.[1] There is little to suggest, therefore
that the long-term performance of the British economy has lagged
seriously behind that of the other countries. In other words, it was
only in the 1950s that the discrepancy in growth between Britain
and the major industrial countries really emerged.

A more detailed temporal breakdown does reveal some differences
however. Before the First World War the United States and certain
European countries were growing more rapidly than Britain. This
was particularly true of the decade or so before 1914 when Britain
was experiencing a retardation in growth. The timing of this
deceleration along with its causes are still the subject of some dispute,
but there can be little doubt that Britain's overall performance was
relatively poor in this period. Nevertheless, the difference between
Britain and other countries was not as great as it was after the
Second World War. On the other hand, between 1913 and 1950
Britain probably gained on balance. The check to income growth
during the two world wars was less serious in Britain than in many
European countries, and in both cases recovery from the effects of
war was more rapid in this country. Moreover, in the inter-war
years Britain's relative performance improved somewhat. This was
especially the case in the 1930s when the United States and many
European countries experienced a very slow recovery from the
depression of 1929–32. In Britain, on the other hand, recovery from
the slump was vigorous and sustained and was assisted by a fairly
rapid rate of technical improvement and a shift of resources to the
newer sectors of the economy.[2]

Though the analysis of growth in the twentieth century is

[1] M. Lipton, *Assessing Economic Performance* (1968) pp. 120–1.
[2] This is treated more fully in D. H. Aldcroft and H. W. Richardson, *The British Economy, 1870–1939* (1969) ch. 1.

complicated by two world wars and a very severe depression, the fact remains that Britain's long-term record has not been especially bad. The real problem seems to have arisen in the 1950s when European growth accelerated considerably while Britain only managed to make a slight improvement on her previous performance. It will be helpful, therefore, to examine briefly some of the main sources of British and European growth during this period.

The sources of growth may be divided into two broad categories. First, there are changes in the resources used to produce the national product. These include the factor inputs of labour, capital and land, the last of which can be excluded on the grounds that its contribution to growth is generally very small. Secondly, growth may result from changes in output per unit of input. This is commonly described as the residual element being that part of the growth of income which cannot be attributed to changes in factor inputs. This category covers a wide range of variables which influence productivity, the most important of which are advances in knowledge and new techniques, improved allocation of resources and economies of scale. Growth may be achieved, therefore, either by raising the inputs of capital and labour or by changes in the residual items which improve the productivity of these factors.

A number of attempts have been made to measure the sources of growth for the post-war period. The most elaborate study is the recent one by Denison which examines nine countries including the United Kingdom. Though, as the author points out, the sources of growth are complex and vary from one country to another it is possible to distinguish some of the main influences at work. A detailed analysis of his findings for each country is not possible here and for convenience we shall compare the United Kingdom with north-west Europe[1] over the period 1950–62.

During this period the national income of Britain rose by 2·29 per cent per annum. To this rate inputs of labour and capital contributed 0·6 and 0·51 percentage points respectively, giving a total factor input of 1·11 points or 47 per cent of the growth of income. The remaining 53 per cent was derived from improvements in the residual. The two most important items here were advances in knowledge and economies of scale which contributed 0·76 and 0·36 points respectively. Combined they accounted for 1·12 points or 47 per cent of the income growth of 2·29 per cent. Improved allocation of resources accounted for most of the remaining 6 per cent.[2]

[1] That is Belgium, Denmark, France, Germany, the Netherlands, Norway and the United Kingdom.
[2] Denison, *Why Growth Rates Differ*, pp. 314–15.

The comparison with north-west Europe provides some interesting contrasts. Here national income rose by 4·78 per cent per annum to which total inputs contributed 1·69 points (36 per cent), divided almost equally between capital and labour. The rate of input growth was higher in both cases than in Britain but the differences were not sufficiently large to account for the big difference in rates of income growth. The major part of Europe's growth, 3·07 points or 64 per cent of the total, came from improvements in the residual. The most important influences were advances in knowledge (0·76), improved allocation of resources (0·68) and economies of scale (0·93). These three items were responsible for nearly 78 per cent of the change in the residual over the period 1950–62.[1]

Though capital and labour inputs grew more rapidly than in Britain it is clear that they were only partially responsible for the much higher rates of growth achieved in European countries.[2] The most important source of growth in Europe was the high value of the residual which was more than twice the British rate. In fact the residual tended to be correlated with growth; the three fastest growing countries, Germany, Italy and France, had high residuals whereas the slow-growing countries, United States and United Kingdom, had low ones. Where European countries gained over Britain was because of the very high contributions they secured from economies of scale and reallocation of resources, especially the shift out of low productivity agriculture, and changes in the general level of efficiency. These three items contributed very little to Britain's growth of income. Given the importance of the residual in the growth process, especially in Europe, it would appear that studies which emphasise unduly the role of capital and labour as sources of growth may be somewhat misleading.[3] A word of qualification is required here however. The technique of apportioning growth between factor inputs and the residual may well underestimate the contribution of capital if, as is often the case, technical advances are embodied in investment, part of which comprises the replacement of assets. Thus it is gross investment, rather than the net additions to the capital stock, that is of greater significance.[4] Moreover, it is quite probable that improvements in many of the other residual items are dependent

[1] Ibid. pp. 300–1.
[2] This is especially true in the case of Belgium and France where the growth of total inputs was only slightly higher than in the United Kingdom. In Norway the growth contribution of factor inputs was slightly less than that of the United Kingdom.
[3] For example, A. Maddison, *Economic Growth in the West* (1964), and C. P. Kindleberger, *Europe's Post-war Growth: The Role of Labour Supply* (1967).
[4] Actually Denison averages the growth rates of the two capital stocks.

on capital accumulation to some degree. In so far as this is the case then there is an inherent danger of underestimating the role of capital in any attempts at measuring the sources of growth in the manner described above. It is also important to point out that too much emphasis should not be placed on the seemingly precise allocations made by Denison, since they are subject to margins of error.

It would be interesting to compare the post-war position with that of earlier years but unfortunately there is insufficient data available for European countries to extend the exercise back in time. However, it is very unlikely that the growth in factor inputs in the inter-war years or even before 1914 was very much lower than the rates achieved between 1950–62. If this assumption is correct then it would follow that a considerable part of the acceleration in growth in Europe in the last decade or so was due to an improvement in the residual element.

The same could not be said for Britain since the residual did not improve appreciably during the post-war period. During the 1950s and early 1960s it contributed about 1·2 percentage points to the growth of income, compared with 0·9 points between 1924 and 1937, and in the latter part of the nineteenth century. Only in the decade or so before the First World War was its contribution markedly different, and then it was negative. Moreover, though capital inputs increased considerably in the post-war years compared with earlier periods, labour inputs were about halved so that total factor inputs were about the same, or possibly slightly below, those achieved previously. In short, the contributions of total inputs and the residual to Britain's growth remained remarkably steady over time.

In the light of her own historical experience Britain's post-war performance can be regarded as satisfactory on all counts. But it still remains poor, of course, in comparison with contemporary achievements in western Europe. The question now arises as to how far the experience of European countries was exceptional in the sense that they derived benefits from conditions not present in Britain. Or an alternative way of looking at the question: whether Britain's capacity for growth was limited by internal constraints.

Europe's post-war growth performance was historically out-of-line since it was more rapid than in any previous period. There are a number of particular factors which partly explain this acceleration. First, special influences associated with recovery from the Second World War no doubt affected the position to some extent. Some countries, notably Italy and Germany, had only just surpassed their pre-war levels of output by 1950 whereas British recovery occurred somewhat earlier. Moreover, in some cases, notably in Germany, extensive reconstruction of productive facilities had to be carried out with the result that the efficiency of the capital stock was higher than in countries less seriously damaged by war activity.[1] However, by the mid-1950s the special circumstances associated with the aftermath of war had probably ceased to operate and they cannot really be used to explain the higher rates of growth in Europe in the later 1950s and 1960s. It is important to note that in more recent years the gap between British and European growth tended to narrow, suggesting that the aftermath of war may have affected the position slightly.

Secondly, some European countries, especially Italy and to a lesser extent France, were less developed than Britain at the end of the war and in the subsequent process of catching up they had somewhat more to gain from improved allocation of resources and economies of scale associated with large-scale industrial development. In such countries there was also greater scope for the adoption of best practice techniques and general improvements in efficiency. It is significant that both France and Italy gained substantially from these influences. For example, 2·64 percentage points (45 per cent of the total) of Italy's income growth between 1950 and 1962 came from reallocation of resources and economies of scale, while a further 0·9 was due to changes in the lag in the application of knowledge, general efficiency, and errors and omissions. In the case of France, 1·95 percentage points (or 41 per cent of the total) was due to the first two factors, 0·65 of which came from the reduction in agricultural inputs.[2] In fact nearly all countries stood to gain more in these directions than did Great Britain where the opportunities for shifting resources out of low productivity agriculture were virtually exhausted[3] and the scope for economies of scale was more limited. However, this argument is less tenable in more recent years since in some countries, e.g. Germany and Sweden, income *per capita* has now exceeded the British level.

Thirdly, some European countries had higher rates of employment growth than Britain. This was partly accounted for by the reduction in disguised unemployment, which in turn was associated with the reallocation of resources, but in certain cases it resulted from additions to the labour force through immigration, for example Germany,

---

[1] Though it is easy to exaggerate the extent of war damage. See K. W. Roskamp, *Capital Formation in West Germany* (1965) p. 36.

[2] Denison, *Why Growth Rates Differ*, pp. 306, 316.

[3] A similar point is made by N. Kaldor, *Causes of the Slow Rate of Economic Growth of the United Kingdom* (1966) p. 31.

and from a relative improvement in the quality of the labour force.[1] Demand for labour remained fairly high in most countries but the factors just mentioned helped to keep the labour supply reasonably elastic so that pressure on the labour market was never quite as severe as in this country.

A fourth influence, though one which is difficult to measure, may have been the greater degree of internal stability in Europe compared with pre-war. The political situations were more favourable and this resulted in the removal of many restrictions especially on trade between continental countries. But perhaps more important has been the fact that economic fluctuations have been much less severe than those experienced in the inter-war years. This is partly due to the fact that governments have been more willing than previously to adopt policies to stabilise the business cycle. Of course Britain has also benefited from a dampening of the cycle, though not to the same extent as in Europe since fluctuations were relatively less severe in this country in the inter-war period.[2] In short the more stable conditions in Europe produced an atmosphere more conducive to growth than before the war.[3]

Finally, nearly all countries experienced high levels of demand which were boosted to a considerable extent by high rates of export growth. The same could be said for Britain though the stimulus from the external side was much weaker. The importance of demand, particularly export demand, has been stressed by a number of economists.[4] One cannot deny that a high level of demand is a necessary condition of fast growth. Buoyant markets raise entrepreneurs' expectations about the future and this in turn encourages investment. But, as Beckerman points out, it is difficult to determine whether demand is the autonomous element which induces changes in supply or whether autonomous changes in the latter govern the rate at which demand increases.[5] Here we shall suggest that a high level of demand has not been as conducive to growth in Britain as in other countries because of the presence of supply constraints. The position is complicated, however, by the different experience in the export trade and we must consider this aspect in a little more detail.

[1] Britain drew more female and part-time workers into the labour force than did other large European countries, which depressed the average quality. See E. F. Denison, 'Economic Growth', p. 243, in R. Caves, *Britain's Economic Prospects* (1968).

[2] See A. Maddison, 'The Post-War Business Cycle in Western Europe and the Role of Government Policy', *Banca Nazionale Del Lavoro Quarterly Review*, XIII (1960), and E. Lundberg (ed.), *The Business Cycle in the Post-War World* (1955).

[3] Though as T. Wilson shows in chapter 11 of this volume there has been little correlation between growth and instability in the post-war period.

[4] Beckerman, *The British Economy in 1975*, ch. 2.

[5] Ibid. p. 65.

It has become very fashionable in recent years to talk about export-led growth and some economists have assigned an independent role to the export component in the growth process.[1] To a large extent the case for the argument is based on empirical experience. Fast-growing countries generally experienced high rates of export growth whereas the reverse was true in slow-growing countries such as Britain. But a positive association between exports and growth does not tell us anything about the causal sequence. It may well be that the line of causation ran from the economy to exports rather than the other way round. Thus rapid growth and improved competitive performance resulted in rapid export expansion. Conversely, slow growth and a low rate of investment in Britain led to competitive weakness and thereby dampened the growth of exports.[2] Certainly competitive weaknesses are far more important than structural maladjustments in the composition of Britain's export trade in explaining the relatively slow expansion in exports.[3] Moreover, past experience does not lend a great deal of support to the export-led growth thesis.[4]

In short, therefore, the potential demand for British exports was high[5] but in part this demand was choked off by competitive weakness and supply constraints. If, as we suggest below, the overall growth of the economy was limited by supply constraints it would have been difficult to have achieved a high rate of export growth without diverting resources from home to export orders.[6] Of course,

[1] See, for example, R. F. Emery, 'The Relation of Exports and Economic Growth', *Kyklos*, xx (1967).

[2] S. J. Wells, *British Export Performance: A Comparative Study* (1964) pp. 69–70.

[3] Political and Economic Planning, *Growth in the British Economy* (1960) pp. 167–8. Since the late nineteenth century competitive rather than structural factors have been the major cause of Britain's declining share in world export trade. See A. Maizels, *Industrial Growth and World Trade* (1963) pp. 198–202, and H. Tyszynski, 'World Trade in Manufactured Commodities, 1899–1950', *Manchester School*, xix (1951).

[4] For example, when Britain's exports were relatively high in the decade or so before 1914 the growth of income was at an all-time low, whereas in the inter-war years, when exports stagnated, income growth was higher than pre-war.

[5] There is no reason to assume that this was not the case, though European countries no doubt gained more from reduction in trade barriers and closer economic integration, especially after the formation of the European Economic Community in the later 1950s.

[6] In which case the overall growth rate would not change appreciably. There has been rather a lot of speculation and controversy as to the precise relationship between the level of domestic demand and exports. A recent econometric study of the problem suggests that exports do tend to slacken when domestic demand is high, whereas a lower level of demand helps to boost exports. See R. J. Ball, J. R. Eaton and M. D. Steuer, 'The Relationship between United Kingdom Export Performance in Manufactures and the Internal Pressure of Demand', *Economic Journal*, LXXVI (1966).

a high rate of export growth would probably have eased the balance of payments situation, and in so far as this was a limiting factor on growth it would have been advantageous. Moreover, the more favourable conditions would have stimulated investment and helped to relieve the supply bottleneck. But since inadequate investment was not the only problem on the supply[1] side a higher rate of exports would not have eliminated supply constraints completely. If this assumption is correct then it is unlikely that the recent government policies to stimulate exports will provide a lasting solution to Britain's growth problem.

It would be wrong, of course, to suggest that rapid expansion in western Europe since the war was due solely to special influences. To do so would merely be to offer an apology for Britain's slow growth. In any case some of the conditions listed above were not enjoyed exclusively by European countries. Nevertheless, certain factors were favourable to European growth which were not operative in Britain to the same extent. In particular the relatively elastic supply of factor inputs coupled with the large gains from the residual, especially those derived from improved resource allocation and economies of scale, made it possible to meet high levels of demand without too much strain being placed on European economies. Some of the sources of growth are of a once-and-for-all type and as they become exhausted it is probable that rates of expansion will decline. In fact the tendency in recent years for European growth rates to diminish slightly may be a sign of things to come.

The British position can be summed up as one of lack of flexibility. Generally speaking, demand conditions were favourable to rapid growth even though exports were less buoyant than in European countries. Where the problem lay was in the conditions of supply. All too frequently the capacity available was insufficient to meet the level of demand since the margin of spare capacity was generally very small. Strong internal demand tended, therefore, to put pressure on the external account, either through a slackening in exports but more usually because of a rise in marginal imports to satisfy domestic demand, and this led the government to impose various restrictions to curb the level of demand.[2] These restrictions reacted unfavourably on investment and by implication on the

---

[1] In fact some economists argue that there has been too much investment and that the real problem has been a shortage of labour. See C. Clark, *Growthmanship* (2nd ed. 1962) and J. R. Sargent, *Out of Stagnation, a Policy for Growth* (1963).

[2] The weakness of the external account was aggravated by other factors as well, particularly by the large overseas transactions of the Government for aid and defence.

rate of technical progress[1] and overall growth. Thus although the
policy measures helped to moderate pressures on the economy in the
short-term, they also affected the growth of capacity adversely so
that by the time the next surge in demand occurred the margin of
under-utilised resources was insufficient to meet it and so the cycle
was repeated once again.

But it would be wrong to assume that government restraints
were solely responsible for the lack of sufficient capacity to maintain
a high rate of growth. Though policy restrictions tended to damp
down the growth of investment the problem was not simply one of
inadequate investment. The labour supply position was tight owing
to a low rate of population growth, while Britain did not gain to the
same extent as some continental countries from inflows of immigrants
and movements of labour out of the primary sector. Furthermore, as
we have seen, Britain was not able to improve her capacity position
very much by reallocating resources or by economies of scale. Thus in
almost every respect the scope for expanding effective capacity was
limited, but only in the case of investment capacity could it be argued
that government measures to regulate the level of demand had a
serious dampening effect. To a large extent the capacity of the
economy was limited by forces beyond immediate control.[2]

This means that the possibilities of achieving faster growth in the
future are somewhat remote unless the supply situation improves
radically. A sharp rise in the rate of investment may help to some
extent, especially if accompanied by rapid technical progress, though
in the short-term it is likely to run up against the same bottlenecks
as before, particularly a shortage of labour.[3] The prospects of reliev-
ing the situation by redeployment of labour are limited, though some
reallocation from low to high productivity sectors is no doubt
feasible. On the other hand, it is quite possible that the high growth

[1] That is in so far as technical advances were dependent upon the rate of capital
accumulation.

[2] This argument, which emphasises supply constraints, seems to be somewhat
more plausible than the argument commonly put forward that growth has been
restrained because of attempts to pursue a series of incompatible objectives,
namely full employment, relative price stability, a favourable balance of payments
and fast growth. Other countries also followed similar objectives, and with greater
success from the point of view of growth, partly because the conditions of supply
were relatively flexible. Admittedly the external account probably exercised a
more restraining influence on the British economy, though there is reason to
believe that internal policy was influenced unduly by unfavourable short-term
movements in the balance of payments. See Wells, *British Export Performance:
A Comparative Study*, p. 200, and A. R. Conan, *The Problem of Sterling* (1966). The
latter is a particularly useful corrective to popular impressions about the balance of
payments.

[3] Cf. F. Paish, *Studies in an Inflationary Economy* (1962) p. 332.

rates achieved by European countries in the last ten or fifteen years
will be moderated in the future as some of the opportunities for
growth eventually exhaust themselves. In which case it might be
unwise to try to emulate their experience by forcing the British
economy on to a growth path which is inconsistent with both its
past performance and its future potential.[1]

This interpretation of the British economy's performance is only
one possible way of looking at the problem. Not everyone would of
course agree with it and no doubt it conflicts with some of the
opinions expressed in the essays in this volume. But the primary aim
of these introductory comments is to provide some idea of Britain's
relative growth performance in the twentieth century. In doing this
it is apparent how little we know about certain aspects of the
economy. The study of long-term growth in Britain has only just
begun and there are still many important details to be filled in. For
example, national income and industrial production estimates for
the later nineteenth and early twentieth centuries are not very
accurate, with the result that the timing of the climacteric still
remains in some doubt. There is still no breakdown of the residual
before 1950 so that we can only surmise that some elements were
more important than others in promoting growth before that date.
Again, though much has been written about the government's
stop–go policy in the post-war years it is far from clear how far this
policy restricted the British rate of growth. Similarly, though the
problems involved in running sterling as a reserve currency have
been stressed frequently, it would be difficult to say precisely what
effect this has had on the British economy. Thus, although in the last
decade or so great advances have been made in our knowledge of
the dimensions and sources of growth—and the selection of writings
on the British economy which follow bear testimony to this statement—there are still large areas which require further investigation
before something approaching a final analysis can be made.

[1] In terms of modern welfare criteria, moreover, it may not always be desirable
to have a high rate of growth. See, for example, E. J. Mishan, *The Costs of Economic
Growth* (1967).

I Production and Productivity 1920–1962*

by C. H. FEINSTEIN

AT a time when so much emphasis is being placed on the need for more rapid growth of the British economy, and, in particular, on the attainment of the target rate of 4 per cent per annum set by N.E.D.C. for the period 1961–6, it may be useful to view this target in the perspective of the long-run rates of growth of the economy over the period since the First World War. It is evident from the historical record that the sustained achievement of a 4 per cent growth rate would represent a very marked improvement on past performance: in both inter-war and post-war years the rate of growth has been between 2 and 2·5 per cent per annum.

In the thirteen inter-war years from 1924 to 1937, when total population was growing at 0·4 per cent per annum, the average annual rate of growth of output was some $2\frac{1}{4}$ per cent; in the post-war period of fourteen years from 1948 to 1962 when the rate of growth of population was similar (0·5 per cent per annum) the rate of growth of output was about 2·5 per cent per annum. These are the rates shown for the gross domestic product at constant factor cost by the estimates in Table 1. These estimates were built up in great detail from the output side by the method outlined in the Statistical Appendix. An alternative estimate (made largely from independent data) from the expenditure side, i.e. by aggregating estimates of total final expenditure on goods and services (less imports) at constant prices, broadly confirms these overall rates of growth.

The inter-war estimates are still provisional, and all the series are subject to a number of qualifications with respect to their accuracy. The probable margins of error in the series are not, however, likely to invalidate the broad long-run comparisons made in this article.

To give a broad indication of the relative size of the sectors the net output and number employed in 1938 are given in Table 2.

The annual estimates for the gross domestic product are graphed in Figure 1. The rates of growth quoted above were calculated by the ordinary compound interest formula and so depend on the level of output in the first and last year of each period without reference

* First published 1963.

TABLE 1   Index Numbers of
(1938 = 100)

Year	Agriculture, forestry and fishing	Mining and quarrying	Total manu-facturing	Construction	Gas, electricity and water	Total industrial production	Transport and communication
1920	84	95	63	39	42	61·7	69
1921	85	68	49	53	38	50·2	62
1922	86	101	57	44	39	58·0	73
1923	89	113	61	37	43	61·4	79
1924	85	110	68	58	46	68·9	82
1925	91	102	70	74	49	71·0	83
1926	94	56	68	86	51	67·2	80
1927	94	106	75	95	54	77·4	88
1928	100	101	74	77	57	75·2	89
1929	100	109	78	83	61	79·0	92
1930	102	104	74	76	62	75·6	92
1931	93	94	69	72	63	70·8	87
1932	98	89	70	68	65	70·5	84
1933	105	89	74	79	69	75·1	86
1934	106	96	82	89	74	82·6	89
1935	103	97	89	91	81	89·0	91
1936	102	100	97	100	89	96·8	96
1937	101	105	103	104	97	102·7	100
1938	100	100	100	100	100	100·0	100
1946	111	78	104	77	134	102·4	114
1947	106	81	111	80	139	107·9	119
1948	114	85	121	87	148	117·2	128
1949	122	88	129	91	158	124·0	131
1950	125	89	138	91	171	131·1	135
1951	128	91	144	87	182	135·5	141
1952	132	92	138	90	188	132·3	141
1953	135	92	146	97	196	139·9	144
1954	136	93	156	100	214	148·4	146
1955	136	92	166	101	224	156·0	149
1956	143	92	165	106	234	156·6	152
1957	146	91	168	106	244	159·5	152
1958	143	88	166	105	255	157·7	150
1959	149	85	176	111	262	165·9	156
1960	158	83	191	116	280	177·4	164
1961	161	82	191	126	295	179·7	167
1962	163	84	191	127	318	181·4	170

Source: See Statistical Appendix for all output estimates. The estimate of G.D.P. from expenditure data for 1920–48 is based on estimates to be published in my forthcoming study *National Income, Expenditure and Output of the United Kingdom, 1855–1964*, and for 1948–62 on *National Income Blue Book, 1968*, Table 8.

Output at Constant Factor Cost[1]

Distributive trades	Insurance banking and finance	Owner-ship of dwellings	Professional and scientific services (2)	Miscel-laneous services (2)	Public administra-tion and defence (2)	Total distribu-tion and other services	GROSS DOMESTIC PRODUCT	
							Estimate from out-put data	*Estimate from expen-diture data*
80	85	75	82	86	116	85	*73·8*	72·4
70	74	75	83	81	95	78	*64·9*	68·2
77	77	75	83	79	84	79	*69·7*	71·0
78	80	76	82	78	79	79	*71·9*	73·4
80	84	77	83	81	79	81	*75·7*	75·5
83	87	77	85	82	79	82	*77·9*	79·6
80	90	79	87	83	79	83	*76·1*	75·6
85	97	81	88	85	79	86	*82·7*	81·1
86	102	82	89	86	78	87	*82·7*	82·6
87	95	84	90	87	79	87	*84·7*	84·6
87	94	85	91	89	81	88	*83·5*	84·4
88	85	87	92	89	82	87	*80·5*	79·8
87	88	88	94	89	82	88	*80·6*	80·4
90	92	89	95	91	82	90	*83·9*	81·2
94	95	91	96	93	83	93	*88·5*	86·9
97	99	93	98	95	85	95	*92·5*	90·2
101	103	95	99	97	88	98	*97·5*	92·9
103	104	98	99	99	93	100	*101·2*	97·0
100	100	100	100	100	100	100	*100·0*	100·0
82	98	106	102	76	240	105	*104·1*	114·0
89	103	107	106	76	176	101	*105·2*	111·1
92	104	108	111	78	153	100	*109·9*	114·3
97	107	108	115	75	148	102	*113·9*	117·8
103	112	109	121	74	144	104	*118·4*	121·6
99	112	109	125	74	152	104	*120·8*	126·0
97	110	109	129	74	156	105	*119·8*	126·0
103	114	110	132	76	158	107	*124·6*	131·8
109	121	113	137	77	155	111	*129·9*	134·5
114	125	115	140	78	151	114	*134·4*	141·2
115	125	118	144	78	149	115	*135·7*	143·8
118	131	120	150	79	146	117	*138·0*	146·6
120	136	123	155	81	141	119	*137·9*	146·2
126	150	125	160	84	138	124	*143·9*	151·3
132	158	128	163	87	136	128	*151·5*	158·9
134	163	130	169	89	136	131	*154·1*	164·7
134	166	132	174	93	139	133	*156·9*	166·3

NOTE: (1) Comparable data for the years 1939–45 are generally not available and the link between 1938 and 1948 is in many cases very uncertain.

(2) The quantity indicators used in the estimates for these sectors consist, to a very large extent, of numbers employed or of deflated wage and salary bills.

to the level in intervening years.[1] In the inter-war years the growth of output was not only a fraction slower but was also very uneven, with a strong downswing in many sectors between 1929 and 1932, followed by more than normally rapid expansion during the early stages of the recovery. In the post-war period the growth of output has been more stable and the annual levels have kept much closer

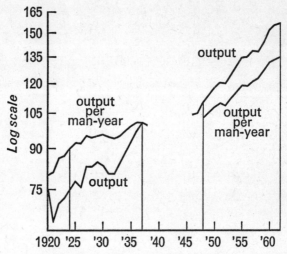

Fig. 1. Index Numbers of Gross Domestic Product: Total and per Man-Year
(*1938 = 100*)

to the long-run trend rate. Bursts of expansion (as in 1953–5 and 1959–60) have been followed by years with little or no growth but not, as a rule, by an actual fall in output.

Figure 2 shows the rates of growth (between the terminal years 1924–37 and 1948–62) in each sector. Perhaps the most interesting point to emerge from this comparison is that the small rise in the overall growth rate in the post-war period is entirely due to the more rapid expansion of agriculture and the service sectors. The long-run rate of growth of industrial production has been much the same in both periods: just over 3 per cent per annum. By contrast, agriculture has more than doubled its rate of growth to some 2·5 per cent per annum; while both transport and distribution and other services, have increased their growth rate from 1·5 to 2 per cent per

---

[1] If the average annual rate of growth of gross domestic product is calculated by fitting a trend line (second degree curve) by the method of least squares (so as to take account of the level of output in each year of the period) the result is very little different.

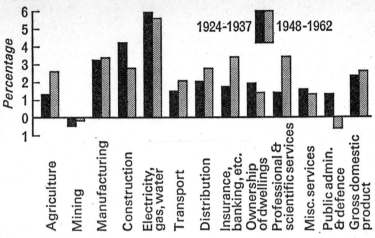

Fig. 2. Percentage Change in Output

TABLE 2

Employment and Net Output in 1938

Sector	Number at work (000s)	Net output* per 1,000
Agriculture, forestry and fishing	1,080	35
Mining and quarrying	890	35
Manufacturing	6,590	325
Construction	1,380	47
Electricity, gas and water	280	24
Transport and communication	1,510	88
Distributive trades	3,330	143
Insurance, banking and finance	540	60
Ownership of dwellings	—	57
Public administration and defence	1,320	52
Professional and scientific services	1,130	66
Miscellaneous services	3,450	79
Total	21,500	1,000†

* Provisional estimates.   † After adjustment for net interest paid.

annum, with particularly marked expansion in insurance, banking and finance and in professional and scientific services. Among the services only public administration and defence shows a lower output in 1962 than in 1948, reflecting the reduction in the size of the armed forces of almost 50 per cent between 1953 and 1962.

The constant long-run growth of industrial production at 3 per cent per annum covers both the persistent decline of coal mining and the very rapid expansion of electricity, gas and water. The latter has achieved the highest growth rate among the sectors shown in Figure 2 in both inter-war and post-war periods, with a rate of some 5·5 to 6 per cent per annum, due mainly to the very rapid expansion in the supply of electricity. Manufacturing industry as a whole has grown at roughly the same pace in both periods but this is, of course, the average of the very different rates of growth of the component industries.

Output per Man-Year

As a first step towards the explanation of the observed differences in rates of growth of output, both over time and between sectors, it is tempting to estimate the corresponding changes in output per man. This is often used as a measure of productivity but as it only allows for changes in one input—labour employed—it cannot tell us how much of the change in output per man is due to the change in efficiency of the labour force, and how much to changes in the quantity and quality of the capital and other factors of production employed together with labour. Even with these qualifications the estimates of output per man are generally of considerable interest. There is, however, one important exception to this: where the measurement of output was based (for lack of other data) on numbers employed (see Table 1), output per man is implicitly assumed to be constant and the subsequent division of output by numbers employed has no significance.

The input of labour may be measured in several ways, with progressively more refinement, but for the present purpose we have taken only the very crude measure of numbers at work, including employers and self-employed. There is no allowance made for such factors as changes in the age and sex composition or in the relative skills of the labour force, in actual weekly hours worked or in length of holidays. It must also be noted that the basic data on employment (described in the Appendix) were not fully comparable in the inter-war and post-war periods, and although an attempt has been made to correct this as far as possible, it is an additional reason why the link between 1938 and 1948 is a good deal less reliable than the estimates for either of the two periods considered separately.

The percentage increases in output per man-year in each sector for which it can be measured are shown in Table 3 for the three periods 1924–37, 1937–48 and 1948–62. The most striking feature is the much larger increase shown in the post-war period (see also

TABLE 3

Output per Man-year

Sector	Percentage change 1924–37 (13 years)	1937–48 (11 years)	1948–62 (14 years)
Agriculture, forestry and fishing	49	− 1	84
Mining and quarrying	36	−15	21
Manufacturing	29	2	35
Construction	20	−27	36
Electricity, gas and water	44	30	78
Total industrial production	33	2	36
Transport and communication	13	5	41
Distributive trades	−16	9	16
Insurance, banking finance	− 5	19	19
Gross Domestic Product	11	1	31

Figure 1). The broadly steady rate of growth of total output noted above is thus the product of differing rates of growth in numbers employed and output per man-year. From 1924 to 1937 the total labour force increased by 20 per cent, whereas the increase from 1948 to 1962 was less than half of this: about 9 per cent. The large rise from 1924 to 1937 was not the result of a fall in unemployment (which was almost 1,500,000 in 1937 and 300,000 higher than in 1924), but of an increase in the proportion of the population in employment. This in turn was largely the result of a fall in the number of children aged 14 or less and a rise of 2·8 million in the number of persons of working age (15–64). The slower growth of the labour force since 1948 was thus offset by the more rapid expansion of output per man-year: about 2 per cent per annum compared with less than 1 per cent between the wars.

Table 3 also suggests that the faster increase in productivity in the post-war period is to be attributed almost entirely to the services. For transport and communication the improvement is almost three-fold and for the other services a downward trend between 1924 and 1937 has been replaced by rising output per man-year. For manufacturing, and for industrial production the long-run rate of growth has been roughly the same throughout: about 2 per cent per annum. Agriculture has achieved the highest rate of growth in both periods, closely followed by electricity, gas and water.

The higher post-war rate is still appreciably below the 3·2 per cent target rate of growth for output per worker set by N.E.D.C. for 1961–6. It may nevertheless be possible to achieve the target rate, given the benefit in 1961–6 of such factors as the high level of fixed investment in recent years and the impetus to growth created by the activities of N.E.D.C. The crucial factor is probably whether or not the present phase of fairly rapid expansion is followed by a pause for one or more years as has been the case previously in the 'stop–go' cycles which have characterised the post-war period. If the target is to be reached it is essential that, on this occasion, there should be no such pause: not simply because these phases of 'restraint' pull down the average rate of growth, but also because they make it far more difficult to obtain the co-operation from labour needed for the introduction of new techniques and the elimination of restrictive practices.

Statistical Appendix

Output Estimates. For the post-war years the estimates in Table 1 are taken from official estimates, linked to each other (and to 1938) by the author.

The link between 1938 and 1948 was based on indicators similar to those described below, including the Lomax index of industrial production. Separate links were calculated with pre-war (1938 or 1935) and 1948 weights and a geometrical mean of the two was taken.

For the inter-war years the estimates for industrial Production are those published in 1959 by K. S. Lomax.[1] For Agriculture new estimates for 1920–38 were made by valuing gross output for each year at the prices of 1936–8 and deducting inputs at 1936–8 prices. The output data were based on the annual *Agricultural Statistics* and the input data on this source and on estimates given by J. R. Bellerby.[2] For transport and communication, the distributive trades and the other services new estimates were made for 1920–38 with 1938 weights. It is not possible here to list all the indicators used, but in the vast majority of cases it was possible to find indicators for the inter-war years which are the same as, or very similar to, those used for the post-war estimates, and listed in *Sources and Methods*, appendix IV.[3]

The base year prices at which the inter-war estimates were valued were those of 1938. For each of the sectors shown in Table 1

[1] 'Production and Productivity Movements in the United Kingdom since 1900', *Journal of the Royal Statistical Society*, A122 (1959).

[2] 'Agricultural Income', *Journal of the Royal Statistical Society*, A118 (1955).

[3] See Central Statistical Office, *National Income Statistics, Sources and Methods*, (1956) ch. III, and appendix IV. Final estimates, and a detailed account of the sources, will be published in *National Income, Expenditure and Output of the United Kingdom, 1855–1964.*

approximate estimates of value added (net output) in 1938 were based on data on wages and salaries in A. L. Chapman[1] and on the Inland Revenue classification of trading profits made in 1938 and assessed under Schedule D.[2] The analysis of the profits data is still provisional and may be appreciably revised. Within the sectors, weights were based either on the above data or on the extrapolation (by means of the quantity indicators) of the 1948 weights given in *Sources and Methods*.

Numbers at Work. For 1948–62 mid-year estimates for the United Kingdom of the total number in civil employment plus the Armed Forces were taken from the *Annual Abstract of Statistics* (1959 and 1962).

For 1920–38 the starting point was the estimates of man-years of employment (for employees only) given by A. L. Chapman.[1] A very approximate adjustment to include employers and workers on own account was made for each sector.

[1] *Wages and Salaries in the United Kingdom, 1920–38* (1953).

[2] *Ninety-Second Report of the Commissioners of His Majesty's Inland Revenue for the year ended 31st March, 1949* (1950) tables 43–76.

2 Growth and Productivity in the United Kingdom*

by K. S. LOMAX

INTEREST in economic growth has developed considerably in recent years. It thus becomes important to measure rates of economic change. When this is done for an advanced country like the United Kingdom, productivity is of vital interest. In such a country prospects of any large increase in the labour force are remote and therefore the major part of any growth in national output must come from productivity increase.

There are several ways in which the growth of an economy can be measured. One is in terms of gross national product. Another is through direct computation of an index of real product. However, for the United Kingdom it can be argued that industrial production plays a predominant role in the economy.

Total Industrial Growth

For the United Kingdom a completely new index of industrial output has been calculated for the hundred years or so from 1860. The most reliable part of this series, from 1900 onwards, has already been published.[1] The new calculations from 1860 to 1900 are necessarily on a rather less secure basis. Nevertheless sufficient data do exist for this period to enable an adequate index to be computed.

Before 1860, the information available concerning industrial output is so meagre that the calculation of an index of industrial output is a most hazardous undertaking. It seems doubtful whether, for the period prior to 1860, there is any alternative superior to using the index calculated some years back by Hoffmann.[2]

So, using the Hoffmann index up to 1860 and the new indices thereafter, the industrial history of the United Kingdom can broadly be summarised as follows:

There was a gradual acceleration in the rate of growth from the

* First published 1964.
[1] K. S. Lomax, 'Production and Productivity Movements in the United Kingdom since 1900', *Journal of the Royal Statistical Society*, A122 (1959).
[2] W. G. Hoffmann, *Structure of British Industry, 1700–1950*, trans. W. H. Chaloner and W. O. Henderson (Blackwell, 1955).

time of the industrial revolution until in the 1780s it reached more than 3 per cent per annum. The rate of growth, generally, continued to run at around 3 per cent right up to 1877. Rates of growth are measured throughout from peak to peak, in order to ensure comparability in degrees of capacity utilisation. In 1877 began a long period of fluctuation with growth at a much slower rate, lasting until the First World War. The average growth rate throughout this time from 1877 to 1913 was only 1·7 per cent per annum.

TABLE 1

Index of Industrial Production: United Kingdom; 1924 = 100

1860	30	1880	48	1900	73·9	1919	81·3	1938	146·4
1861	30	1881	47	1901	73·6	1920	90·3		
1862	29	1882	50	1902	76·4	1921	73·5	1946	149·4
1863	30	1883	51	1903	76·4	1922	85·0	1947	158·7
1864	32	1884	50	1904	75·7	1923	90·0	1948	171·7
1865	33	1885	49	1905	78·3	1924	100·0	1949	182·0
1866	34	1886	48	1906	80·2	1925	103·9	1950	193·5
1867	34	1887	49	1907	81·6	1926	98·4	1951	199·9
1868	36	1888	54	1908	77·1	1927	113·4	1952	194·7
1869	36	1889	57	1909	78·9	1928	110·2	1953	206·4
1870	38	1890	56	1910	80·6	1929	115·8	1954	219·9
1871	41	1891	58	1911	83·0	1930	110·8	1955	231·1
1872	43	1892	56	1912	84·2	1931	103·7	1956	232·3
1873	44	1893	55	1913	90·5	1932	103·2	1957	236·3
1874	44	1894	60	1914	84·8	1933	110·1	1958	233·5
1875	46	1895	61	1915	86·4	1934	121·1	1959	245·6
1876	48	1896	65	1916	81·8	1935	130·3	1960	262·5
1877	49	1897	68	1917	76·4	1936	142·0	1961	265·7
1878	44	1898	71	1918	73·8	1937	150·5	1962	268·4
1879	46	1899	74						

In the inter-war period, again, we had violent fluctuations but a substantial improvement in the rate of growth to around 3 per cent per annum or a little over, once more.

Since the Second World War there have not been oscillations of the pre-war type with successive booms and slumps and periodically heavy unemployment but we have had, while maintaining apparent full employment, spurts of rapid growth followed by periods of stagnation. In other words, fluctuations there have been but of a different type, consisting of oscillations in the rate of growth. Nevertheless, on average, since 1948, the rate of growth has still further improved to a level not far short of being the highest in our industrial history.

The intra-industry growth pattern

Now, a brief summary of the pattern within industry. In the last
three or four decades of the nineteenth century there were few rapid
growers. Only steel, gas supply, paper and shipbuilding showed an
average growth rate, from 1860 to 1900, exceeding 3 per cent per
annum. Railway construction was stagnating. Coal and cotton
output, while still increasing, was doing so at a decreasing rate.

TABLE 2

Rates of Growth in Total Industrial Output of the United Kingdom

1738–1748	1·2 per cent per annum
1748–1767	0·8
1767–1782	1·6
1782–1792	3·8
1792–1811	2·6
1811–1839	3·1
1839–1860	3·2
1860–1877	3·0
1877–1883	0·5
1883–1891	1·6
1891–1902	2·4 } 1·6 per cent per annum
1902–1913	1·6
1920–1929	2·8
1929–1937	3·3 } 3·1 per cent per annum
1948–1960	3·7

There were the usual fluctuations in building with booms in the
mid-1870s and late 1890s. The new industries of the twentieth
century had not yet developed sufficiently to appear in significant
statistical form.

In the present century, since 1900, we have had *relative stagnation*
in mining, shipbuilding, textiles, clothing, china and earthenware
and drink; *moderate expansion* in mechanical engineering, ferrous
metal manufacture, building materials and timber; and *great
expansion* in electrical engineering, electrical supply, vehicles,
chemicals, non-ferrous metal manufacture, glass, paper and printing,
food and tobacco.

It is seen that the stagnating trades are the 'older' industries
which had enjoyed rapid growth and prosperity in the eighteenth
and nineteenth centuries. Most of the greatly expanding industries
are the 'newer' trades of the twentieth century owing their origin
in large part to the technical change and innovation occurring in

the twenty or thirty years around the turn of the century; and their expansion, the large rise in demand for their products, partly to increased incomes, partly to shifts in consumer tastes, as, for example, with tobacco, but perhaps most of all to the lowering of costs and prices through increased scale of production.

The pattern of growth rates presented above clearly suggests that, in considering the economic climate in which the modern industrial history of the United Kingdom has taken shape, the 1870s would, perhaps, form the most meaningful starting point. Also, both from the viewpoint of economic experiences as well as political history, the period since then divides naturally into three sub-periods.

First Period: From the 1870s up to the First World War

During this sub-period, the first part of which, from 1873 to 1896, coincides with the 'Great Depression' the rate of growth of industrial output seems to have been lower than at any other time. Indeed from the viewpoint of growth rates the period from 1877 to 1913 was quite unique in the whole of our industrial history. Apart from the early years of the industrial revolution, rates of industrial growth have generally fluctuated between about $2\frac{1}{2}$ and $3\frac{3}{4}$ per cent per annum. Yet between 1877 and 1913 the rate averaged only 1·6 and only between 1891 and 1902 did it rise above 2 per cent annually.

The slackening in our rate of growth is usually associated with the decline in Britain's predominant position in world production and trade and the beginnings of the rise of other industrial nations, particularly Germany and the United States, generally behind tariff walls. It has been argued that the falling off in the rate of exports would react adversely, through the accelerator mechanism, on the level of home investment and productivity. There is substance in this argument but, in fact, Britain had had to withstand increasing competition from abroad and, indeed, had suffered a decline in the rate of increase of exports long before 1877 when there was such a marked change in the rate of growth in industrial output. The rate of increase in export volumes had actually begun to fall off more than a quarter of a century earlier, in the early 1850s. Thus the slackening in the output growth rate seems more closely to be associated in timing with the great depression period of 1872–96 than with the rise of Britain's competitors. It is true that while the long period of decline in the growth rate of British exports, due no doubt to increasing competition from rising nations abroad, is clear and unambiguous, in fact, it was during the great depression period that our 'gains' from trade suffered a sharp and striking blow. The rate of growth of exports was falling off from the 1850s up to the turn of the century. The growth rate of import volumes, too, was decreasing at pretty well the same pace. What appears to have been crucial, however, was the rapid deterioration in the net barter terms of trade during the first part of the period of the great depression, from 1873 to 1883. This, coupled with the falling volumes of trade, meant that our gain from trade suffered a severe set-back during this ten-year period. Whereas from 1863 to 1873 our total gain from trade had been increasing at 6·2 per cent per annum, over the decade 1873 to 1883 the rate fell sharply to 1·4 per cent per annum. Then from 1883 to 1890 there was something of a recovery to 3·7 per cent per annum. The above figures refer, of course, only to merchandise trade, and during the period of rapidly decreasing rates of growth in the volumes of goods traded we were developing vigorously the invisible side of our trade. We were investing heavily abroad and during the whole of the period up to the First World War we were never in the slightest difficulty in balancing our overseas account.

The twenty or thirty years around the turn of the century was a time of considerable, far-reaching and rapid technical progress; the end of the coal, steam and iron era; the period of birth of vast industrial sectors depending on electricity, the internal combustion engine, steel, non-ferrous metals, chemicals, etc. Partly no doubt because of tradition, conservatism and, perhaps, some scientific and technological backwardness, some legal impediments and, certainly, serious economic barriers, we seemed slow, compared with other countries, in our progress with these new developments.

These changes, increased competition from abroad, and rapid technical change, came at a particularly unfortunate time for this country. It has been said that 'we had been coasting effortlessly forward in expansion from the time of the industrial revolution' and this had, no doubt, induced certain rigidities, inflexibilities, and some complacency in the system. Certainly there was some maldistribution of resources from the viewpoint of the new developments. Then, the rate of population increase in the United Kingdom was slowing down. Probably most important of all, however, the period from 1873 up to 1896, the great depression, was a time of continuously falling prices, stable wages, falling profit margins, and hence low investment at home. To summarise: falling prices, slowing down of population rise, slowing down of export growth, were all factors inhibiting investment at a time when technical progress was providing the opportunity of expansion in new directions, expansion which was also hindered by the rigidities of a traditional society with its resources distributed largely in a pattern becoming increasingly out-of-date. In the years before the First World War there was, too, an institutional bias in the capital market tending to inhibit home investment as against investment abroad. It is clear that institutional factors, particularly the policy of the banks, were much more favourable to home development in Germany, for example, in this period, than they were in the United Kingdom. The traditional means of financing expansion through the ploughing back of profits in industries such as cotton in Britain was completely inappropriate in the new situation requiring heavy investment in industries producing entirely new products. It could well be that difficulties of financing was a most important constraint hindering rapid development. There were well-established institutions for channelling savings abroad. Employment of savings in large-scale development of new industries at home was not so well provided for.

Second Period: The inter-war years

The inter-war years were characterised by violent economic fluctuations with very severe depressions in 1921 and 1932. These depressions, like the relative stagnation before 1914, were to a predominant extent generated through international trade. The overall economic position, however, was by no means as black as has been painted although unemployment remained a serious problem throughout. The new index-numbers of industrial output show a much less depressing picture than that exhibited by older currently-published indices. Certainly industrial output growth showed a big improvement compared with pre-First World War. The cumulative rate of growth of output from 1920 to 1926 was 2·8 per cent per annum and from 1929 to 1937, 3·3 per cent per annum. What were the factors underlying this progress which contrast with the generally held view of an economically depressing experience in the inter-war period?

Firstly, there was a slight tendency for the terms of trade to move in our favour. More strikingly significant, however, was the direct result of the very substantial fall in import prices. The great majority of wage and salary earners in work were thus better off than ever before. Demand for imports did not prove to be elastic which is not surprising as Britain's imports consisted largely of food and raw materials. Purchasing power was therefore released for other goods. This stimulated demand for houses and for many of the new durable consumer goods coming on to the market. Home industry benefited, the tariff introduced in 1932 being, of course, a contributory factor.

Then, there was very considerable innovation in the twenties and thirties in the newer industries, making up in some measure for Britain's slow start in steel, motor-vehicles, electricity, electrical engineering and chemicals. This further generated expanding demand for a wide range of engineering products, machine tools, etc., and for metals. Rapid technical progress in the processes of manufacture for the new products meant reducing costs and prices and, in consequence, expanding demand. The most striking examples of this are motor vehicles and electricity supply.

In parallel with the technical progress on the supply side there were, on the demand side, changes of tastes on the part of consumers; a move away, with increasing incomes, from traditional products such as textiles to consumer durables. Also, apart from changes of tastes, it is probably true to say that, with a new product, there is probably at first high income elasticity of demand. So, with rising incomes it is not surprising to observe rapidly expanding demand for electricity, electrical products, motor-cars, radio, etc.

Another factor which perhaps played some part in aiding the recovery of home industries was the decline and, ultimately, virtual disappearance of foreign lending. Now the preponderant causal influences in such a situation could proceed from trade, and not from the capital side, that is, for a weak balance of current payments position, and this may well have been the case in the twenties. Later, however, it seems more likely that investment at home in the expanding industries providing for rising consumer demand behind a tariff wall appeared much more attractive than investment abroad; in other words, the capital side became dominant and trading relations had to adjust to the situation where investment opportunities at home led to a reduction of foreign lending. Home investment in money terms in the inter-war period seemed low but, in fact, capital goods were then relatively cheap and, in real terms, domestic investment was in consistent relationship to growth compared with the state of affairs since the Second World War.

Some commentators have stressed the importance of the building booms of the twenties and thirties. Cheap money, low interest rates, and low building costs must have exerted considerable influence in stimulating demand for houses as well as the purchasing power released by falling import prices.

Another factor which contributed to the rapid growth from the mid-thirties on was, of course, rearmament. And so we come to government policy. There is doubt about its influence and effectiveness but we can certainly point to many stimulating measures which were taken:

i The devaluation of the currency following the abandonment of the gold standard in 1931. Yet, of course, on the other side of the account has to be placed the deliberate deflation in the early 1920s culminating in the return to gold in 1925.

ii Tariffs introduced in 1932. This cannot have influenced the building boom or the rearmament drive but may have helped development elsewhere.

iii Cheap money policy after 1932.

iv Direct help to certain industries such as coal, cotton, shipbuilding and steel, in the form of subsidies, loan guarantees, and measures to encourage reorganisation. It has been suggested that these measures were more successful in restricting capacity than in encouraging growth.

Perhaps the most striking fact about British internal economic policy was that almost alone among the major industrial nations, we did not resort to deficit financing. The suggestion has even been made that this loyalty to orthodox budgetary policy may well have made a positive contribution to recovery by generating confidence in the business community!

Third Period: The post-war years

The outstanding feature of the period since the war is the supreme role the government now plays. Through its monetary and fiscal policies, through its direct control of a large part of the investment taking place, through indirect influences of many kinds, the government now exerts a strong effect on growth if not, indeed, we may say, specifically controlling it. But growth itself has not, until very recently, really been the predominant aim. The main object has been stability, that is, balance of payments equilibrium and conservation of the reserves of gold and foreign exchange. The establishment of the National Economic Development Council (N.E.D.C.) in 1962 was really the first indication of a possible change of outlook in official circles.

The broad post-war picture is one of short periods of rapid industrial growth followed by spells of stagnation. We have certainly not achieved *steady* growth even at a relatively low rate. In fact, though we no longer have the pre-war trade cycle we have had fluctuations of a different type, namely, variations in the rate of growth.

The periods of stagnation have, to a large extent, been induced by government policy measures designed to damp down home demand. What has happened is that whenever we have run into serious balance of payments difficulties, that is, in 1951, 1955 and 1960, the government has applied the brakes in the form of credit restriction, dear money through high interest rates, wage restraint, increased taxation and hire-purchase restrictions.

The main instruments of government policy have been monetary and fiscal measures and such stand-bys as the hire-purchase regulations. The method has been to damp down home demand in order to check price rises, encourage exports, and discourage imports, and thus correct balance of payments disequilibrium. Higher interest rates in addition to inhibiting home investment have also served to attract foreign funds into London and so aid the building up of reserves. These measures of government policy impinge directly on demand, and with export demand not rising sufficiently to offset the cut in home demand we can, therefore, summarise the situation by saying that in order to maintain the economy in balance, growth has had to be restrained.

Apart from wages restraint, the measures adopted have been indirect in their application, not operating directly on costs, which are at the root of the trouble. In fact, by creating much spare capacity the result of the government policy of dampening down demand has been to raise the unit costs. There have been many other criticisms of official policy:

i Monetary and fiscal measures do not make their impact swiftly enough to bring the quick relief which balance of payments disequilibria need.

ii The general financial controls—high interest rates and credit restrictions—do not operate primarily on the right strands of demand. From the viewpoint of growth and particularly in regard to costs, investment is of fundamental importance in the British economy. Thus in operating on demand, policy ought, as far as possible, to encourage investment spending and discourage consumer expenditure. In fact, since the war, when the brakes have had to be applied, policy measures have seemed to impinge more on investment than on consumption.

Further fundamental criticisms of the way successive governments have approached the post-war economic problem arise from more detailed charting of the progress of the economy. At the outset, however, it is as well to remember that, by and large, we cannot complain about external conditions in considering Britain's difficulties. The period since the war has been one of buoyant demand all over the world. Re-equipment of war-damaged territories and industrialisation of underdeveloped areas generate demand for the products and equipment in the production of which the United Kingdom should be at an advantage. Financing of development has been, of course, a major constraint here. In regard to the terms of trade things could have been far worse for us. There was a deterioration from 1949, through 1950 to 1951, owing first to the 1949 devaluation and then to the Korean boom in prices of primary products. Thereafter, however, there was continuous improvement in the terms of trade until 1960 when a slight deterioration once again set in. The present level is still only slightly above that for 1948. Thus, apart from a short spell up to 1951, the volume of exports needed to pay for a given volume of imports has not seriously been tending to increase. If this had not been the case, the problem of stabilising the balance of payments would have been even more acute.

We ran serious deficits on the current balance of payments in 1951, 1955 and 1960 and, if the account is divided into its components, it is seen that these were attributable to large visible deficits in these years, together with a continuous decline over the whole period from 1950, of most serious proportions, in invisible earnings.

While much of government policy has been orientated towards the encouragement of exports, examination of the trade figures draws attention particularly to the import side. Now it is true that a lower level of home demand will mean, *ceteris paribus*, reduced demand for imports, but it appears that the fluctuations in imports have been far greater than could possibly be countered by manipulation of the level of home demand. For one thing changes in import prices have to be taken into account. They can have a considerable effect. A large part of the serious deficit in the 1951 balance of payments was contributed by the enormous rise in prices of primary products resulting mainly from the scramble following the outbreak of the Korean war. Since 1951 import prices have not really been a problem. Far more serious have been volume changes. The crisis years of 1951, 1955 and 1960 were years in which there were exceptional rises in import volumes. Moreover, quite apart from these, the volume of imports rises with rising output and since about 1954 there has been an undoubted tendency for import volumes to rise rather faster than the production index. This has been attributable, mainly, to the fuels and manufactured goods categories. Several factors have made their contribution here: the switch from coal to oil as a primary source of fuel and power; the continuing increase in road traffic; greater liberalisation of trade and, perhaps, most significant of all, declining competitiveness of Britain's home production.

The various trends already mentioned had their effects in 1951, 1955 and 1960. For instance, in 1951, our invisible earnings suffered a severe decline due, partly, to the Persian seizure of the oil refineries at Abadan and the beginning of servicing of American and Canadian loans. However in the crisis years there were certainly other specific causes present which must be stressed. One particular volatile element in final demand which causes wide fluctuations in imports and consequently is often an important contributor to balance of payments difficulties is the matter of stock-piling. This was certainly one of the principal factors behind the 1951 situation and, partly, 1960, too. Stocks were heavily run down in 1950 so that quite apart from the post-Korean scramble we would have expected to find a build-up again in the following years. Korea added further impetus to this movement. Stock-piling was then very important in 1951. This factor also played a strong part in 1960 but not in 1955.

The key to 1955 and partly to 1960 is the very large increases in imports under the heading of manufactured goods — 25 per cent in 1955 and 34 per cent in 1960 — on the previous years, respectively. The term 'manufactured goods' covers not only finished manufactures but also many semi-manufactures for further processing. In these marked jumps in imports of manufactures two factors appear to have been at work. Firstly, we have the clear trend for manufactured imports to increase both absolutely and relatively. Liberalisation of trade has played some part here but the main reason lies in the decline in competitiveness of British products. Secondly, and more specifically important, we have the problem of shortages and bottlenecks appearing at particular points in the economy. These latter might well be obviated in the future through planning of the kind now being undertaken by the National Economic Development Council. In a free economy there is always the danger of temporary shortages and bottlenecks occurring. Forecasting techniques are never perfect. Even a relatively short time ahead it is frequently difficult to foresee detailed needs and implications with any certainty. At these times, demand may have to be met from abroad and it may be necessary to step up the level of imports of particular commodities even though the price advantage lies with home production. Delivery dates may be the crucial issue. This seems to have happened with steel, particularly in 1955 and 1960. The volume of imports under the heading of 'iron and steel' in 1955 was more than $3\frac{1}{2}$ times the level in 1954 while in 1960 it was 2¼ times the 1959 level. The inability of home producers fully to meet the needs of home industry, if it arises, is likely to be most acute after a period of rapid growth and it may be significant that 1951, 1955 and 1960 were just such years. It may be, then, that in the crisis years, superimposed on substantial stock-piling, and a declining trend in competitiveness, there was heavy importing because of capacity shortage in key sectors of the economy.

Now consideration must be given to government policy in face of these recurrent balance of payments crises and its effects because it is this, largely, which has determined the rate of industrial growth in the post-war period. With the establishment of N.E.D.C. in 1961 came a new outlook and the expectation that Britain's economic problems could be solved in some manner other than through the stop–go policies adopted in the past. Before N.E.D.C., however, each time we ran into a serious balance of payments deficit, government reaction was to damp down home demand in order to check price rises, encourage exports and discourage imports. The brakes have been applied through credit restriction, dear money through high interest rates, increased taxation, stiffening of hire-purchase regulations and wages restraint. By inhibiting the excessive growth of home demand the government hoped both to discourage imports and encourage exports. Higher interest rates would also attract funds into London and thereby increase the reserves of foreign currency. The aim of government policy too was to keep down costs and so still further generate correcting movements to the balance of payments, although the only part of official action directly impinging on costs was wages restraint. Indeed a policy of holding back home demand since it causes spare capacity is likely to tend to raise costs. Particularly has this proved to be so since the measures of restraint have affected investment just as much as consumption. From the viewpoint of cost reduction investment is vital. A high level of investment means much new plant, equipment and buildings, a lowering of the average age of the capital stock, *and* more power, on average, at the worker's elbow.

When the results of government policy are examined it is seen that we have ultimately emerged successfully from each successive crisis although specific anticipated effects in particular sectors hardly seem to have been completely achieved. For example, the stagnation years when government policy was designed to encourage exports turned out to be most depressing in export performance. On the costs side we find that the rate of increase in home costs per unit of output in the United Kingdom was appreciably greater in the years when demand was stationary than it was in the years of rapid growth. On the import side the picture is more favourable. When the government has damped down home demand and imposed restraints on output and incomes, the rate of importing has tended to fall. Now, undoubtedly, when output is stagnant and incomes are restrained, demand for imports will be inhibited and, without question, government policy has been successful, in this way, on the import side. It is doubtful, however, that this is the whole story. A strong contributor to the balance of payments crises of 1951, 1955 and 1960 was the exceptionally heavy importing in these years. This was due to a particular conjunction of circumstances certain not to persist. When stock-piling had been achieved and the serious bottlenecks eased, it would inevitably be expected that the importing position would rectify itself. Fluctuations of import levels imply the existence of troughs as well as peaks.

Government policy cannot then be said to have failed in that we have corrected balance of payments disequilibria but it has been only partly successful in achieving specific aims, limited though they have been. We have certainly not enjoyed *steady* growth within the constraint of external stability. However, desirable though this may always be, it is only since the establishment of N.E.D.C. that it has become the expressed intention of government policy.

What alternative courses could post-war governments have pursued in face of the economic situation since 1948? In the first place, within the broad confines of the kind of approach accepted, it would have been preferable to encourage investment at the expense of consumption. Then, perhaps, there has been excessive preoccupation with export stimulation and too little attention given to the possibilities of import substitution. What other proposals have been made? There have been suggestions for changes in taxation policy which would provide more incentives to export and would encourage firms to economise as much as possible on labour. A payroll tax, for example, would possibly achieve this. One of the oddest features of economic behaviour in the fifties has been that when demand was inhibited and much spare capacity induced in the economy, firms generally held on to their labour so that productivity suffered and costs increased. It is true that the Selwyn Lloyd measures of 1961 appeared to have effects more in the right direction. Nevertheless it is still true that a taxation policy orientated more towards payrolls and less towards profits would both encourage investment and discourage the hoarding of labour and should stimulate the rapid advance of productivity.

If we consider radically different courses open to the government, there are really five broad alternatives which could have been pursued. These will now briefly be considered in turn:

1. *Devaluation.* This was the solution adopted in 1949 when it had become clear that we were to be faced, following the war, with the long-term problem of stimulating exports sufficiently to achieve balance in our overseas account. In the fifties this alternative would have required International Monetary Fund approval which would probably have not been forthcoming until more 'orthodox' policies of restraint through credit restriction, high interest rates, etc., had been tried. It would also have been a very unpopular policy internally as indicating national weakness. Again, fear of retaliatory devaluations by other countries which might have left us pretty well where we were before was always a deterrent.

2. *Free exchange rates.* A policy favoured by several eminent economists but unlikely to be achievable and even it if were, almost certain to produce international payments chaos and confusion.

3. *Physical controls.* Diagnosis of the causes underlying the recurrent balance of payments crises immediately suggests the remedy of direct physical import controls. This was not really open to governments, however, in this period. In the first place physical controls had become politically most unpopular and had been speedily dismantled following their use in the immediate post-war period by the Labour government. Secondly, their adoption would have been an infringement of GATT and would have run counter to the trend towards greater liberalisation of trade throughout the fifties. Thirdly, again, even if practicable there would have been inhibiting retaliatory fears concerning the attitudes of other countries.

4. Perhaps a more promising approach would have been to eschew measures impinging specifically on demand and to operate directly on costs. This would have involved, on the one hand, the achievement of some kind of wage bargain with the trade unions and, on the other, encouragement of the raising of productivity. The first of these still remains a serious barrier to a more rational economic policy; the second could have been pursued more vigorously. The effects of the Monopolies Commission and the Restrictive Practices Court in controlling the worst abuses of monopoly and restrictive practices have made a contribution, but a rather leisurely one. Reform of the taxation system to increase the rate of obsolescence and replacement and to encourage firms in the economical use of labour would also have helped greatly. There is indeed much scope for the joint tackling of the problem of productivity on the part of employers, trade unions and government.

5. *Economic planning.* After a decade in which planning has been regarded as discredited in the United Kingdom there is now much revival of interest and a belief that, perhaps after all, the right way to tackle our economic problems is through some kind of concerted effort. The French example, where a form of flexible planning appears to have been highly successful, has clearly been in people's minds. Economic planning in the immediate post-war sense of a detailed control by centralised agencies of the operations of the economy is no longer thought of as appropriate or practicable for the United Kingdom. However, some loose form of planning through joint investigation and discussion of economic problems by both sides of industry and the government, as exemplified by the establishment of the National Economic Development Council, might achieve the desired but elusive steady growth with stability. We have already pointed out that there is much scope for headway to be made in the sphere of productivity advance along co-operative lines, and in other areas, too, much could be achieved. The phasing of investment plans, the levelling out of fluctuations in investment in stocks are important potentialities. Investment in stocks is particularly important. This is the most volatile element in final demand. The N.E.D.C. will, however, be devoting its energies not only to the phasing of economic movements but also to the long-term problems of the U.K. economy. At any long-term rate of growth, there are problems of keeping developments in line and avoiding bottlenecks, shortages, and undue fluctuations; averting the need to import steel, for example, by keeping steel-making capacity at the level necessitated by activity in the steel-using industries. The overriding problem of all, however, is the need to step up the rate of growth and deal with such matters as declining competitiveness, the long-term tendency for invisible earnings on our overseas account to decline, etc. Almost certainly the most serious barrier to the achievement of N.E.D.C.'s aims is the matter of incomes policy. The trade union leaders have usually reacted violently against talk of incomes policy because they have been suspicious that this meant simply wages restraint. They have always argued that wages cannot be considered in isolation, apart from other forms of income, particularly profits. This attitude has until now stultified N.E.D.C. operating in this important area of policy, while the National Incomes Commission has never from the start had trade union blessing. Now there are signs of more enlightenment. The Chancellor of the Exchequer, prior to the meeting of N.E.D.C. on 4 December 1963, raised this thorny issue without there being quite the hostile reaction which might have been ex-

pected. There were subsequent signs, both from the trade union and employers' side, of some willingness to compromise. If the N.E.D.C. could develop an incomes policy which included some mechanism for confining wage-rate advances within the limits set by productivity advances this would be the most vital step towards a rational economic policy.

Industrial productivity

So far, although productivity has necessarily been involved in the argument from time to time, there has been concentration on the growth of output. It is now necessary to examine productivity changes from as far back as they can be taken. Productivity is, in fact, a vital matter in considering the growth of an economy. There are, however, formidable difficulties, both conceptual and practical, in measuring anything more sophisticated than the simple concept of labour productivity through some measure such as output per man-hour. Productivity measurement in this sense can be carried back to 1907 — the time of the first Census of Production. During this time, of course, there have been fluctuations during which the degree of capacity utilisation has varied. Hence it is important in measuring productivity change either to correct for varying capacity utilisation or to confine comparisons as far as possible to times of comparable utilisation. The latter has been the approach here, measurement being made, as far as possible, from peak to peak in economic activity. Results are given in Table 3 below.

The two most outstanding features of Table 3 are the marked quickening in pace of productivity advances since the Second World War and the considerable variety of experience in productivity record between different industries. Both of these are to some extent part of the general picture of a notably close association between production change and productivity movement. The rate of output growth, for example, has been higher since the war than ever before it. Also the industries with the most impressive productivity records are the rapid growers; chemicals, motor vehicles, electricity supply, etc. The implications of the observed correlation between rates of output and productivity growth will be discussed below. It is possibly the crucial issue.

There is, however, a multitude of factors which affect productivity levels and changes, by no means all or even most of them quantitatively measurable. It is, then, almost impossible to test the various hypotheses which can be put forward to explain the behaviour observed. In fact, the results will be the combined effect of very

TABLE 3

Annual Average Percentage Rates of Productivity Change in the U.K.
(Output per Operative-hour Basis)

	1907 to 1924	1924 to 1935	1935 to 1949	1949 to 1955	1955 to 1960
Building materials, etc.	1·9	2·1	2·5	2·7	2·4
China and earthenware	2·4	0·3	1·7	1·2	3·2
Glass }	1·7	2·5	3·7	1·4	3·7
Bricks, cement, etc. }		2·2	2·2	3·5	1·1
Chemicals and allied trades	1·3	2·3	2·5	6·1	5·9
Metal manufacture	1·1	1·7	1·2	3·6	2·1
Ferrous metals	1·1	1·5	1·1	3·9	1·9
Blast furnaces }	2·0	1·9	1·6	2·9	–
Smelting and rolling }					
Non-ferrous metals	0·5	2·6	1·6	2·1	1·6
Engineering, shipbuilding and electrical	1·3	1·3	1·0	2·1	2·6
Mechanical engineering }	1·5	1·3	1·2	1·6	2·3
Electrical engineering }		1·1	0·6	2·9	–
Shipbuilding	1·3	–	−0·9	0·3	0·7
Vehicles	5·1	3·7	4·3	4·7	3·7
Motors, cycles, etc.	6·2	5·2	2·6	5·1	6·0
Metal goods not elsewhere specified	2·4	1·7	1·4	1·8	2·4
Precision instruments	0·6	3·3	2·2	1·3	–
Textiles	0·7	2·3	1·9	1·5	2·3
Cotton	0·2	0·9	1·0	1·6	2·6
Wool	1·1	1·4	2·4	0·3	1·0
Leather	2·1	0·7	1·2	−0·6	0·2
Clothing	1·8	1·5	0·3	1·4	4·2
Food, drink and tobacco	1·2	1·0	1·6	0·8	3·2
Food	2·0	2·0	1·7	1·1	3·1
Drink	0·9	−0·2	0·7	1·2	3·7
Tobacco	3·8	1·8	1·8	4·0	3·9
Timber trades	2·4	1·0	0·1	4·7	0·8
Paper and printing	3·2	1·0	2·4	4·0	2·1
Other manufacturing	1·3	3·6	2·0	3·8	3·0
Total manufacturing	2·0	2·0	1·9	3·0	2·9
Coal mining	−0·6	2·6	−0·1	0·7	2·5
Construction	1·7	1·2	−3·5	3·3	2·2
Gas, water and electricity supply	1·9	3·0	3·6	4·5	3·9
Gas supply	0·9	0·4	3·1	1·9	0·8
Electricity supply	4·8	5·9	4·4	5·4	7·6
TOTAL: ALL INDUSTRIES	1·6	2·2	1·3	3·0	2·9

many tendencies and events. The climate of industrial relations, the extent of restrictive practices, the degree of monopoly, the quality of effort input, management quality and outlook, the degree of mechanisation, the average age of plant, plant size, market size, natural resources and materials used and many other variables are involved. These all vary in their effects from industry to industry and from time to time. Many of them have possibly been more favourable to productivity advance since 1946. There has, indeed, been a much greater cost and productivity consciousness since the war in the United Kingdom. The economic position of the country, the vital necessity of balancing our overseas account, of exporting in larger and larger volumes, has necessitated the giving of considerable attention to cost and productivity questions. The setting-up of such bodies as the Anglo-American Productivity Council and the European Productivity Agency, as well as the institution of a National Productivity Year, are indications of the importance with which governments and international economic institutions regard such matters.

We know that labour productivity is vitally influenced by investment levels. The close association observed between productivity change and output growth naturally reinforces this view. Further, the variety of experience exhibited in the productivity table rather points to the importance of such matters as growth and capital investment, technical change, and the tendency towards increasing or decreasing returns which we know to be differential in their influence on different industries. In fact, it is clear at the outset that a good deal of technical change must be fairly general in its effects. The results of much innovation would be expected to spread from sector to sector throughout the economy, even though with time lags of varying duration. There may be barriers and impediments, funds for the associated necessary investment may not always equally be available, but there is no reason why the benefits arising from technical development of a cost-reducing kind should not have rapidly permeated, at any rate, a wide range of industry. This has been true of the use of electric power, motorised transport, mechanical handling and a host of less spectacular productivity-raising innovations. When we explore explanation of the really high rates of productivity advance, however, we come to innovation of the far-reaching type which leads to the establishment and growth of new sectors in the economy such as has happened in the industries deriving from the development of electricity, the internal combustion engine, the aeroplane, or many new chemical products. Technical change of this kind is highly differential in its impact. Its connection with productivity change is, however, indirect. The position is that this type of technical change and innovation provides the initial stimulus, basis, and scope for output expansion, and rapid growth of output usually, though not always, means rapidly rising productivity. Thus, for example, the discovery and development of electricity, of the internal combustion engine, provided scope for completely new sectors in the economy and, indeed, for vast changes in the whole of our industrial system. The rapidly rising productivity in electricity supply and in motor vehicle production, however, would not have arisen from technical change alone. Other factors, both on the demand and supply sides, were necessary. Technical change provides the initial stimulus and opportunity for growth. The connection with productivity change is no more direct than that. The figures in the table, indeed, suggest that technical change is not enough; it must be associated with other factors, to cause rapid productivity change. Logically it seems reasonable to expect that without expansion and rapid output growth the result of technical change and innovation is liable to be marginal and productivity for the industry is not likely rapidly to increase. Old equipment cannot be replaced overnight and the average age of plant will remain high. Without the heavy capital investment associated with expansion the gap between the best and the average technique is certain to remain wide. But this cannot be all. The experience in engineering shows most strikingly that technical change, even together with output expansion, is still insufficient to guarantee rapid productivity increase. This sector has experienced much technical innovation and considerable growth in output yet the productivity advance has been relatively modest. So it is certainly necessary to look beyond technical change and probably beyond output growth as well.

A very clear feature of the figures in Table 3 is the tendency for productivity movements to be highly correlated with output changes. This is true as between industries. It is also true, within industries and industry groups, between different periods. There are few cases of productivity rising rapidly with output static, even though the competitive pressures on declining industries might have been expected to stimulate search for any methods of reducing costs. The most outstanding instance of an impressive productivity advance in an industry where output is static, or even declining, is the recent record of the coal-mining industry. An enlightened policy of mechanisation and concentration on the most productive mines and seams has produced there, under Lord Robens's leadership, as impressive a productivity record as for any sector. Over the last three years productivity at the face in coal mining has been rising at the astonishing rate of 7·2 per cent per annum. Another declining industry where considerable concentration has been achieved and where there have been far-reaching technical developments, such as automatic looms, is in the cotton industry. The recent productivity record here too, while nothing like so impressive as in coal mining, is an exception to the generalisation of only modest productivity rise with static or declining output. It is, of course, not surprising that a rapidly growing industry such as motor vehicles or electricity supply generally experiences a high rate of productivity advance. In such an industry there will be heavy investment, the latest techniques and equipment will be characteristic of a much larger proportion of the industry than will be true of a stagnant or declining trade. The range from average to best current technique will be relatively small. The average age of plant and equipment will be comparatively low. There should be a spirit of enterprise and initiative, and ability easily to recruit the better type of trained personnel. It is the continuous and rapid growth of the American economy over a long period which has probably been one of the most important factors behind the rate of productivity advance there. Another is the fact that having to attract labour into industry by high wage-rates, the degree of mechanisation and level of capital investment have always been higher in the United States than in the United Kingdom.

It is, then, not surprising that rapid growth of output means, usually, high productivity rate advance. The high rate of productivity rise which tends to be associated with expansion itself makes an important contribution to the rate of economic growth. As productivity advances, costs fall relatively, and demand is stimulated. This has certainly been a significant factor, for example, in the advance of the electricity supply industry and in motor vehicles. The continuous relative fall in the price of electricity as the industry has expanded has strongly stimulated the widespread use of electricity in industry and in the home. With motor vehicles it is only necessary to estimate what the price of a car would be if the industry had not been able to adopt mass production methods on a large scale and had not been in a position to benefit from the realisation of increasing returns to scale, in order to appreciate the importance of this factor.

Indeed a characteristic which probably more than any other on the technical side distinguishes industries capable of enjoying rapid growth of labour productivity is the degree to which the production processes operate under conditions of increasing returns to scale of output. When demand for the products of an industry is growing, if the technical structure is such that increasing returns are realised with expansion of the scale of output, then the figures of labour productivity and, indeed, of capital productivity, too, will show rapid advance. This has certainly been true of electricity supply, motor vehicles, paper, and, more recently, chemicals. Benefits from increasing returns tendencies can only arise when demand is expanding, but all industries do not enjoy these advantages even when growth is occurring. The engineering group of industries and the metal trades have increased very considerably in output, but do not possess the same scope for increasing returns as do motor vehicles and electricity supply. Nor, possibly, has there been quite the same degree of technical advance. The machine-tool industry in the United Kingdom has, for example, been strongly criticised for its rather slow pace of technical progress. The argument concerning returns to scale can be illustrated, in particular, by reference to electrical engineering. The rate of growth of output in electrical engineering has been surpassed only by motor vehicles and electricity supply, yet the productivity rise in electrical engineering has consistently been below the average for all industry. This must be associated with the fact that in the construction of heavy electrical machinery, generating plant, transformers, and the like which form the predominant part of the industry, the nature of the productive processes is such that scope, both for factor substitution and for increasing returns, is limited. In heavy electrical engineering production the process is that of building a relatively limited number of large pieces of equipment. Mass production in the normal sense is just not feasible. This is likely to continue to be the case because the trend in demand is for fewer and fewer but larger and larger (in the sense of power output though not in physical dimensions) machines. Very often these large pieces of engineering equipment are built to individual specifications with regard to physical size, power output, etc. The limitation in scope for increasing returns is imposed by limitations on the degree to which production processes can be subdivided and is, to some extent, a function of demand. If we had to produce diesel locomotives in the same numbers as motor-cars no doubt we should have increasing returns there as well.

It should be mentioned here, too, to be quite fair, that output indices are perhaps at their most vulnerable in engineering. It is very difficult to be certain that substantial improvements in quality do not fail to be reflected in measures of output change. A complicated piece of electrical generating equipment or switchgear, for example, may be entered in output returns under the same description as in years past but may, in fact, have incorporated many more man-hours of effort input. Nevertheless there is clearly a big difference in the technical nature of the production process in large parts of engineering and, say, in motor vehicles. Of course, in electrical engineering (the same will not be true of mechanical engineering to anything like the same extent) there are considerable sections of the industry producing small-scale electrical goods, domestic appliances, radio, television, and the like, in which the benefits of mass-production methods have been enjoyed. This would explain the rather better productivity record in electrical engineering in more recent years.

A broad generalisation seems to be, then, that productivity rises most rapidly where and when output is expanding and, consequently, investment is high and there is scope for increasing returns to scale of output. Rapid expansion of output has usually followed a significant break-through in technical development in some new area. We see, therefore, the importance of factors on both the demand and supply sides. The final figures of output for an industry over a period are, in fact, the final resultant effect of both dynamic demand and supply influences. For output and productivity to grow rapidly it is necessary not only that technical supply factors are favourable but also that there is buoyant demand for the product. What has happened in the twentieth century is that technical innovation provided the initial impetus, or at any rate, the potentiality for growth. Demand for the new products, the motor car, electricity, the radio, chemicals, etc. expanded, at first, slowly. Then, when there was appreciation of the benefits these new developments were bringing and the needs they were satisfying plus the fact that, most important, real costs were reduced through realisation of increasing returns to scale of output, demand and productivity rapidly increased. For rapidly growing output and productivity for an industry we must have buoyant demand *and* increasing returns to scale of output.

Appendix

TABLE 1

Index-numbers of Industrial Production:

Manufacturing

Year	Total All industries	Total Manufacturing industry	Building materials	Chemicals	Metal manufacture			Engineering, shipbuilding and electrical goods				Vehicles	Precision instruments etc.
					Total	Ferrous	Non-ferrous	Total	Mech. eng.	Elec. eng.	Ship-bldg.		
1900	73·9	71·3	–	60·6	76·1	77·7	66·8	79·5	87	28·7	112·2	28·2	–
1901	73·6	71·2	–	60·3	72·7	73·2	67·8	81·8	85	30·3	130·1	28·3	–
1902	76·4	73·0	–	61·6	78·8	79·4	75·0	79·6	87	31·8	108·3	28·4	–
1903	76·4	72·9	–	67·4	79·3	80·9	69·5	79·2	87	34·0	102·9	30·8	–
1904	75·7	73·0	–	70·7	81·6	81·9	78·9	78·8	88	35·4	96·2	30·9	–
1905	78·3	77·2	–	72·1	87·3	91·0	67·2	90·4	97	38·4	128·0	32·2	–
1906	80·2	78·6	–	74·0	88·6	92·4	67·8	90·7	93	41·9	139·6	32·5	–
1907	81·6	79·9	80·7	79·0	87·9	91·3	69·1	84·3	85	44·3	126·9	35·1	83·9
1908	77·1	75·3	–	79·0	84·3	84·9	79·8	72·9	82	43·7	71·0	31·1	–
1909	78·9	77·6	–	78·2	88·7	92·7	66·8	78·1	87	45·5	82·1	29·9	–
1910	80·6	80·1	–	81·6	94·9	99·9	81·1	84·2	92	51·4	93·1	30·6	–
1911	83·0	83·9	–	84·0	94·3	96·2	83·4	94·0	90	55·7	152·4	33·9	–
1912	84·2	86·3	77·4	84·8	91·4	94·1	76·4	89·9	85	59·7	141·3	36·0	–
1913	90·5	92·2	–	90·0	101·3	105·5	78·3	104·2	103	64·6	156·5	43·3	–
1914	84·8	85·9	–	86·6	94·7	94·7	93·9	95·3	92	68·1	138·5	–	–
1915	86·4	90·4	–	88·3	95·9	92·3	114·0	94·4	99	74·8	100·4	–	–
1916	81·8	84·6	–	91·7	93·1	91·7	99·8	101·4	100	80·0	132·2	–	–
1917	76·4	78·4	–	92·3	96·1	90·1	126·3	110·9	112	85·7	139·2	–	–
1918	73·8	76·1	–	93·3	98·0	92·6	125·9	118·5	115	91·4	166·8	–	–
1919	81·3	85·0	–	94·1	85·0	87·5	72·1	100·3	92	94·4	148·2	42·9	–
1920	90·3	93·6	87·2	101·3	93·5	97·1	74·5	104·9	95·4	94·0	154·9	70·7	98·2
1921	73·5	72·8	84·4	72·9	45·5	45·4	45·6	78·2	62·7	80·4	125·0	62·7	89·0
1922	85·0	84·8	73·3	86·3	65·6	67·1	57·4	73·4	76·2	63·2	88·2	71·5	92·6
1923	90·0	90·8	83·8	94·1	92·6	95·2	73·4	87·3	95·6	83·0	73·6	85·9	99·3
1924	100·0	100·0	100·0	100·0	100·0	100·0	100·0	100·0	100·0	100·0	100·0	100·0	100·0
1925	103·9	103·1	113·7	96·6	92·7	89·4	111·2	108·1	114·0	113·2	70·1	107·6	104·6
1926	98·4	99·8	116·1	89·0	64·2	57·0	103·7	98·2	99·7	103·6	52·7	113·1	103·5
1927	113·4	110·4	128·7	101·9	108·5	106·7	118·2	110·4	110·9	112·7	105·7	125·1	117·1
1928	110·2	110·8	118·9	106·8	101·3	96·0	129·8	111·4	116·9	117·5	93·3	123·7	123·7
1929	115·8	114·5	127·9	112·2	106·4	104·3	117·8	115·9	120·9	120·2	109·9	133·4	129·0
1930	110·8	109·6	122·1	106·6	95·9	93·0	111·6	107·9	107·2	121·6	95·8	127·8	123·2
1931	103·7	102·2	114·9	102·3	74·6	70·5	97·5	87·6	87·6	116·9	36·2	109·3	110·9
1932	103·2	102·7	110·7	109·1	76·4	74·7	85·8	79·5	77·4	126·1	11·3	106·4	110·9
1933	110·1	109·4	126·2	114·2	89·5	86·9	103·4	80·1	79·0	127·0	13·9	118·8	117·1
1934	121·1	120·4	146·6	123·3	110·0	106·3	129·9	99·5	92·7	155·9	48·2	139·8	123·9
1935	130·3	131·3	157·8	133·9	121·4	116·4	148·7	117·2	110·4	181·0	59·1	166·6	136·0
1936	142·0	143·5	171·7	139·6	136·1	130·9	164·3	132·9	119·8	202·9	91·0	199·4	145·1
1937	150·5	152·2	179·7	148·7	152·9	146·9	185·8	146·0	128·0	219·0	117·8	221·2	154·3
1938	146·4	147·8	168·5	141·0	127·0	118·3	174·6	145·2	130·2	215·5	96·4	224·7	158·3
1946	149·4	153·6	168·7	209·8	157·5	138·6	264·7	179·2	–	–	–	244·9	175·2
1947	158·7	164·3	194·3	213·3	168·6	145·0	304·2	202·9	–	–	–	255·8	203·9
1948	171·7	178·4	213·0	232·9	187·1	167·4	297·7	220·1	–	–	–	279·9	208·1
1949	182·5	190·5	223·2	253·6	191·0	174·8	279·8	233·7	–	–	–	309·8	221·6
1950	195·1	206·6	237·3	289·3	201·5	182·8	304·5	256·0	–	–	–	339·2	229·7
1951	201·2	215·2	247·9	313·9	212·7	189·2	345·3	279·7	–	–	–	348·2	234·9
1952	195·9	206·2	245·8	310·5	217·8	195·2	344·1	279·3	–	–	–	347·6	208·3
1953	207·9	219·8	256·0	356·1	213·5	198·2	295·3	284·4	–	–	–	385·4	225·4
1954	222·5	237·6	263·7	392·4	230·1	208·6	349·2	308·4	–	–	–	434·7	256·6
1955	234·5	253·1	274·1	415·7	249·2	224·1	388·8	340·5	–	–	–	480·9	262·8
1956	234·4	249·9	271·1	431·1	251·1	229·5	369·4	331·5	–	–	–	449·0	249·3
1957	237·6	254·4	264·3	448·1	255·2	235·5	361·4	342·9	–	–	–	461·8	254·5

United Kingdom, 1900–57 (1924 = 100)

Industry

Metal goods n.e.s.	Textiles	Leather	Clothing	Food, drink and tobacco				Timber	Paper and printing	Other manufactures	Mining and quarrying	Building and contracting	Gas, water and electricity supply
				Total	Food	Drink	Tobacco						
–	88·7	96·6	104·7	76·0	47·7	128·3	52·5	89·1	49·0	–	86·0	108·0	39·1
–	91·0	92·3	104·2	76·0	48·8	126·9	51·2	87·1	46·1	–	83·4	108·5	41·6
–	92·0	84·2	106·1	78·2	52·8	126·6	52·9	94·2	50·6	–	86·7	119·0	43·7
–	86·4	76·2	105·9	79·7	56·5	124·8	54·1	90·3	52·0	–	87·8	115·4	46·1
–	88·7	76·9	102·1	80·3	59·1	121·9	55·3	82·7	53·6	–	88·8	105·7	44·3
–	99·1	71·5	104·1	80·3	60·2	120·0	56·4	87·6	54·1	–	90·2	95·2	48·3
–	101·8	77·5	107·0	81·2	61·3	120·7	57·2	91·0	55·3	–	95·4	94·1	51·6
84·1	108·5	79·8	108·3	82·9	63·9	120·7	59·7	84·4	60·7	67·3	100·9	87·4	55·2
–	96·5	84·2	105·5	81·5	62·4	118·4	61·1	84·9	63·7	–	98·2	75·0	57·1
–	102·4	82·6	104·9	82·4	65·1	117·2	60·4	84·9	62·8	–	98·8	74·9	58·5
–	99·0	91·1	109·3	85·8	70·3	118·0	63·1	81·6	68·5	–	98·8	70·8	60·1
–	111·0	82·5	111·5	88·6	71·7	122·7	66·3	78·2	64·9	–	101·2	59·9	63·6
–	119·2	93·0	114·3	92·0	77·0	123·9	67·6	79·1	71·4	–	96·6	57·9	67·1
–	121·7	89·3	116·8	94·1	78·4	127·2	69·9	85·9	74·6	–	106·3	64·0	70·6
–	102·6	100·5	114·6	92·5	78·0	121·7	74·4	84·8	75·5	–	98·7	58·0	75·6
–	137·7	129·7	105·3	91·4	80·8	112·0	80·2	83·6	70·5	–	93·5	45·0	77·3
–	122·9	101·9	92·5	89·7	82·7	105·2	77·1	60·4	49·9	–	93·8	35·2	80·6
–	110·0	121·5	82·9	76·2	75·9	75·7	79·6	35·3	30·7	–	91·1	24·5	85·3
–	94·4	130·5	70·9	72·7	69·7	74·5	81·7	41·8	33·4	–	84·3	20·8	89·3
–	122·9	121·4	78·7	91·7	78·2	106·2	110·2	57·2	67·7	–	84·9	29·8	92·8
115·1	107·8	75·7	80·4	101·2	89·3	117·3	106·9	71·9	89·9	–	86·1	66·2	90·5
71·4	71·6	63·5	86·0	93·4	85·7	103·5	97·9	66·8	53·3	–	61·7	91·7	82·8
81·3	102·8	79·7	94·9	93·3	93·2	92·1	97·2	79·6	84·1	–	91·7	75·9	84·9
95·4	86·7	91·6	94·2	97·5	97·4	97·7	97·4	91·1	94·5	–	102·1	63·1	92·0
100·0	100·0	100·0	100·0	100·0	100·0	100·0	100·0	100·0	100·0	100·0	100·0	100·0	100·0
106·3	99·4	99·0	103·3	102·7	103·5	100·8	105·0	107·2	102·2	–	92·2	127·7	105·3
107·9	95·6	95·6	104·7	103·2	106·2	97·1	108·7	112·3	105·8	–	51·1	148·5	109·5
113·8	101·0	104·0	111·9	106·7	110·4	99·3	113·6	125·4	110·6	–	95·9	163·4	117·3
117·2	95·0	107·3	112·9	109·8	115·0	98·7	121·8	129·6	110·5	–	91·2	131·6	123·6
124·1	96·0	94·3	114·1	110·7	117·9	99·9	130·2	142·0	116·7	–	99·1	142·2	131·0
119·3	83·9	103·4	113·7	113·8	120·5	98·5	131·8	143·5	117·4	129·2	94·2	131·3	133·4
107·4	88·4	102·3	112·7	110·7	123·3	89·2	123·0	132·5	116·8	–	84·9	124·1	136·9
109·0	95·8	103·1	112·8	110·5	131·2	79·1	118·7	120·9	122·2	–	80·6	117·0	140·4
113·9	104·1	107·2	119·3	114·1	133·3	84·4	123·8	138·5	125·4	150·5	80·7	136·0	148·7
135·7	107·3	108·2	120·8	121·0	140·1	91·5	130·1	148·3	129·5	165·7	86·6	153·4	159·8
150·1	111·6	117·2	123·8	129·3	151·1	96·7	136·9	163·4	132·5	177·3	87·5	157·0	174·4
167·2	121·7	127·6	128·6	135·0	157·2	101·2	144·4	180·0	139·5	–	90·5	171·9	192·5
182·5	122·5	125·9	131·0	142·7	163·7	109·3	155·7	184·7	142·9	200·3	95·4	179·2	208·7
180·5	111·3	110·0	129·5	146·7	168·3	112·7	159·3	178·7	141·7	–	90·7	171·8	216·3
208·9	86·5	102·1	85·2	162·8	182·8	124·2	216·2	133·0	132·9	208·7	70·6	131·9	289·8
222·6	93·5	116·2	90·9	162·1	183·5	125·1	194·1	126·0	141·5	256·5	72·7	137·6	300·6
232·1	108·3	166·5	95·3	168·9	196·3	126·9	184·5	139·7	147·7	306·4	76·9	149·9	319·5
232·8	117·3	117·5	103·9	175·5	207·7	124·4	182·7	157·2	170·3	314·7	79·4	156·9	341·2
242·5	128·2	119·8	109·9	180·7	219·9	122·1	184·7	169·9	196·7	357·9	80·1	157·1	371·6
262·5	128·4	113·0	105·8	177·5	213·0	118·4	191·0	178·1	207·2	376·3	82·9	150·9	395·5
257·4	104·2	110·0	108·9	182·4	223·0	119·4	188·4	160·8	174·9	341·0	83·8	155·4	407·4
239·5	123·4	110·3	108·9	192·5	241·6	118·8	193·5	173·6	196·3	371·4	83·5	166·7	427·8
257·9	127·1	112·1	108·8	196·3	246·6	121·1	201·1	203·0	229·1	426·8	84·4	173·0	462·6
289·2	125·0	111·8	112·7	198·3	248·2	131·0	204·1	204·8	249·3	469·1	83·4	174·3	488·2
285·5	124·3	106·1	114·9	204·0	251·3	134·0	204·1	196·0	246·4	453·8	84·0	184·5	511·5
269·9	123·9	106·8	114·1	206·9	251·3	142·4	209·8	200·3	250·4	486·6	84·1	184·5	519·5

3 Economic Growth in Britain in the Inter-War Years: A Reassessment*

by DEREK H. ALDCROFT

THE view is still firmly held that the inter-war years were depressed and rather wasted years as far as Britain's economy was concerned. This is certainly the layman's impression of the period and many scholars have continued to pass unfavourable judgement on these years.[1] In many respects this interpretation is not altogether surprising since this period was notable for its high unemployment and stagnating exports. Throughout the period one million men or more were out of work, while even in the best years the volume of exports was no more than 80 per cent of the 1913 level. Furthermore, a number of basic industries, such as cotton, coal and ship-building, were seriously depressed or in decline. But it is probable that the depressed sectors have attracted too much attention in the past and this has resulted in a failure to recognise the important gains achieved in these years. There is a good deal of truth in the remark made by G. C. Allen some years ago, to the effect that it was the persistence of heavy unemployment that gave the inter-war years such a bad name.[2] Recent work on the growth and structure of the British economy suggests, however, that Britain's economic performance was by no means as black as often painted and that a revision of the traditional view is required. Not only does it appear that the growth of the British economy was better than before 1914, but also that the performance compared quite favourably with other industrial countries. Furthermore, important structural and technical changes were taking place in industry which were of vital significance for the long-term growth of the economy. In the following discussion we will attempt to show that there was a brighter side to the British economy in these crucial years.

There are two main ways of assessing an economy's economic

---

* First published 1967.

[1] For a review of these see D. H. Aldcroft, 'Economic Progress in Britain in the 1920s', *Scottish Journal of Political Economy*, XIII (1966). Reprinted in D. H. Aldcroft and H. W. Richardson, *The British Economy 1870–1939* (1969).

[2] G. C. Allen, 'Economic Progress, Retrospect and Prospect', *Economic Journal*, LX (1950) 464.

potential in any particular period; it can be compared with the achievements of other similar countries over the same time period or comparison can be made with the past, and if possible future, performance of the particular country in question. Recent statistical material gathered for a number of countries including Britain make it possible to adopt both these methods for the inter-war years. For the first part of our inquiry we have computed rates of growth of total output and industrial production for twelve countries on the basis of statistical indices assembled by Maddison, Lomax and O.E.E.C.[1] The choice of base year on which to calculate the growth rates was not as difficult as might be imagined. In part the decision was made for us since Maddison's indices of output and productivity (Gross Domestic Product) are only available for key years, namely 1913, 1929 and 1938, which meant that it was impossible to calculate growth rates for the 1920s alone. But the absence of data for the early 1920s is no great hardship, since the selection of a suitable base year for all countries would have been difficult on account of the differences in speed with which each country recovered from the effects of the war. On the other hand, 1913 and 1929 were fairly normal years (in so far as any year can be classed as normal) and it seemed most appropriate to judge British performance on the basis of pre-war and pre-depression levels of output. The availability of annual data for industrial production made possible a more detailed breakdown. Although 1920 was used as an additional base year, there is no doubt that it is unsuitable for the purposes of inter-country comparisons. Many countries were only just beginning to recover from the war and their levels of industrial production were quite low, so that the use of 1920 as a base year would tend to inflate the growth rates of those countries artificially. By 1924, levels of output in most countries had returned to pre-war dimensions and so it seemed an appropriate year for comparison. The terminal date was fixed at 1937 rather than 1938 as with total output, since the impact of the temporary recession of 1937–8 varied considerably from country to country and it would have been unfair to introduce an unnecessary element of bias into the calculations.

Tables 1–4 present the results of the calculations for twelve countries, the first three of which refer to Gross Domestic Product while the fourth covers industrial production for a rather wider

---

[1] A. Maddison, *Economic Growth in the West* (1964); K. S. Lomax, 'Production and Productivity Movements in the United Kingdom since 1900', *Journal of the Royal Statistical Society*, A122 (1959) and O.E.E.C., *Industrial Statistics, 1900–1959* (1960).

range of countries. Taking the period as a whole (1913–38) it can be seen that Britain's rate of growth of total product and output per man-year or man-hour was higher than the unweighted average of the twelve countries including Britain. The difference in favour of Britain was most noticeable for output per man, and in fact only two countries, namely Norway and Switzerland, experienced a rate of productivity growth higher than this country. A more detailed breakdown into two separate periods, 1913–29 and 1929–38, produces some interesting results. In the 1920s total output grew more slowly in Britain than elsewhere, though in terms of productivity (output per man or man-hour) the British performance was no worse than the general average. The position was quite different in the following decade; most countries then experienced sluggish growth rates apart from Britain and one or two other countries. In fact, between 1929 and 1938 Britain was near the top of the growth league table and in terms of output per man only two countries, Germany and Sweden, recorded higher rates of growth than Great Britain. Moreover, the inter-war period was the only time in which British growth rates were above the general average. As can be seen from Tables 1–3, in the pre-1914 period and the years after the Second World War (1950–60) Britain's performance compared unfavourably with the general average of the group of countries in question.

The position as regards industrial production is less clear cut, but even here the comparison is not unfavourable to Britain. Over the period 1913–37 her rate of growth of industrial production was above the average for all O.E.E.C. countries (2·0 as against 1·6), though a number of members achieved growth rates well above the British average. If 1920 is used as a base year the British performance appears very poor indeed in relation to other countries. In fact in the years 1920–9 the rate of growth was less than half that of the combined average. This result is not, however, altogether surprising since British industrial production had attained the pre-war level very rapidly (in fact by 1920) whereas in the European countries as a whole production was nearly one-third below the 1913 level. Hence growth rates worked out with 1920 as a base would tend to favour those countries whose recovery from the war was slow. By 1924 most of the O.E.E.C. members had attained their pre-war position and this year provides a more satisfactory base from which to operate. Over the period 1924–37 industrial production in Britain grew at a rate similar to the general average. During the 1930s (1929–37) the tide ran strongly in Britain's favour; with a growth rate of 3·4 per cent she was one of the best

TABLE 1

Growth rates of Total Output

(*percentages per annum*)

	1870–1913	1913–38	1913–29	1929–38	1950–60	1870–1938
Belgium	2·7	0·8	1·6	−0·5	2·9	2·0
Denmark	3·2	1·9	1·8	2·1	3·3	2·8
France	1·6	0·3	1·6	−2·2	4·4	1·1
Germany (F.R.)	2·9*	1·6	0·3	3·9	7·6	2·4
Italy	1·4	1·7	1·8	1·6	5·9	1·5
Netherlands	2·2†	2·1	3·3	0·1	4·9	2·2§
Norway	2·2*	2·9	2·8	2·9	3·5	2·3
Sweden	3·0	1·7	1·3	2·6	3·3	2·5
Switzerland	2·4‡	2·0	2·8	0·6	5·1	2·2‖
U.K.	2·2*	1·9	1·6	2·3	2·6	2·1
Canada	3·8	1·4	2·4	−0·2	3·9	2·9
United States	4·3*	2·0	3·1	0·0	3·2	3·5
Unweighted average	2·7	1·6	2·0	1·1	4·2	2·3

* 1871–1913.   † 1900–13.   ‡ 1890–1913.   § 1900–38.   ‖ 1890–1938.

Source: Based on A. Maddison, *Economic Growth in the West* (1964) pp. 201–2.

TABLE 2

Growth rates of Output per Man-hour

(*Percentages per annum*)

	1870–1913	1913–38	1913–29	1929–38	1950–60	1870–1938
Belgium	2·0	1·5	2·0	0·6	2·5	1·8
Denmark	2·6	1·3	1·7	0·4	2·9	2·1
France	1·8	2·3	2·8	1·6	3·9	2·0
Germany (F.R.)	2·1*	1·3	0·8	2·1	6·0	1·7
Italy	1·2	2·6	2·3	3·2	4·1	1·7
Netherlands	1·1†	1·5	2·6	−0·3	3·7	1·4§
Norway	1·8*	2·7	3·0	2·2	3·9	2·1
Sweden	2·7	1·6	0·9	3·0	3·5	2·3
Switzerland	1·6‡	2·4	3·2	1·1	4·2	2·1
U.K.	1·5	2·1	2·1	2·1	2·0	1·7
Canada	2·1	0·8	1·3	0·0	2·5	1·6
United States	2·4*	3·0	2·8	3·3	2·4	2·6
Average	1·9	1·9	2·1	1·6	3·5	1·9

* 1871–1913.   † 1900–13.   ‡ 1890–1913.   § 1900–38.

Source: Based on Maddison, *Economic Growth in the West*, p. 232.

TABLE 3

Growth rates of Output per Man

(Percentages per annum)

	1870–1913	1913–38	1913–29	1929–38	1950–60	1870–1938
Belgium	1·6	0·9	1·1	0·5	2·5	1·3
Denmark	2·1	0·7	0·9	0·2	2·3	1·6
France	1·4	0·9	2·0	−0·7	4·0	1·2
Germany (F.R.)	1·6*	0·8	−0·2	2·7	5·3	1·3
Italy	0·8	1·5	1·5	1·6	4·1	1·1
Netherlands	0·7	0·9	1·6	−0·4	3·7	0·8
Norway	1·4*	1·9	2·2	1·4	3·2	1·6
Sweden	2·2	0·9	0·1	2·5	2·7	1·8
Switzerland	1·1	1·8	2·4	0·7	3·8	1·5
U.K.	1·1*	1·5	1·3	1·6	1·9	1·2
Canada	1·6	0·1	0·7	−0·8	2·0	1·1
United States	1·9	1·2	1·5	0·8	2·1	1·7
Average	1·5	1·1	1·3	0·8	3·1	1·4

* 1871–1913.

Source: Based on Maddison, *Economic Growth in the West*, p. 231.

TABLE 4

Growth rates of Industrial Production (excluding building)
for U.K. and O.E.E.C. countries

	U.K.	All O.E.E.C. countries	U.S.	Canada	Norway	Belgium	Sweden	Denmark	Germany	France	Italy
1901–13	2·3	3·9	4·9	n.a.	4·4	3·3	n.a.	n.a.	4·7	4·2	5·2
1913–37	2·0	1·6	2·9	n.a.	2·3	1·5	3·5	3·9	1·2	0·8	2·4
1913–29	1·3	1·4	4·2	n.a.	1·9	2·1	2·4	3·9	0·9	2·0	2·8
1920–37	2·8	3·7	2·3	4·2	2·8	3·7	5·2	3·6	5·4	3·4	4·0
1924–37	3·0	3·1	2·7	4·7	3·4	2·3	5·9	3·5	5·3	0·9	2·8
1920–9	2·3	5·1	4·0	6·5	2·4	6·6	5·0	3·2	7·6	7·9	6·0
1929–37	3·4	2·2	0·4	1·6	3·3	0·5	5·4	4·0	3·0	−2·8	1·7
1950–9	2·7*	5·7	3·5	4·1	4·2	3·4	2·8	3·0	9·2	6·3	8·4

*Includes building.

Source: Based on K. S. Lomax, 'Production and Productivity Movements in the United Kingdom since 1900', *Journal of the Royal Statistical Society*, A122 (1959) 196, and O.E.E.C., *Industrial Statistics, 1900–1959* (1960) p. 9.

industrial performers, being surpassed only by Denmark and Sweden Comparing Britain's performance with that of other countries over different time-spans we find again, as with output, that the inter-war years and especially the 1930s were more favourable to this country than periods either before or after. For example, the combined growth rates of the O.E.E.C. members exceeded those of Britain by a large margin in the years 1901–13 and again in 1950–9.

The alternative way of assessing the potential of the British economy is to judge it in terms of its performance over time. Here again the inter-war years show up remarkably well, particularly in relation to past trends. The annual rate of growth of domestic product per man or man-hour between 1913 and 1937 was considerably higher than before 1913 and compares favourably with the long-term trend (see Table 5). At first sight the rate of industrial production growth would appear to be in accordance with the long-term trend before 1914. If, however, the war years are excluded from the calculation, the inter-war years register a sharp break with past trends. During the period 1920–37 industrial production increased by 3·1 per cent per annum and in the 1930s by 3·3 per cent as against 2·1 per cent in 1870–1913. Moreover, if pre-1914 estimates are taken from the late 1870s, when the retardation in industrial growth really began to set in, the long-term growth trend is 1·6 to 1·7 per cent per annum which is considerably below the rates recorded for any of the inter-war periods.

But perhaps the most remarkable break in trend occurred in industrial productivity. As Table 5 shows, the pace of productivity growth accelerated enormously in the inter-war years, especially in the 1920s, and contrasts markedly with the very slow progress made between 1880 and 1914. It is quite probable that the data on which these calculations are based tends to exaggerate the break in trend of productivity growth. The pre-1914 estimates of productivity are probably slightly on the low side since they are based on the Hoffmann production index, the precise accuracy of which is open to question on the grounds of weighting and coverage.[1] Moreover, these estimates, unlike the post-war ones, have not been corrected for unemployment, though a revision to take account of this factor would not make a great deal of difference to the long-term trend of productivity growth.[2] On the other hand the estimates

[1] The Hoffmann industrial production index, on which the pre-1914 productivity rates are based, has been criticised by a number of scholars for its inaccuracy. In fact, however, recent reworking of the data suggests that the margin of error is quite small. The biggest discrepancies lie in the building sector (which we have excluded from our calculations) and in the later part of the period, that is from 1890 onwards, when insufficient account was taken of the newer industries. Adjustments to take account of this factor would tend therefore to raise slightly the productivity rates for later years, but it would not affect to any great extent the long-term trend of decelerating growth. Comparison of the Hoffmann index and the new Lomax index of industrial production suggests that the differences are quite small. Between 1900 and 1913, for example, the Hoffmann index produces an annual rate of growth of 2·0 per cent per annum as against 2·1 per cent on the basis of the Lomax index (excluding building).

[2] See D. J. Coppock, 'The Climacteric of the 1890s: A Critical Note', *Manchester School*, XXIV (1956) 7, 8 and 12.

for the post-war period are more comprehensive, since they are based on the Lomax index and allowance has been made for unemployment. The rate of productivity growth for the 1920s may be rather on the high side because of the inclusion of the immediate post-war years when productivity levels were fairly low. But the trend rate of growth is still 2·7 per cent for the years 1922 to 1930, and 2·2 per cent 1924–35. Despite these reservations,

TABLE 5

Rates of Growth of Production and Productivity
in the U.K. 1870–1960

	Rate of growth of industrial production (including building)	Rate of growth of industrial productivity per man-year	Rate of growth of total output per man-hour	Rate of growth of output per man
1870–80	2·3	1·2	0·9	0·4
1880–90	1·6	0·5	3·8	3·3
1890–1900	2·8	0·2	1·3	0·8
1900–13	1·6	0·2	0·6	0·2
1870–1913	2·1	0·6	1·5	1·1
1913–37	2·1		2·1*	1·5*
1920–37	3·1	3·0		
1920–9	2·8	3·8	2·1†	1·3†
1929–37	3·3	2·2	2·1‡	1·6‡
1950–60	3·0	2·2	2·0	1·9

* 1913–38.   † 1913–29.   ‡ 1929–38.

Source: Based on E. H. Phelps Brown and S. J. Handfield-Jones, 'The Climacteric of the 1890s: A Study of the Expanding Economy', *Oxford Economic Papers*, IV (1952) 294–5; London and Cambridge Economic Service, *Key Statistics of the British Economy, 1900–1962*, p. 9; K. S. Lomax, 'Growth and Productivity in the United Kingdom', *Productivity Measurement Review*, XXXVIII (1964) 6 and Maddison *Economic Growth in the West*.

therefore, it would still be safe to say that productivity growth was substantially higher than before 1914 and compares favourably with the trend after the Second World War. Even on the most generous estimation the rate of productivity growth was no more than 0·5 to 0·6 per cent per annum in the three or four decades before 1914 and rarely rose (even in the short term) above 1·0 per cent per annum, whereas during the inter-war years it rarely fell below 2·0 per cent and the average for the period as a whole was around 3·0 per cent (see Table 5).

On the basis of the statistical evidence now available it would appear that Britain's economic growth performance in the inter-war years was much more impressive than is often imagined. In comparison with other countries Britain did not do at all badly, especially in the 1930s when she was near the top of the growth league table, while on the basis of past performance the showing was very satisfactory indeed. The evidence does in fact suggest that there was a sharp break with past growth trends in the 1920s and 1930s. The acceleration is most noticeable in productivity, though most indices of economic growth except exports show a distinct shift upwards in comparison with earlier periods. Real incomes and wages also rose fairly steadily throughout this period in contrast to their rather sluggish movement in the decade or so before the war.[1] If anything, therefore, there is every indication that the inter-war years saw a return to the growth rates which characterised the early and middle decades of the nineteenth century. In this respect, then, these years can be regarded as the beginning of a new period of relatively high growth rather than a period of economic decline.

If, as we suggested, the inter-war growth pattern of the U.K. economy was comparatively respectable, some further comment is necessary on the mechanics of growth. Why did the rate of growth improve in this period when the general impression is one of depression and decline? Obviously some important qualitative changes were taking place in the structure of the economy which counteracted the adverse effects of the collapse of the export markets and the decline of the basic industries. Some of these changes — for example, the development of the newer industries — are well known, though their importance and contribution to the growth process is perhaps insufficiently appreciated. Before discussing the nature of the shifts in structure let us first examine the role of the two main determinants of economic growth, investment and technical progress. Few economists would deny the importance of these two factors as growth-producing agents, though controversy remains as to which is the most important.[2]

[1] In the inter-war years real income per head rose by about 1 per cent per annum compared with 0·3 per cent 1900–13 and 0·6 per cent 1895–1913. Real wages rose by slightly less than 1 per cent per annum whereas in the couple of decades before 1913 they were stationary or falling slightly.

[2] The choice of these two factors does not imply that they are the only ones. There are four main factors in a classic production function: land, labour, capital, and a residual or technical progress. In a mature economy land as a production factor is of negligible importance, and following Meade we have therefore ignored it. Labour is more important and we shall introduce this in due course. Some would argue that the number of production factors is greater than four, but in reality this is a confusion between variables which determine the nature of the production factors and those factors themselves. Enterprise is a difficult case and might be included as a fifth, though for the sake of simplicity it has been included in the labour compound.

Until recently, capital was accorded a central role in the growth process, but of late, doubt has been expressed on this score though some economists would still adhere to the former judgement. It is very unlikely, however, that the capital variable provides the major explanation of the improved growth performance of the inter-war years. It is true that gross fixed investment as a proportion of gross national product was greater in the inter-war years. On the other hand much of the increase is attributable to residential construction which was running at a much higher level than in the pre-war period. If the residential sector is excluded on the grounds that its contribution to general growth was fairly small,[1] then the investment proportions for the 1920s and 1930s are only marginally above those of the pre-war decades (see Table 6) apart from the 1880s. What is perhaps most significant is that the rate of investment in the inter-war years was no higher than in the 1870s and the first decade of the twentieth century, whereas the growth performances in each case were markedly different. Furthermore, by international standards, Britain's investment ratio was very modest indeed in the inter-war period.[2]

TABLE 6

Gross Domestic Fixed Capital Formation as a Proportion of
G.N.P. at current prices U.K.

	Total	*Excluding residential construction*
1870–9	8·0	6·3
1880–9	6·1	4·9
1890–9	6·9	5·5
1900–9	8·4	6·9
1920–9	9·0	6·7
1930–8	10·1	6·9

On balance, therefore, the evidence does not suggest that the improvement in growth rates can be attributed simply to a marked shift upwards in the investment ratio during the period in question. No doubt the growth of the economy would have been better still had the rate of investment been appreciably higher, but that is a different matter altogether and not one we are particularly con-

[1] This must not be taken as implying that the building or construction industries were unimportant in the growth process. In fact later on we shall argue that building was an important item in the new growth sector. However, capital formation in residential construction does not provide the economy with wealth-producing assets and therefore must be excluded from calculations relating to the proportions of growth-producing capital.

[2] See Maddison, *Economic Growth in the West*, pp. 239–40.

cerned with here. This conclusion is confirmed by recent work done
by Matthews. He attempted to allocate the growth derived from
the main factor inputs, that is labour, capital and technical progress
(or residual) for the British economy during the past century.
His findings show that variations in growth rates over time have
been largely the result of changes in the technical progress function.
Before 1914 (1899–1913) and during the inter-war years the
amount of growth attributable to changes in employment and
capital per man was fairly constant (see Table 7).[1] It follows
therefore that the rise in the rate of growth must have been largely

TABLE 7

Annual Percentage Rates of Growth of Output and Input in the U.K.

	Real Gross Domestic Product	Employment	Growth due to changes in capital per man	Technical progress
1899–1913	1·1	1·0	0·3	−0·2
1924–37	2·3	1·2	0·2	0·9

due to changes in the technical progress factor. Thus, of the increase of 1·2 percentage points in the rate of growth of real G.D.P.
after the war, no less than 1·1 was due to the improvements which
took place in techniques.

In aggregate, then, the capital component was not the major
factor in the acceleration of growth in the inter-war years. But
this provides no reason for dismissing it without further discussion.
The distinction between capital accumulation and technical progress as growth agents is often a fine one, and it is doubtful whether
it is practicable to separate the two factors and allocate so much
growth to each, since for most of the time they are interacting
or interdependent variables in the process of growth. It is of
course possible to have one without the other. Capital may be
replaced or new capital added to the stock which has little impact
in terms of growth (at least productivity growth) largely because it
takes place in traditional or static techniques. Much of the investment in Britain's basic industries before 1914, for example, was
based on unchanged techniques and as a result productivity growth
was very slow indeed.[2]

[1] R. C. O. Matthews, 'Some Aspects of Post-War Growth in the British Economy
in Relation to Historical Experience', *Transactions of the Manchester Statistical
Society* (1964), and below, Ch. 5.
[2] See D. H. Aldcroft, 'Technical Progress and British Enterprise, 1875–1914',
Business History, VIII (1966). Reprinted in Aldcroft and Richardson, *The British
Economy 1870–1939* (1969).

What this implies, therefore, is that it is not the absolute amount of capital investment which is so important but the way in which it is utilised and deployed. Thus a low investment ratio may well produce a relatively high rate of growth, providing the investment is used in the most productive way possible. The inter-war years provide confirmation of this. Although the investment ratio was not markedly different from the pre-1914 pattern, rates of growth were appreciably higher in the latter period. This suggests that the available capital resources were being used more productively, a point which is confirmed by the fact that there was a tendency for the capital–output ratio to decline in this period.[1] Three main factors were responsible for this improvement. First of all, there was a noticeable shift in the pattern of investment resources towards the new high growth sectors of the economy. Secondly, important productivity gains were being realised as a result of technical improvements which necessitated little additional capital, e.g. the rationalisation of production methods, a type of technical progress which had been sadly neglected before the war. And thirdly, replacement investment became an important vehicle of new techniques.

The last of these points is especially important in regard to manufacturing industry, since there was very little net addition to the capital stock in this sector throughout the period.[2] On the other hand, gross investment increased fairly rapidly and there is evidence that it was being concentrated in more productive techniques than before 1914, when the chief tendency had been routine replacement in static techniques. An obvious example is the rapid shift from steam to electrical power; between 1912 and 1930 the proportion of power applied electrically to industrial operations rose from 25 to 66·2 per cent.[3] Not only was electrically-driven plant more efficient than steam but it also often involved a rearrangement of the layout of factory plant and equipment which increased overall

[1] For fixed assets other than dwellings, the capital–output ratio fell from 2·6 in 1920–4 to 2·3 in 1935–8. C. H. Feinstein, *Domestic Capital Formation in the United Kingdom, 1920–1938* (1965) p. 56. Comparable data are not available for the pre-war period, but it is probable that the capital–output ratio was somewhat higher before 1914. See P. Deane and W. A. Cole, *British Economic Growth, 1688–1959* (1964) p. 274.

[2] Even for the economy as a whole, fixed capital per head of the employed labour force remained fairly stationary during most of the inter-war period. See C. H. Feinstein, *Domestic Capital Formation in the United Kingdom, 1920–1938* (1965) p. 53. This is in marked contrast to the period 1895–1914 when physical equipment per head rose fairly rapidly yet produced very small gains in productivity. E. H. Phelps Brown and B. Weber, 'Accumulation, Productivity and Distribution in the British Economy, 1870–1938', *Economic Journal*, LXIII (1953) 27.

[3] L. Rostas, *Comparative Productivity in British and American Industry* (1948) p. 55.

efficiency. A number of other examples can be cited where replacement investment produced important gains in productivity. By the beginning of the twentieth century the cement industry had begun a vast programme of plant replacement which was completed in the 1920s. The rotary kiln was substituted for the fixed kiln while at the same time much larger kilns were installed. In addition, greater use was made of labour-saving devices such as hydraulic drying and mechanical conveyance for weighing and packing.[1] The net effect of these changes was that output per operative rose by nearly 80 per cent between 1924 and 1937.[2] Similarly, the output per head in blast furnaces rose by over 50 per cent during the same period and this again can be largely attributed to technical improvements, such as the adoption of larger blast furnaces and the improvement in auxiliary equipment, e.g. mechanical charging.[3] Examples such as these do suggest that replacement investment brought in new techniques though how important and extensive it was is difficult to say. Some economists consider it to be a crucial factor in the productivity growth of this period. Colin Clark, writing in the 1930s, observed that 'without new investment the replacement of obsolete capital ... appears to give all the scope necessary for the introduction of technical and organisational improvement and to bring about the rapid increase in productivity under which we are now living.'[4] Certainly the most recent capital formation estimates show that for the economy as a whole net investment was quite small, while replacement investment formed a much larger share of the total domestic investment than before 1914. It can be seen from Table 8 that net investment was less than a third of the total in the inter-war years, whereas before 1913 it had accounted for two-thirds or more. Though not conclusive proof, such figures go some way towards confirming the general impression that replacement investment was an important vehicle for introducing new techniques in these years.

Whether in fact the existing capital stock was being utilised more effectively is a much more debatable point. Certainly as far as some industries were concerned there does seem to have been a greater willingness and effort to rationalise production methods, to economise in the use of factors of production, and to replan factory

[1] L. Rostas, *Productivity, Prices and Distribution in Selected British Industries* (1948) pp. 80–4.
[2] W. E. G. Salter, *Productivity and Technical Change* (1960) p. 178.
[3] L. Rostas, *Productivity, Prices and Distribution in Selected British Industries* (1948) pp. 117–19.
[4] Colin Clark, *National Income and Outlay* (1937) p. 272.

layouts in order to get the best out of fixed equipment. The rapid spread of electric motor power was a reflection of such tendencies, since as we have seen its adoption often resulted in a revision of a firm's methods of production. Rationalisation schemes designed to eliminate excess capacity and improve the performance of the equipment remaining were a prominent feature of this period, and although they did not always achieve spectacular results it was a step in the right direction. Some of the schemes were, however, quite successful. The reorganisation of the electricity supply industry culminating in the establishment of the national grid might be cited as a case in point. Many of the improvements stemmed directly from the war when government control forced industrialists to co-operate and rationalise their methods of production. After hostilities the benefits of wartime co-operation were

TABLE 8
Total Fixed Capital Formation
(Annual averages at constant prices)

	Gross capital formation	Net capital formation	Net as a percentage of gross capital formation
1870–9	102·5	72·8	71·0
1880–9	92·4	58·9	63·7
1890–9	130·5	85·9	65·8
1900–9	179·8	127·5	70·9
1920–9	349·8	87·4	25·0
1930–8	467·2	148·7	31·8

Based on C. H. Feinstein, 'Income and Investment in the United Kingdom, 1856–1914', *Economic Journal*, LXXI, (1961), and *Domestic Capital Formation in the United Kingdom, 1920–1938* (1965).

often retained and even extended. The reorganisation of the railways into four main groups in 1921 was a specific attempt to secure the economies which had been achieved when the railway system was under unified direction. Many of the changes which occurred in peacetime were carried out by industry on a voluntary basis. This is particularly true of the machine tool and engineering trades where the process of rationalisation which had proved so successful in the war was continued and extended during the 1920s. The Associated British Machine Tool Makers, a body comprising eleven firms set up in 1916–17 to assist the government with its rationalisation plans, was continued, and by 1922 a further nine firms had joined it. Each member firm agreed to specialise in a narrow range of non-competing lines and to take steps to standardise the design of their tools. As a result the production programmes of the constituent firms were considerably reduced and eventually each firm was restricted to producing only a few types of tools.

The scheme proved to be a considerable success and great improvements in workshop organisation and efficiency resulted from it.[1]

Despite what has already been said, it seems unlikely that the greater utilisation of capital and its productive efficiency via new techniques were responsible for more than a modest proportion of the improvement in growth in these years. Measurement is difficult and we may be underestimating the impact of these two factors, but it would seem more plausible to argue, at least on the evidence available, that by far the most important factor was the shift of resources to the newer sector of the economy, and the higher productivity of the new capital installed therein. It is not always appreciated fully just how extensive and rapid was the shift to this new or high growth sector in the inter-war years. A few figures will make the point clear. The net output of the newer industries accounted for just over 16 per cent of total manufacturing production in 1930 and probably approaching one-quarter by the end of the 1930s, as against around 8 per cent in the immediate pre-war years.[2] Reliable investment data is not available to make accurate comparisons with the pre-war period, but calculations made on the basis of Feinstein's capital investment figures for the period 1920–38 produce some interesting findings. By the 1930s seven rapidly expanding industries accounted for nearly 45 per cent of the gross domestic fixed investment in manufacturing (in real terms) compared with 37·6 per cent in the early 1920s. If building work and electricity, gas and water are included, then the proportion of total investment devoted to these industries amounts to 70 per cent in the 1930s compared with around 58 per cent in the early post-war years (see Table 9). Although comparative data are not available, there seems little doubt that these proportions were much smaller before the war when investment was still heavily concentrated in the older basic sectors of the economy. Employment figures show a similar pattern of readjustment of productive factors. Between 1923 and 1929 employment in industries classified by the Ministry of Labour as expanding[3] increased by 22·2 per cent as against a fall of 10·7 per cent in the contracting industries, while during the same period the proportion of industrial workers employed in the former sector rose from 57·3 to almost 66 per cent.[4] These figures suggest that not

[1] For details see D. H. Aldcroft, 'The Performance of the British Machine Tool Industry in the Inter-War Years', *Business History Review*, XL (1966).

[2] The new industries included here are electrical goods and electricity supply, automobiles and cycles, aircraft, chemicals and allied goods, scientific instruments and rayon and silk.

[3] Largely composed of newer industries.

[4] *Ministry of Labour Gazette*, Nov 1929, pp. 394–5.

TABLE 9

Allocation of Gross Investment in Real Terms

	Investment in seven rapidly expanding industrial groups as a percentage of total manufacturing investment	*Investment in seven rapidly expanding industrial groups and in building and electricity and gas as a percentage of all investment*
1920–4	37·6	57·9
1925–9	44·4	64·8
1930–4	44·8	70·0
1935–8	44·6	69·1

Source: Feinstein, *Domestic Capital Formation in the United Kingdom* (1965).
The seven industries are chemicals, non-ferrous metals, vehicles, food, rayon and silk, electrical engineering, and wood, cement, bricks and glass.

only was a fairly high proportion of Britain's productive resources already located in the newer and rapidly expanding sectors of the economy but also that this proportion was increasing steadily throughout the years in question.

Clearly, then, these sectors were a potent force in the growth of the United Kingdom economy of the inter-war years. It can be

TABLE 10

Annual Rates of Growth in Selected Industries

	1920–38
Total all industries	2·8
Total manufacturing industries	2·6
Vehicles	6·6
Building and contracting	5·4
Gas, water, and electricity supply	5·0
Non-ferrous metals	4·8
Electrical engineering	4·7
Building materials	3·7
Food	3·6
Metal goods	2·5
Chemicals	1·9

Source: Lomax, *Journal of the Royal Statistical Society*, A122 (1959).

Note: Between 1929 and 1938 metal goods expanded much faster than the average for all industries, while the chemical industry experienced a rate of growth similar to the national average in the 1920s.

seen clearly from Table 10 that these industries expanded much more rapidly than the national average and had the shift of resources not taken place the British economy would have been much less buoyant. Many of these industries witnessed a constant stream of innovations in the inter-war years and under the influence of rapid technical progress and economies of scale, productivity increased rapidly and prices were reduced. Some of the most outstanding changes occurred in the electrical and automobile industries where techniques and methods of production and organisation were transformed out of all recognition to those prevailing before 1914.[1] Furthermore, many of these newer industries had important repercussions on other branches of economic activity because of their strong inter-industry relationships. The development of the motor-car industry stimulated or brought into being a whole range of industries including oil-refining, rubber, electrical goods, glass, metallurgy and mechanical engineering. It has been suggested that *in toto* the newer industries formed an interdependent block which markedly assisted economic recovery from the depression of the early 1930s.[2]

One of the most buoyant sectors of the economy was the building industry, largely on account of the sustained housing development in the inter-war years. Although much of the investment in residential construction can be regarded as unproductive in terms of future growth, since it adds little to the stock of wealth-producing assets, the building industry itself cannot be ignored in any discussion of inter-war growth. Not only did it become an increasingly important sector of the economy in this period but, in view of its sustained and almost uninterrupted growth and its widespread inter-industry transactions, it provided a powerful stimulus to many other parts of the economy.

There is no doubt that the building industry formed an expanding sector of the economy. Its rate of growth was twice the national average (5·4 per cent per annum as against 2·7 per cent) and it accounted for a much larger share of the nation's total productive resources than before 1914. By the 1930s nearly one-half the total gross domestic investment was taken up by building work compared with about one-third prior to 1914, while the industry's share of gross national product was nearly double that of pre-war by the 1930s. The impact on the labour market was equally substantial. Employment in building and related trades (mainly building materials) rose by about half a million, equivalent to

[1] See, for a discussion of these, D. H. Aldcroft in *Scottish Journal of Political Economy*, XIII (1966). Reprinted in Aldcroft and Richardson, *The British Economy 1870–1939* (1969).

[2] H. W. Richardson, 'The Basis of Economic Recovery in the Nineteen-Thirties: A Review and a New Interpretation', *Economic History Review*, XV (1962–3). Reprinted in Aldcroft and Richardson, *The British Economy, 1870–1939* (1969).

about one-quarter of the total increase in employment between 1923 and 1938, and by the latter date nearly 13·5 per cent of the national labour force was engaged in these trades. This of course takes no account of the indirect effects of the increased volume of building activity. An input–output analysis based on the 1935 census of production provides some indication of the demand created by the building industries for products of other industries. Altogether the building industry bought products from 24 of the 36 main industrial groups classified by Barna.[1] The total inter-industry transactions on behalf of building amounted to nearly £213 million in 1935. Admittedly this was a fairly small proportion of the total industrial output of Great Britain, while apart from one or two exceptions the proportion of total output of any one industry that was acquired by the building industry was quite small. But what is important is the fact that only two other industrial groups, food processing and the distributive services, had a wider range and a larger volume of transactions with other industries. In other words, building had a greater impact on the rest of the industrial economy than practically any other industry. Moreover, if we consider some of the less quantifiable indirect effects of increased building activity the importance of this sector is enhanced even further. In particular, the vast housing programme—over four million houses were constructed in these years—generated a demand for a wide range of new consumer durables mainly based on electricity, and additional transport facilities in many of the new residential suburbs. It is difficult, of course, to separate cause and effect in some cases, especially in the relationship between transport and building. Nevertheless, there can be no question that had building activity not been so buoyant during these years the rest of the economy would have suffered accordingly.[2]

Clearly, then, the new or expanding sector of the economy was an important factor making for an improvement in Britain's economic performance compared with the pre-1914 period. The steady shift of resources towards this sector—one might almost call it rapid—more than counteracted the adverse effects of the decline or contraction in the old basic sector. The question might be asked why the first really sustained growth in these industries occurred in the inter-war years rather than in the decades before 1914. This is a complex matter and cannot be resolved fully here. Briefly it will

---

[1] T. Barna, 'The Interdependence of the British Economy', *Journal of the Royal Statistical Society*, A115 (1952).

[2] Much of the material relating to building is drawn from H. W. Richardson and D. H. Aldcroft, *Building in the British Economy between the Wars* (1968).

be argued that the chief reason is simply that conditions were generally more favourable to new developments in the inter-war years than they were before 1914. Obviously this line of reasoning runs counter to popular impressions of the period, but it is hoped that the following points will clinch the case for the view expressed here.

In the first place one has to remember that the large-scale production of many newer goods only really became technically and commercially possible around the second and third decades of the twentieth century. This is certainly true, for example, of the motorcar, rayon goods, and many of the consumer durables based on electricity. The First World War in particular provided a sharp stimulus to the introduction and use of new products and to the adoption of more modern and scientific methods of production. Thus it was not until the early 1920s that the time was really ripe, at least in a technical sense, for the rapid commercial exploitation of new products. But the release of technical constraints was not the only factor which made possible the growth of such industries in the twenties and thirties. An important consideration was the rise in real incomes, particularly in the latter decade, which gave a boost to the demand for new products at the very time when their prices were falling due to improved methods of production. In contrast, real incomes had risen only very slowly, if at all, in the couple of decades before 1914, and although even earlier (1870s to the early 1890s) real incomes and wages were rising fairly rapidly, technical constraints were still holding back the developments of the new industries. In fact, right down to 1914 the techniques for producing new products for the mass market had still not been perfected. Furthermore, there is evidence that in the inter-war years consumers' tastes and preferences changed in such a way as to favour the development of new products and better services. This is certainly reflected in the demand for better housing accommodation and new domestic gadgets.[1]

Probably a further factor delaying the technical perfection and commercial exploitation of new products before 1914 was the fact that a disproportionate amount of attention was being devoted to the still profitable basic industries, while some of the new products, such as electricity, ran foul of vested interests in older competing products, in this case gas. But whatever the causes for the delay in the development of new products before 1914, there is no

---

[1] It is recognised of course that a shift in consumer preferences may in fact simply be a response to rising real incomes and the entry of new products into the market.

doubt that the decline or partial collapse of the older basic industries after 1920 made adaptation to a new industrial structure far more urgent than it had ever been before the war.

It was the latter sector, of course, which was mainly responsible for the high unemployment and decline in exports after the war. It has been estimated that in 1929 unemployment in the six leading staple export trades caused by a fall in exports since 1913 amounted to no less than 700–800,000 workers, or practically the whole of the core of unemployment.[1] Apart from the early 1930s, when conditions were universally bad as regards unemployment owing to the general depression, this holds true for the inter-war years as a whole. In fact, given the high level of unemployment and disastrous decline in exports, what is really remarkable is the narrow range of industries which were affected and the small number of industries which actually failed to increase their output substantially over pre-war. Apart from textiles, shipbuilding and mining, there were few industries which experienced an absolute check to production in this period. And in any case, as we have already pointed out, in terms of absolute growth the contraction of these industries was more than compensated for by the rapid growth of the expanding sectors.

The question might be raised as to why the new or rapidly expanding sectors of the economy were unable to absorb the resources (especially labour) displaced from the old basic industries and why they failed to make up for the loss in exports. There are a number of possible explanations. For one thing the demand structure of the two sectors was somewhat different. The older basic industries had been primarily export-predominant industries, whereas the newer sectors never became so heavily committed to selling abroad. Their products were of a fairly sophisticated nature and hence were less acceptable to our main customers abroad, the primary producing countries, while the products of the newer industries found a fairly buoyant market at home and therefore could afford to neglect outlets abroad. Rapidly rising real incomes coupled with a shift in consumer tastes boosted the effective demand for the new consumer durables in Britain and as a result it was possible for these industries to develop fairly rapidly, largely on the basis of the internal market. Moreover, because the techniques of production spread more rapidly than in the case of the old staples, many of the richer industrial countries were able to satisfy their own demand for new products, while the fact that they had often got off to an earlier start in this respect meant that they were in a

[1] E. V. Francis, *Britain's Economic Strategy* (1939) pp. 55–6.

better position than Britain to capture the most lucrative export outlets. On the question of labour resources one has to remember that, apart from building, most of the new and rapidly expanding sectors were less labour intensive than the old staples and so their impact on the labour market was less than might be expected. In any case, the hard core of unemployment was centred around a few industries in selected areas, and the difficulties involved in the movement and re-training of labour from these regions reduced the rate at which labour resources were reallocated, and hence made the unemployment problem seem really worse than it actually was. Only this factor can explain why at times industries in the south and Midlands were suffering from shortages of workers while the more northerly regions were heavily overstocked with unemployed men. Even within depressed regions it was not uncommon to find expanding industries suffering from a shortage of skilled labour. The building industry, for example, was affected in this way in the mid-1920s and later 1930s.

There is one further general point to bear in mind. Since the development of the newer industries was somewhat belated in Britain, at least that is before 1914, many of them were still in their teething stages in the early post-war period. It is somewhat unreasonable, therefore, to expect them to have filled all the gaps left by the sudden and violent contraction of the basic industries, the causes of which were often outside this country's control. In an economy which had neglected adjustment in the past there was bound to be a period of dislocation while the necessary changes were taking place. Moreover, the problems of adjustment were bound to be acute in view of the fact that the new growth sector was structurally different from the old one. In any case, it can be argued that such difficulties as occurred merely reflected the rate at which the process of adjustment was progressing rather than an indication of the bankruptcy of Britain's industrial system. Indeed, it was the rapid progress made by the new industries which laid the foundations of a new growth sector for the future. What is important, then, is not the fact that the new industries failed to take the place of the old but that they were, as Richardson has observed, 'a potent force making for permanent structural change in British industry, and to place an arbitrary time limit ... for the readjustment to be made is to ignore the difficulties involved'.[1]

Although one cannot deny that some sectors of the economy were

[1] H. W. Richardson, 'The New Industries in Britain between the Wars', *Oxford Economic Papers*, XIII (1961) 366. Reprinted in Aldcroft and Richardson, *The British Economy 1870–1939* (1969).

depressed in the inter-war years, the economy as a whole was much more dynamic than often imagined. Growth performance was respectable whatever standard of measurement or comparison is employed, and in terms of past achievements British growth indices showed a noticeable improvement. It would be profitable if scholars in future devoted more attention to examining the factors underlying this growth pattern rather than discussing the economic disasters which characterised the period. We have suggested that one of the major determinants was the rapid shift of resources towards the new and expanding sectors of the economy, and it could be argued that Britain benefited in these years from the fact that adjustment of the economic structure had been delayed in the past.[1] But much more detailed work is required on the nature of these changes and the interrelationships between different sectors of the economy. In many respects the inter-war years were unique, particularly on account of the fact that fairly rapid growth took place at a time when the economy was inherently unstable and subject to random and often violent shocks. To those prepared to devote time and energy to the study of the mechanics of growth in the period the results might well be quite rewarding.

[1] In America, on the other hand, where the shift or readjustment occurred earlier and more rapidly, the economy overshot itself at the end of the 1920s and as a result the 1930s were years of very protracted growth indeed.

4 Growth in the Inter-War Period: Some More Arithmetic*

by J. A. DOWIE

THIS paper is concerned with the similarity (or otherwise) of the growth performance of the British economy during the 1920s and 1930s and with the usefulness of the 'new–old' industry dichotomy in illuminating the trends of the inter-war period: two of the main topics which have attracted the interest of economic historians in recent years. But because an adequate historical perspective seems to be lacking in some of their writing, we begin by seeing how the inter-war period as a whole emerges from recent statistical work on long-term growth.

I. THE INTER-WAR PERIOD IN HISTORICAL PERSPECTIVE

The emergence (in preliminary form) of the Matthews–Feinstein findings on the historical experience of growth means that three central aggregates have now been extended back to the middle of the nineteenth century: those for output (real G.D.P.) and the two main conventional inputs, employment (in man-years) and capital (gross stock of reproducible fixed assets).[1] Other variants of the output aggregate are also available and it is possible to bring in foreign investment and income, but the primary focus of the exercise is domestic productivity rather than national welfare. While the results so far presented are provisional there seems little chance that the broad picture will be altered by later refinements.

The most meaningful trends to identify in the newly extended

---

* First published 1968.

[1] R. C. O. Matthews, 'Some Aspects of Post-War Growth in the British Economy in Relation to Historical Experience', *Transactions of the Manchester Statistical Society* (1964). Basic data for project prepared largely by C. H. Feinstein (see the note on Statistical Sources which follows the appended tables).

series are not unambiguous, especially in the nineteenth century, as Matthews admits in his cautious periodisation:

> ... an initial phase of fairly rapid growth, terminating in the 1870s or in 1900 as the case may be; a doldrums period, running from then until the early 1930s; and a concluding period of faster growth, beginning in the 1930s, interrupted by World War II, and carrying on up to the present time.[1]

At the present stage the statistics underlying the published graph (see chart) and rates of change are not available, and we can only risk the personal judgement that the extent (and probable quality) of the pre-1870 figures is insufficient to permit a confident decision regarding the existence of a trend change about that date. However, the case for a trend break about the turn of the century—with or without the Coppock 'flash in the pan' of 1897–1902 — seems convincing. There was a decade or more before the First World War in which productivity (labour or 'total') was declining fairly consistently and when output was rising much more slowly than it had in the last thirty years of the nineteenth century, 'Great Depression' and all. Since there is presumably no longer any doubt about the *historical* respectability of the post-1945 performance, the important question which emerges is, when during the three decades following 1914 did the rate of growth of output regain its previous level and productivity begin to rise again? This question clearly has implications for the long-run picture, although we leave main consideration of it until the following section of the paper.

Allowing for the departure of Southern Ireland and particularly for the effects of post-war recovery has always bedevilled quantitative discussion of the inter-war period, especially attempts to establish and assess its growth performance. Growth is the Matthews–Feinstein, and our, interest and we support their decision to use the 1924–37 period. Ideally we seek a calculation of potential (i.e. capacity) growth, to which the actions of decision-takers both public and private can be related and against which they may be 'judged'. The second-best solution is a measure of actual growth over a period when it can reasonably be expected that the realised trend approximates that of potential. This, in practice, normally boils down to choosing as termini years in which the level of unemployment of one factor, labour, was equal or nearly so. Usually this means periods when almost full utilisation was approached, with unemployment levels of 1 or 2 per cent. In the inter-war period the meaning of the calculations must inevitably seem more doubtful (even if we accept

[1] Ibid. p. 4.

the internal representativeness of the unemployment data) because the peaks of activity still leave unemployment around the 10 per cent mark. But little can be done about this, and the resulting difficulty of comparing any useful post-war year with a pre-war one means that discussion of the wider setting of the inter-war period must be conducted in terms of *trends*, the difference between the *levels* of 1914 and 1924 being largely, albeit reluctantly, disregarded in growth discussions.

The inter-war years emerge as a period of growth almost as rapid as any of comparable length in British measured history (post-1856). The exact rating of the performance naturally varies slightly with the growth criterion adopted (aggregate, *per capita*, per man-year of employment, per unit of 'total' input) and the termini used for the other periods; the simplest way to establish the validity of the conclusion and at the same time leave it open to the reader's judgement is to draw in the inter-war (1924–37) trends on the Matthews graph.

The earlier Lomax industrial product series provide some basis for an independent check on the income/expenditure-based Matthews–Feinstein aggregate, though without the inclusion of other sectors the check can never be more than partial. Lomax's revisions of previous industrial output series for the post-1900 period were first published in 1959.[1] A revised aggregate (but not components) for 1860–1900 was published in 1964, along with labour productivity growth rates for individual industries over five periods: 1907–24, 1924–35, 1935–49, 1949–55 and 1955–60.[2] Arguing that industry played a predominant role in the United Kingdom economy and could therefore be used as an acceptable indicator of growth, Lomax began the quantitatively based resurrection of the inter-war period which has been confirmed in the later, more aggregative, work:

> The overall economic position . . . was by no means as black as has been painted although unemployment remained a serious problem throughout. The new index-numbers of industrial output show a much less depressing picture than that exhibited by older currently-published indices. Certainly industrial output growth showed a big improvement compared with pre-first world war.[3]

[1] K. S. Lomax, 'Production and Productivity Movements in the United Kingdom since 1900', *Journal of the Royal Statistical Society*, A122 (1959) 185–210. The more detailed indexes mentioned, which would be of great interest, have not yet appeared.

[2] K. S. Lomax, 'Growth and Productivity in the United Kingdom', *Productivity Measurement Review*, xxxviii (1964) 5–22, and above, ch. 2.

[3] K. S. Lomax, in *Productivity Measurement Review*, xxxviii (1964) 9.

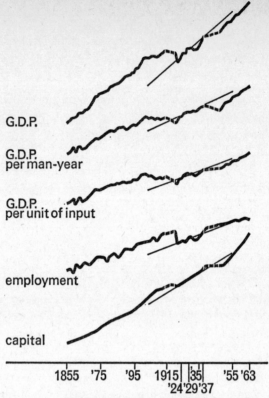

G.D.P.

G.D.P.
per man-year

G.D.P.
per unit of input

employment

capital

1855   '75   '95   1915| |35| '55 '63
                       '24'29'37

Output and Inputs 1855–1963
(log. scale, 1939 = 100)

Source: Matthews in *Transactions of the Manchester Statistical Society* (1964) (inter-war trends added: fine lines).

Industrial output grew, he suggests, at 3·1 per cent per annum between 1920 and 1937: double the rate of the 1877–1913 period and as fast as in the 1811–60 period (according to Hoffmann in the latter case). And output *per operative-hour* grew at 2·2 per cent per annum between 1924 and 1935, considerably above the rates for the neighbouring periods—1·6 (1907–24) and 1·3 (1935–49)—although slower than the 3 per cent per annum achieved in the 1949–60 period.

But apart from the limitations imposed by the restriction of the output estimates to industry and of the productivity calculations to the twentieth century, Lomax's choice of periods makes it difficult to accept his interpretation unreservedly. He is emphatic about the need to measure rates of growth from peak to peak 'in order to insure comparability in degrees of capacity utilisation'.[1] It is surprising, therefore, firstly, to find him using, in the inter-war years, the period 1920–37 for the measurement of output and 1924–35 for productivity. The rate of unemployment was almost certainly several times higher in 1937 than it had been in 1920 and it was perhaps 50 per cent higher in 1935 than it had been in 1924. Information on hours and earnings was admittedly not available for 1937 (when unemployment was at approximately the same level as in 1924), but it was available for 1938, which had a level of unemployment closer to 1924 than did 1935. (Ironically, he rejected 1938 as a time of recession, 'and it might have been misleading to include in a comparison of this kind, years at different phases of the trade cycle'.)[2] It is surprising, secondly, to find 1877 used not only as a peak (by the unemployment criterion it is midway between the peaks of 1872 and 1882) but also as the beginning of the lengthy period of stagnation seen as extending until the outbreak of war. With a little aid from the choice of sub-period within 1877–1913 this dating effectively distracts attention from the possibility of a trend break about the turn of the century. We would not want to argue that such a break is as clear in the Lomax industrial product series as it is in the Matthews real G.D.P. and, especially, G.D.P. per man-year series, but it is at least a worthy candidate for discussion.

The general effect of Lomax's processing of his industrial production data is to take the resurrection of the inter-war period somewhat beyond what is justified. This is, of course, largely excusable on the grounds that he was writing before Matthews and Feinstein. Less understandable is Aldcroft's recent affirmation that between the wars 'in terms of past achievements British growth indices showed a remarkable improvement indeed'.[3] Aldcroft does quote Matthews at one point but does not appear to have taken the Matthews graph seriously, preferring to rely instead on the calculations of Maddison.[4] The latter are unfortunately in terms of standard decades — 1870–80, 1880–90, etc. — and it is clear from the Matthews graph that this procedure and the underlying data result in a quite different picture of the pre-1914 period. Aldcroft, like Lomax, treats the three or four decades before the First World War as a unit, whereas the implication (already noted) of the Matthews graph (and his Table 1) is that an important distinction must be drawn between

[1] Ibid. p. 6 and again on p. 17.

[2] K. S. Lomax, in *Journal of the Royal Statistical Society*, A122 (1959) 202.

[3] D. H. Aldcroft, 'Economic Growth in Britain in the Inter-War Years: A Reassessment', *Economic History Review*, xx (1967) 325, and above, Ch. 3.

[4] Angus Maddison, *Economic Growth in the West: Comparative Experience in Europe and North America* (1964).

the late nineteenth century and the decade or so before 1914: there
is a trend break somewhere around the turn of the century. Aldcroft,
talking in terms of consistently slow growth for the several decades
before the war, finds 'a sharp break with past growth trends in the
1920s and 1930s' and sees this accelerated growth in the inter-war
period as 'a return to the high growth rates which characterised the
early and middle decades of the nineteenth century'.[1] A look at the
modified Matthews graph, on the other hand, suggests that what
was occurring in the inter-war years was really a return to the
growth rates which had characterised the economy in most of the
second half of the nineteenth century. Aldcroft would have also
noticed this if in his Table 7, which relates to the periods 1899–1913
and 1924–37 and is drawn directly from Matthews's Table 1, he had
inserted the previous line from that table: that for the period 1856–
99. The equivalent growth rates here are real G.D.P. 2·0, employment 0·9, growth due to changes in capital per man 0·2, and
technical progress 0·9 — virtually identical to those for 1924–37.
The faster rate of 'technical progress' which he is keen to emphasise
in the inter-war period emerges as only equivalent to that of the late
nineteenth century, and the small increase in the rate of growth of
output between the 1856–99 and 1924–37 periods as attributable to
a small rise in the rate of growth of employment.

II. THE PRESENT EXERCISE: THE INTER-WAR PERIOD IN ISOLATION

The inter-war period is the earliest for which it is reasonably easy
to reproduce the main Matthews–Feinstein calculations from published sources, both at the aggregate and sector/industry levels. It
seemed desirable to do this for two reasons. Firstly, the results so far
presented at the disaggregated level are tantalising, but in so far as
they are in the form of unweighted component trends, they do not
convey much sense of relative importance. We can get some ideas
of structure after reconstruction. Secondly, the recent literature
on the period, including the contributions by Richardson[2] and

---

[1] D. H. Aldcroft, in *Economic History Review*, xx (1967) 316.
[2] H. W. Richardson, *Economic Recovery in Britain, 1932–9* (1967). See also the
earlier articles: 'The New Industries Between the Wars', *Oxford Economic Papers*,
xiii (1961) 360–84; 'The Basis of Economic Recovery in the Nineteen-Thirties:
A Review and a New Interpretation', *Economic History Review*, xv (1962) 344–63;
'Over-Commitment in Britain Before 1930', *Oxford Economic Papers*, xvii (1965)
237–62. All reprinted in Aldcroft and Richardson, *The British Economy, 1870–1939*
(1969).

Aldcroft[1] as well as that of Matthews, seems to raise a reasonably interesting question: if there was a significant break in the growth performance of the British economy between that of the Edwardian years and that of the post-depression period (interpreted as a war-interrupted entity on the lines of the Matthews quote[2]), did it occur during the 'war and recovery' decade (1914–24), during the 'normal' twenties (1924–9), or during the 'depression and recovery' (1929–37)?

Matthews, we have seen, favours the last: Britain was in the doldrums until the early thirties (from at least 1900, possibly earlier). From Richardson's earlier articles one could never be quite sure whether the discussion was about the origin of cyclical recovery or the sources of more sustained growth. In his recent book the focus on one cyclical upswing is clear and explicitly stated, in the preface as well as the title. But the whole tenor of the book still appears to suggest that the recovery of the thirties was so vigorous and sustained that it represented—or brought about—a significant improvement in the trend performance of the British economy. This is symbolised at one level by the different attitude adopted towards the same 10 per cent rate of unemployment which characterised the peaks of the 1929–37 cycle (with the emphasis on the high 'structural' content in both cases):

> In 1929, the economic situation could initially be described as moderately healthy. . . . Yet the British economy showed no signs of boom: unemployment remained about 10 per cent, excess capacity remained high in the staple industries and labour was being transferred into the newer industries at a painfully slow rate.[3]
>
> . . . The strength of the recovery is not contradicted by continued high unemployment for the unemployment remaining at the peak in 1937 was non-cyclical.[4]

But it is revealed especially in his attitude to the events of the twenties:

---

[1] D. H. Aldcroft, 'Economic Progress in Britain in the 1920s', *Scottish Journal of Political Economy*, XIII (1966) 297–316. Reprinted in Aldcroft and Richardson, *The British Economy, 1870–1939*.

[2] Perhaps we should *not* accept the Matthews picture of a single growth period from the thirties to the present, but argue for an (upward) trend break in the second 'war and recovery' decade of the century. The conclusions of this paper would certainly be sympathetic to such an approach, although, as the chart shows, the acceleration since the Second World War has been relatively slight and it would not be impossible to maintain that the break under discussion has been the only substantial one this century.

[3] H. W. Richardson, *Economic Recovery in Britain*, p. 8.   [4] Ibid. p. 313.

... there was no strong upswing in the British economy in the second half of the 1920s, therefore the slump cannot be described as the inevitable reaction from an extensive boom.[1]

and most expressly:

The economy was therefore subject to two successive trend influences: a depressive trend in the 1920s as external events forced the need for readjustment upon a recalcitrant economy, and an upward trend in the 1930s as these readjustments got clearly under way.[2]

Aldcroft, on the other hand, has pleaded the case for the twenties, particularly the early twenties:

... in many respects the 1920s formed a watershed between the old industrial regime of the pre-1914 era and the new industrial economy of the post-1945 period. For, as a result of the progress made in the 1920s, a viable base was created which ensured that steady growth would take place in the future. Taken all round, and considering the difficult circumstances prevailing in these years (e.g. unfavourable international factors and overvaluation of the £) we might go so far as to suggest that this was a period of fairly rapid economic progress.[3]

It is possible to have some qualms about the exact meaning of the middle sentence and to suspect that it would be possible to find enough difficult circumstances of the sort mentioned to prove that most periods were ones of 'fairly rapid economic progress'. But the claim is supported statistically by both intertemporal and (less convincingly) international comparisons, and our general conclusion on the twenties is fairly much in line with that of Aldcroft.[4]

What we now try to do is look at both the 1920s and 1930s in Britain, with the object of seeing in what senses, if any, the growth performance of the economy differed. Aldcroft's latest article (referred to in the first section of this paper) has surprisingly little to say on this question. Some statistics relevant to it are presented but only a few isolated comments made. At the aggregate level rates of

[1] Ibid. p. 9.   [2] Ibid. p. 97.

[3] D. H. Aldcroft, in *Scottish Journal of Political Economy*, XIII (1966) 298–9.

[4] The response by Neil K. Buxton, 'Economic Progress in the 1920s: A Reappraisal', *Scottish Journal of Political Economy*, XIV (1967) 175–86, and 'Rejoinder' by Aldcroft, 187–91, confuse as much as advance the debate. Buxton seems over-worried about the need to take the twenties literally and emphasises the rates of growth between 1920 and 1929, 'years not too dissimilar in terms of capacity utilisation' (p. 182). Leaving aside the more diffused problems of using a year as close to the end of the war as 1920, the simple unemployment rates—about 2 and 10 per cent respectively—hardly support Buxton's position.

growth for both output and productivity are offered for the 1913–38 period and for the sub-periods formed by breaking it at 1929; there is accordingly nothing on either the twenties or inter-war period as a whole as far as the whole economy is concerned. At the more restricted industrial level exclusively inter-war calculations *are* presented: for 1913–37, 1920–37 (both broken at 1929), and 1924–37 (not broken) as far as output is concerned; for only 1920–37 (and its sub-periods) of these as far as productivity is concerned, although additional productivity growth rates are quoted in the text for 1922–30 and 1924–35. Since, as Aldcroft virtually admits, calculations involving 1920 are fairly valueless—and those involving 1913 include the war—only 1924–37, 1922–30, 1929–37 and 1924–35 are left. In view of the favour with which the 1924–37 period is regarded and of the use of 1929 as the breaking point in the other two cases, it is strange that the 1924–29–37 sequence was not employed; especially since it has the additional advantage of comparing years in which the level of activity was similar, the rates of unemployment being 10·3, 10·4 and 10·8 per cent respectively according to the most widely used series.[1] The present paper does use this sequence and attempts analysis at the aggregate and component levels as well as the industrial. It suggests that there is an interesting aggregate similarity between the twenties and thirties, but also interesting sectoral and component differences.

The appended series of tables presents the resulting growth arithmetic of the inter-war period: firstly, the rates of change between the three years (including those for the whole period, which can be compared with the Matthews–Feinstein figures) and then structural pictures for each as far as they are possible. The first pair give the aggregate and sector results, the second pair the results, again as far as possible, for individual manufacturing industries. The precision of the printed figures belies, of course, their conceptual and statistical inadequacies, which are particularly great with the capital stock and residual calculations. The source note which follows the tables outlines the major problems but we are reasonably confident that the main points made in the text avoid them satisfactorily. Individual figures from the tables should clearly not be used in isolation without further investigation of their origin. Many of the criticisms which may be levelled at these calculations will be legitimate, but one point particularly relevant to this exercise should

[1] London and Cambridge Economic Service, *The British Economy: Key Statistics 1900–1966* (1967) p. 8. The rate in 1929 was 10·4 per cent and, while the 1928 rate was the same as that in 1937, the need to select one year favoured 1929 because the extent of the difference had to be considered in relation to the duration of the intervening period.

be borne in mind: the results become invalid as indicators of comparative trends only to the extent that the *relative* inadequacy of the data changes (for the better or for the worse) during the period. No matter how inadequate the underlying data are in an absolute sense, this will not be fatal, in many instances, as long as the bias is consistent.

(a) *Aggregate and Goods–Services trends*

The case for an early break, probably before 1924 and therefore in the 'war and recovery' decade, rests fundamentally on the similar aggregate performance of the economy in the 1924–9 and 1929–37 periods: similar rates of growth of total output (2·2–2·3 per cent per annum) of total employment (1·3 per cent per annum) of total capital stock (1·6–1·7 per cent per annum) and, consequently, insignificant differences in the rates of increase of the productivity of either factor taken singly or both taken together under the familiar residual assumptions. (The population of the United Kingdom grew slightly faster in the second period—0·43 per cent per annum against 0·34 per cent per annum—but not, obviously, sufficiently to make any substantial difference to the rate of improvement in product per head. Improvements in product per head have, of course, to be distinguished from improvements in income per head in a period when the terms of trade shift.)[1] Given the assumptions upon which the present measures are constructed there seems to be little case for maintaining that the *growth* performance of the British economy *as a whole* was any better, or worse, in the thirties than it had been in the twenties. Attenuating the influence of short-term variations yields a picture of fairly steady change after 1924 and suggests that the 'growth recovery' from the poor performance of the early twentieth century occurred during the war and/or post-war readjustment periods. There may not have been, as Richardson would maintain, a strong *upswing* in the late twenties, but this does not mean that there was no *growth*.

The similarity of the growth performance in the twenties and thirties is largely maintained even when activity is divided into goods production and service production. The merits of such a division are arguable and those who employ it usually have in mind a service/non-service dichotomy, the unity of goods production (cf. the

---

[1] The net terms of trade moved against Britain in the 1924–9 period (at an average of about 0·7 per cent per annum) and more strongly in her favour between 1929 and 1937 (at an average of 1·3 per cent per annum). Over the whole period the average improvement was about 0·5 per cent per annum.

Fisher–Clark subdivision of it into primary and secondary) being of an essentially negative character. Services get their unity partly from their physical intangibility as final products, partly from supposed differences in income demand elasticities or productivity improvement possibilities, partly, and increasingly, from the statistical difficulties of arriving at satisfactory real output series. Both goods and services output grew at the same rate in the two periods, though goods at not far short of twice the rate of services. There was some tendency for both labour and capital inputs in goods production to increase faster in the thirties than in the twenties (at least 'as measured', without allowing for possible changes in the effective length of a man-year, for example). On the other hand, there was a definite slowing down in the rate of increase of service employment, if not in capital employed in services. In both periods, however, services were absorbing factors at a much faster rate than goods, so that in terms of productivity improvement the performance of the two sectors was in marked contrast—as measured, services actually showed a decline in both periods, with the slightly better performance of the thirties in terms of labour productivity 'explained' largely by a *relatively* faster growth of capital per employee. Since the service sector accounts for just under half the work-force, about two-thirds of fixed assets, and over half of output in the inter-war period, the amount of attention it has so far received has been negligible, whether or not there is any justification in treating it as a largely 'dependent' area of the economy.

(b) Sector trends

The similarity in growth trends ends as soon as we move to the more detailed, nine-sector breakdown. On the goods side a substantial deceleration in the growth of both output and productivity took place in the primary industries and construction. The output of the utilities tended to become more capital-intensive but neither the output, labour productivity, nor residual trends show any significant change in this sector. The growth which accordingly offset these decelerating (though not generally declining) trends was in manufacturing, a reasonable if unspectacular acceleration of output in the thirties being achieved with no increase in the growth rate of employment and perhaps a small decline in the rate of fixed capital expansion.

With services we are frequently dealing with absolute declines in both periods, especially on the productivity side. But in comparative terms the overall similarity of the two periods arises in a similar way to that in goods. The equivalent to manufacturing here is distribution, which managed to raise its rate of output growth in the thirties while halving the massive (nearly 5 per cent per annum) rate of employment growth it had displayed in the late twenties and maintaining the same rate of capital expansion. The very bad (measured) productivity performance of the distributive trades in the twenties (−2·1 per cent per annum) became almost respectable (marginally positive) in the thirties. Transport and communication and 'other services' are the service areas where productivity performance deteriorated comparatively in the thirties to offset the distribution gains; but the deterioration was from a relatively high figure in the former case (about 1·5 to about 0·6 per cent per annum), whereas in the latter it was from a slightly negative to an even more negative figure (−0·2 to about −0·9 per cent per annum).

To summarise at this level, the persistence into the thirties of the growth rate achieved in the twenties was based on acceleration in manufacturing and distribution, which offset deceleration in most other sectors. This statement holds true whether we are referring to output, labour productivity, or to the residual. Even introducing the 'ownership of dwellings' sector does not alter the comparative picture, because neither its output nor capital expansion trends are very different in the two periods.

It is probably necessary to re-emphasise that these conclusions do not relate to the actual growth achievement in either of the two periods or the 1924–37 period as a whole. It can be seen from Table 1 that in terms of productivity growth manufacturing ranked only sixth or fifth out of eight in the twenties; its relative acceleration raised it to second place in the thirties and to fourth or third overall. (Where two rankings are mentioned the first refers to labour productivity and the second to 'total' productivity.) And despite its relative improvement in the thirties distribution only raised itself from last to second last and remained last overall (much farther behind 'other services' in labour than 'total' productivity terms because of the discrepancy in capital expansion rates). Emphasising the positive improvement in manufacturing and distribution must not, therefore, lead to an overlooking of the fact that many of the sectors which displayed a slowing down in the thirties were coming back from very high levels in the twenties and were still going to turn in good performances both in the thirties and overall. This is particularly true of the primary activities. Agriculture had the second fastest rate of productivity improvement in the twenties, the third highest in the thirties, and was first or second overall. The mining and quarrying industry did not, like agriculture, succeed in reducing the capital-intensity of production—capital per employee grew very rapidly in the twenties—and the results of the two productivity calculations here are farther apart; but the fact that this sector was first or third in the rankings for the twenties, fourth or fifth for the thirties, and third or fifth overall suggests that its positive contribution was far from negligible. The modest positive role of transport and communications and the generally negative picture in the other two service sectors have already been noted. Construction and utilities remain. Both have received considerable attention as sources of expansion between the wars. This is firmly supported in the case of utilities by the present figures, where the similar rates of expansion in both periods—nearly 6 per cent per annum in output and almost 3 per cent per annum in productivity— give them second or first ranking overall. But the achievements of construction, in addition to those of the primary industries, push utilities down to only fourth place in the twenties, as against their top ranking in the thirties. Construction is, however, the sector where the absolute change between the component periods is most striking —productivity grew rapidly in the twenties at around 4 per cent per annum but showed almost no change in the thirties—and over the whole period it had the slowest improvement of all the goods sectors.

This wide variety of sectoral rates of change is, of course, offsetting in the aggregate because of the differing sector weights. Table 2 shows that manufacturing accounts for twice (or more than twice) the output and employment of the other four goods components together, though for only slightly more of the fixed assets. Distribution and miscellaneous services are two other large sectors, and there is a considerable *a priori* case for doubting that the most meaningful level of disaggregation has been reached in any of these three areas. Unfortunately, the two service areas are virtually closed books at the moment and we are restricted to examining the established manufacturing breakdown. This does, however, enable some discussion of the 'new–old' issue, if largely in terms of upper limits quantitatively. Qualitatively, one real issue is whether the new industry 'explanation' of growth—cyclical or longer term—is not dangerously close to becoming a tautology.

(c) *Component trends in manufacturing*

Labour productivity in manufacturing, as measured by output per man-year of employment, rose 50 per cent faster in the thirties than it had in the twenties (2·4 against 1·6 per cent per annum). Table 3 confirms the suspicion that this is the arithmetic resolution of a wide variety of component trends: eleven of the identified industries accelerated, but eight decelerated. Table 4 indicates the input shares for each component, in terms of national totals, which produce the overall manufacturing result.

The following appears to be a useful rough-and-ready classification of the components according to the extent of their performance change; the three sectors which are conventionally combined with manufacturing to form 'industry' are included, in parentheses, for easy comparison:

1. Substantial acceleration (a change of +2 per cent per annum or more): textiles, leather, ferrous metals, electrical engineering.
2. Moderate acceleration (+0·5 to +1·9 per cent per annum): chemicals, other manufactures, vehicles, precision instruments, drink, paper and printing.
3. Little change (−0·4 to +0·4 per cent per annum): non-ferrous metals, food, tobacco, (electricity, gas and water).
4. Moderate deceleration (−0·5 to −1·9 per cent per annum): building materials, metal goods n.e.s., clothing.
5. Substantial deceleration (−2 per cent per annum or more): timber and furniture, shipbuilding, mechanical engineering (mining and quarrying, construction).

Employing the residual produces a perceptibly greater acceleration (or smaller deceleration) in shipbuilding, mechanical engineering, electrical engineering, leather and tobacco. It operates in the reverse direction with vehicles and 'other manufacturing' (in particular), but in no case does the use of this alternative criterion require any change in the above groups.

There would appear to be no simple conclusion to be drawn about the source of the improved manufacturing growth performance of the thirties—the improvement which was a crucial factor in the *maintenance* of the overall growth rate achieved in the twenties. No simple conclusion, except perhaps that simple conclusions in terms of 'new' and 'old' industries must be suspect. Taking those industries which approximate to those conventionally coming within the 'new' group would give us chemicals, electrical engineering, vehicles, precision instruments, paper and printing (and utilities, if the scope is broadened from manufacturing to industry). All these are certainly to be found in the first three groups (none showed deceleration), but they are not there alone and, with textiles (especially) among them, they account for less than half of the work-force in these groups. It seems beyond the bounds of possibility, therefore, that all or nearly all of the acceleration in manufacturing productivity in the thirties can be traced to them.

Obviously we are far from having the ideal degree of disaggregation: it is not possible to isolate the rubber, rayon, or radio industries, for example. But even if detail on narrower 'new' *product* performance were available—and this surely changes the argument radically—the substantial acceleration in important components such as cotton, wool and metal production would almost certainly match them in total effect. And is there not danger in excessive *dis*aggregation anyway? It seems questionable, for example, whether the rayon industry should be separated from textiles and proclaimed 'new'. If all new products are removed from the equivalent old staple area, then it becomes impossible for the latter to transform themselves in the way called for by, above all, the economic historian. If an old industry does not develop new products it is berated for not doing so. If it does develop one with success it runs the risk of having it removed and proclaimed a new industry—the greater the success the higher the risk, in fact—and as a result finding itself still the whipping stick.[1]

Clearly, the implication is not intended to be that the 'new industries' (and probably even more so the 'new products') played no part in the improved manufacturing performance of the thirties. It is merely that even if the important definitional problem is solved they certainly cannot provide an exclusive explanation, probably something more like half an explanation. Several of the 'old' industries were able to meet a rapid growth of demand in the thirties (following negligibly upward or negative output trends in the twenties) with a much less than proportionate expansion of inputs, and accordingly achieved substantial increases in their rates of productivity change. If the price of referring to the 'new' industries is the enforced aggregation of the 'old', then it is clearly too high a price to pay.

Apart from the empirical weaknesses of the 'new–old' division and the difficulty of defining an 'industry', the time may also be ripe for drawing attention to the danger of circularity which the use of the 'new industry' argument creates at the analytical level. The assertion that a structural shift from 'old' towards 'new' was a prominent source of growth can easily degenerate into a tautology. It seems to have done so in Aldcroft's recent work when he says that

[1] The process has a beautiful simplicity which echoes that of Joseph Heller's *Catch-22*. Cf. Sir Stanley Raymond: 'A business must be allowed to live and breathe and expand. British Rail have pioneered air services, shipping services, road services, bus services, travel agencies and they have all at various times been hived off'. *Sunday Times*, 7 Jan 1968, p. 22.

'Clearly . . . the new or expanding sector of the economy was an important factor making for an improvement in Britain's economic performance compared with the pre-1914 period.'[1] There is, here, possibly a tendency to define 'new' in terms of 'expanding' and certainly a failure to recognise the importance of distinguishing clearly between the two. If the 'new industry' argument is to have significant explanatory power it is essential not only that 'new' is defined in a way which avoids expansion being in any way a criterion but also that it be shown that all (or most) truly defined new industries were expanding. It is not sufficient to demonstrate that all (or most) expanding industries were new; this is an interesting descriptive discovery and can add to our knowledge of the form growth took, but not to our knowledge of why it occurred.

Again the discussion has so far focused on *comparative* performance in the 1924–9 and 1929–37 periods. Acceleration may, of course, partly offset previous deceleration, and vice versa. Did the older industries mentioned, despite their acceleration, contribute negatively overall? Did other older industries mentioned, despite their deceleration, contribute positively? Though these questions are not our main interest, some comment is needed, partly to illuminate the previous argument and partly to offer a further modification of what seems to be the received wisdom. Aldcroft has already drawn attention to the achievements of the mining, iron and steel, cement, and other older industries in the twenties (though not in a systematic quantitative way).[2] But perhaps the time has come for a more direct assertion of the importance of some older industries.

Table 3 shows that over the whole period 1924–37 the growth of manufacturing productivity (at about 2 per cent per annum) was broadly based and that there is little chance of using 'old' and 'new' as a ranking device. Vehicles rank second and precision instruments third, but shipbuilding is sixth and textiles eighth. And chemicals, paper and printing, and electrical engineering, for all their acceleration in the thirties, rank thirteenth, sixteenth, and seventeenth (out of nineteen) overall, according to the present calculations. Even without taking into account the heavy weighting of several of the older industries, the relative importance of their performance is obvious. It is accordingly difficult to agree with Richardson's 1961 contention that

> It is obvious that without the new industries — motor-cars, rayon, household appliances, radio and electrical engineering, for example — the increase in productivity and real income would

[1] D. H. Aldcroft, in *Economic History Review*, xx (1967) 323.
[2] D. H. Aldcroft, in *Scottish Journal of Political Economy*, xiii (1966) 307–8.

only have been very small compared with what was actually achieved in the inter-war period.[1]

Difficult to agree, unless a convincing case can be made out that the productivity improvements in the 'old' industries were somehow a direct response to the improvements in the 'new'. If they were a response to either a general, undifferentiated pressure on the British economy or to direct pressure on themselves, then the difficulty remains. It would seem to us that in an age of heavy unemployment the latter are more plausible hypotheses, although clearly there was some competition between 'old' and 'new' products.

It is relevant to ask, in conclusion, how this claim on behalf of older industries, or *some* of them, fits in with the Verdoorn hypothesis. There is considerable consensus among such writers as Richardson, Lomax and Matthews about 'Verdoorn's Law'—the suggestion that there is a significant (positive) correlation between the rate of output growth and the rate of productivity growth. All three writers, though in varying degrees of explicitness, see this correlation as one of the best insights into growth, particularly manufacturing growth, so far arrived at. No one-way causation is suggested; in fact the two main reasons usually suggested as having been responsible, in combination, for the existence of the correlation act in reverse directions: rapid output growth produces economies of scale and hence rising productivity, while rising productivity lowers prices and hence raises sales and output. Does the relationship hold with the present figures?

Matthews, taking all goods industries, in fact arrived at a coefficient of only 0·36 for the 1924–37 period, insignificant at the 5 per cent level; his faith in the relationship rests on the significant result he found for the 1948–62 period and on the belief that the relationship is probably an essentially manufacturing one anyway. Salter's finer (but selective) analysis of industry yielded the significant value of 0·67 for 1924–35.[2] In view of the intermediate level of the present

---

[1] H. W. Richardson, in *Oxford Economic Papers*, XIII (1961) 365. His recent book makes it much clearer that it is in relation to the timing and origin of cyclical recovery that the importance of the 'new' industries was emphasised. The substantial productivity improvements in some older industries over the whole 1929–37 cycle are now freely admitted though there still seems some reluctance to make full acknowledgement of their contribution in the thirties, given their weight.

[2] W. E. G. Salter, *Productivity and Technical Change* (Cambridge, 1960) p. 126. Salter's calculations generally refer to the 1924–50 period and are far more sophisticated than those made here (incorporating study of earnings, price and cost—but not investment—trends, as well as of output and employment). But the price of this sophistication is a restricted coverage: 28 'industries' covering about 30 per cent of industrial production. This does not, however, lessen the importance of Salter's discussion which, despite being pre-Lomax and Feinstein, is the most thorough and informative yet produced.

exercise, the intermediate results achieved are perhaps not surprising. The coefficients are 0·71 (1924–9), 0·51 (1929–37) and 0·47 (1924–37), all significant at the 5 per cent level. An elevation of the older industries is consistent with the relationship for three main reasons. Firstly, the coefficients indicate far from perfect association, especially in the thirties, and while the observations showing most deviation from the regression line include textiles and shipbuilding on the one hand and electrical engineering on the other, these deviate in such a way as to support the argument. Secondly, some 'new' industries conform to the pattern at relatively low levels of output and productivity growth; some 'old' industries conform at relatively high levels (e.g. chemicals and building materials respectively). And, thirdly, the elevation *is* partly a question of weighting, whereas the essence of these correlations is that all identified industries are weighted equally, irrespective of their size.

III. Summary

1. The quantitative work of Matthews, Feinstein and Lomax has established reasonably firmly the respectable growth achievement of the British inter-war economy in historical terms. The present danger, seen in Aldcroft, is that the resurrection will be overdone. The unemployment problem remains, but it clearly did not prevent significant growth, especially in the productivity sense. Whether it was partly the price of this growth is the interesting question which remains (but is well beyond the scope of this paper).

2. Assuming that the trends between the years 1924, 1929 and 1937 (when unemployment levels were approximately the same) will exclude both short-term and 'post-war readjustment' influences, growth was as rapid in the twenties as it was in the thirties. This is an aggregative statement (though having considerable truth at the goods–services level also) and suggests that writers who are excited by Britain's performance in the thirties are either (*a*) paying too much attention to one sector, viz., manufacturing; (*b*) thinking in international rather than historical terms; or (*c*) talking, intentionally or otherwise, about cyclical recovery.

3. The similar aggregate trends in the twenties and thirties concealed significant shifts at the sector level, accelerated improvement in manufacturing and distribution offsetting slower improvement in most other areas. In terms of actual growth there

is, however, a danger of neglecting the achievements of many of the smaller sectors in the twenties and, despite their deceleration, over the 1924–37 period as a whole.

4. Any attempt to explain the acceleration in manufacturing productivity in terms of a 'new–old industry' division seems to break down on empirical grounds. The 'new industries' clearly contributed significantly, but it is unlikely that even more disaggregation of manufacturing and concentration on 'new products' would reduce the real improvement in important old industries to quantitative insignificance. Still less can the manufacturing growth achievement of the inter-war period as a whole be explained adequately in 'new industry' terms.

5. The Richardson investigation into the sources of cyclical recovery is not affected by the present conclusions. The 'new' industries were quite probably the leaders in the upturn of the thirties; attention is here focused on through-cycle performance.

6. There are, however, serious definitional problems with the 'new industry' argument, in whatever form it appears. Unless both 'new' and 'industry' are defined carefully its explanatory power must be negligible.

STATISTICAL APPENDIX

TABLE I

United Kingdom: Rates of Change of Output, Employment, Capital Stock, Output per Employee, Capital per Employee, and 'Total Factor' Productivity, 1924–9, 1929–37 and 1924–37 (per cent per annum)—by Sector

	Output			Employment			Capital stock			Output per employee			Capital per employee			Residual		
	1924–29	1929–37	1924–37	1924–29	1929–37	1924–37	1924–29	1929–37	1924–37	1924–29	1929–37	1924–37	1924–29	1929–37	1924–37	1924–29	1929–37	1924–37
Agriculture, forestry and fishing	3·3	0·1	1·3	−0·8	−2·2	−1·7	−0·2	−0·1	−0·1	4·1	2·3	3·0	0·6	2·1	1·5	3·9	1·7	2·5
Mining and quarrying	−0·2	−0·5	−0·4	−4·6	−1·5	−2·7	0·5	0·5	0·5	4·4	1·1	2·4	5·1	2·0	3·2	2·9	0·5	1·4
Manufacturing	2·8	3·5	3·3	1·2	1·2	1·2	0·6	0·4	0·5	1·6	2·4	2·1	−0·6	−0·8	−0·7	1·8	2·6	2·3
Construction	7·4	2·9	4·6	3·6	2·8	3·1	1·5	2·1	1·9	3·9	0·0	1·5	−2·1	−0·7	−1·2	4·5	0·2	1·8
Electricity, gas and water	5·8	6·0	5·9	2·9	3·0	3·0	3·3	3·8	3·6	2·9	3·0	2·9	0·4	0·8	0·6	2·8	2·7	2·8
Goods	3·1	3·1	3·1	0·6	0·8	0·7	1·0	1·2	1·1	2·5	2·3	2·4	0·5	0·3	0·4	2·4	2·2	2·2
Transport and communications	2·3	1·1	1·5	0·7	0·5	0·6	1·2	0·3	0·6	1·7	0·6	1·0	0·5	−0·2	0·1	1·5	0·6	1·0
Distributive trades	1·7	2·1	2·0	4·8	2·2	3·2	1·3	1·4	1·3	−3·1	−0·1	−1·3	−3·6	−0·9	−1·9	−2·1	0·2	−0·7
Other services	1·5	1·4	1·4	1·8	2·2	2·0	1·6	2·5	2·2	−0·3	−0·8	−0·6	−0·2	0·3	0·1	−0·2	−0·9	−0·6
Ownership of dwellings	1·8	2·0	1·9	—	—	—	3·1	3·2	3·2	—	—	—	—	—	—	—	—	—
Services	1·7	1·6	1·6	2·3	1·9	2·1	1·9	1·9	1·9	−0·6	−0·3	−0·4	−0·4	0·0	−0·1	−0·4	−0·3	−0·4
G.D.P.	2·3	2·2	2·2	1·3	1·3	1·3	1·6	1·7	1·7	0·9	0·9	0·9	0·3	0·3	0·3	0·8	0·8	0·8
G.D.P. excluding dwellings	2·3	2·3	2·3	1·3	1·3	1·3	1·2	1·1	1·1	0·9	0·9	0·9	−0·2	−0·3	−0·2	1·0	1·0	1·0

Sources: See below, pp. 77–9.

TABLE 2

United Kingdom: Shares of Output, Employment, and Capital Stock, 1924, 1929 and 1937 (Percentages)—by Sector

	Output			Employment			Capital		
	1924	*1929*	*1937*	*1924*	*1929*	*1937*	*1924*	*1929*	*1937*
Agriculture, forestry and fishing	4·0	4·1	3·5	6·2	5·6	4·2	5·2	4·8	4·1
Mining and quarrying	4·0	4·4	3·7	7·4	5·5	4·4	3·1	2·9	2·7
Manufacturing	28·5	29·3	32·8	35·9	35·7	35·2	18·0*	17·2*	15·4*
Construction	3·4	4·4	4·7	4·9	5·5	6·1	0·4*	0·4*	0·5*
Electricity, gas and water	1·5	1·8	2·3	1·2	1·3	1·5	6·5	7·1	8·3
Goods	42·4	44·0	46·9	55·7	53·6	51·5	33·2	32·3	31·0
Transport and communications	9·4	9·5	8·6	8·8	8·5	8·0	23·1	22·6	20·3
Distributive trades	15·1	14·7	14·4	10·2	12·0	12·9	11·9	11·7	11·4
Other services	27·4	26·4	24·6	25·4	25·9	27·7	7·7	7·7	8·2
Ownership of dwellings	5·7	5·6	5·4	–	–	–	24·0	25·7	29·0
Services	57·6	56·0	53·1	44·3	46·4	48·5	66·7	67·7	68·9

Sources: See below, pp. 77–9.

* Estimated; Feinstein data combine construction with manufacturing.

TABLE 3

United Kingdom: Rates of Change of Output, Employment, Capital Stock, Output per Employee, Capital per Employee, and 'Total Factor' Productivity, 1924–9, 1929–37 and 1924–37 (per cent per annum) — Manufacturing Industries

	Output			Employment			Capital stock			Output per employee			Capital per employee			Residual		
	1924–29	1929–37	1924–37	1924–29	1929–37	1924–37	1924–29	1929–37	1924–37	1924–29	1929–37	1924–37	1924–29	1929–37	1924–37	1924–29	1929–37	1924–37
Building materials	5·2	4·4	4·7	2·6	2·2	2·4	-0·2	0·5	0·2	2·6	2·2	2·3	-2·7	-2·7	-2·7	3·5	3·0	3·2
Chemicals	2·4	3·6	3·1	1·8	1·1	1·4	1·4	1·5	1·5	0·7	2·5	1·8	-0·4	0·4	0·1	0·8	2·3	1·7
Ferrous metal manufacture	0·7	4·4	3·0	-0·1	1·3	0·8	-0·1	0·6	0·4	0·8	3·1	2·2	0·0	-0·7	-0·4	0·8	3·3	2·3
Non-ferrous metal manufacture	3·6	5·7	4·9	1·1	3·1	2·4	0·4	1·7	1·2	2·5	2·6	2·5	-0·7	-1·5	-1·2	2·7	3·0	2·9
Shipbuilding	1·9	0·9	1·2	-2·6	-0·6	-1·4	-0·3	-1·3	-0·9	4·5	1·5	2·6	2·3	-0·7	0·5	3·8	1·7	2·5
Mechanical engineering	3·9	0·7	1·9	1·4	2·2	1·9	-0·1	0·4	0·2	2·5	-1·5	0·0	-1·5	-1·8	-1·7	2·9	-1·0	0·5
Electrical engineering	4·0	7·8	6·3	4·8	6·1	5·6	2·1	1·7	1·9	-0·8	1·7	0·7	-2·7	-4·4	-3·8	0·0	3·0	1·8
Vehicles	5·6	6·6	6·2	3·3	2·6	2·9	2·5	4·4	3·7	2·3	3·9	3·3	-0·8	1·8	0·8	2·6	3·4	3·1
Precision instruments	5·2	2·4	3·5	2·5	-1·1	0·3	—	—	—	2·7	3·5	3·2	—	—	—	—	—	—
Metal goods, n.e.s.	4·7	4·9	4·8	2·1	3·0	2·7	0·8	0·9	0·9	2·6	1·8	2·1	-2·5	0·2	-0·9	3·4	4·3	4·0
Other manufactures	5·9	5·1	5·4	3·3	0·7	1·7	-0·2	-4·0	-2·6	2·6	4·3	3·7	0·8	-1·1	-0·4	—	—	—
Cotton	—	—	—	-1·0	-3·0	-2·2	-0·4	-0·4	-0·4	—	—	—	2·0	0·1	0·8	—	—	—
Woollen and worsted	—	—	—	-2·4	-0·5	-1·2	11·3	5·1	7·4	—	—	—	-0·4	4·1	2·5	—	—	—
Rayon and silk	—	—	—	11·7	1·0	5·0	-0·5	-0·6	-0·6	—	—	—	-1·4	-0·8	-1·1	—	—	—
Other textiles	—	—	—	0·9	0·2	0·5	-0·5	-0·9	-0·8	—	—	—	-1·4	-0·8	-1·1	—	—	—
Textile finishing	—	—	—	-0·1	-1·7	-1·1	0·1	-1·6	-0·9	—	—	—	-0·4	0·8	0·3	—	—	—
Textiles	-0·9	3·1	1·6	-0·2	-1·2	-0·8	2·3	1·6	1·9	-0·7	4·3	2·4	0·3	-0·4	-0·1	-0·8	4·4	2·4
Leather	-1·1	3·7	1·8	-0·6	1·3	0·6	2·6	1·4	1·9	-0·5	2·4	1·2	2·9	0·3	1·3	-1·4	2·3	0·9
Clothing	2·7	1·7	2·1	0·5	0·4	0·5	0·2	0·6	0·4	2·2	1·3	1·4	2·1	1·0	1·4	1·6	1·0	1·2
Food	3·5	4·2	3·9	1·2	2·2	1·8	0·5	0·3	0·4	2·2	2·0	2·1	-1·1	-1·5	-1·3	2·6	2·5	2·5
Drink	0·0	1·1	0·7	0·6	1·0	0·8	2·5	1·4	1·8	-0·6	0·1	-0·2	0·0	-0·7	-0·4	-0·5	0·3	0·0
Tobacco	5·4	2·3	3·5	2·5	-0·5	0·6	2·0	1·8	1·9	3·0	2·8	2·9	0·1	1·9	1·2	3·0	2·2	2·5
Paper and printing	2·9	2·6	2·7	2·4	1·4	1·8	1·5	2·1	1·9	0·6	1·2	1·0	-0·3	0·3	0·1	0·7	1·1	0·9
Timber and furniture	7·4	3·2	4·8	2·9	1·3	1·9	—	—	—	4·5	1·9	2·9	-2·0	-0·5	-1·0	4·5	0·2	1·8
(Construction)	(7·4)	(2·9)	(4·6)	(3·6)	(2·8)	(3·1)	—	—	—	(3·9)	(0·0)	(1·5)	—	—	—	—	—	—
Manufacturing	2·8	3·5	3·3	1·2	1·2	1·2	0·6	0·4	0·5	1·6	2·4	2·1	-0·6	-0·8	-0·7	1·8	2·6	2·3

Sources: See below pp. 77–9.

TABLE 4

United Kingdom: Shares of Employment and Capital Stock, 1924, 1929 and 1937 (Percentages) — Manufacturing Industries

	Employment			Capital		
	1924	1929	1937	1924	1929	1937
Building materials	1·4	1·5	1·6	0·8	0·7	0·6
Chemicals	1·4	1·4	1·4	1·6	1·6	1·6
Ferrous metal manufacture	2·2	2·0	2·0	2·4	2·2	2·0
Non-ferrous metal manufacture	0·3	0·3	0·4	0·3	0·3	0·3
Shipbuilding	1·2	1·0	0·9	0·4	0·4	0·3
Mechanical engineering	3·2	3·2	3·4	1·5	1·4	1·3
Electrical engineering	1·0	1·2	1·7	0·6	0·6	0·6
Vehicles	2·5	2·7	3·0	0·4	0·4	0·6
Precision instruments	0·6	0·7	0·5	—	—	—
Metal goods, n.e.s.	1·5	1·5	1·8	—	—	—
Other manufactures	0·8	0·9	0·9	0·4	0·3	0·3
Cotton	3·2	2·8	2·0	2·2	2·0	1·3
Woollen and worsted	1·9	1·5	1·3	1·0	0·9	0·8
Rayon and silk	0·3	0·5	0·5	0·2	0·3	0·3
Other textiles	1·9	1·9	1·7	0·6	0·5	0·4
Textile finishing	0·8	0·7	0·5	0·8	0·7	0·6
Textiles	8·0	7·4	6·1	4·7	4·4	3·4
Leather	0·5	0·5	0·5	0·2	0·2	0·2
Clothing	3·9	3·7	3·5	0·6	0·6	0·6
Food	2·7	2·7	2·8	1·7	1·5	1·4
Drink	0·7	0·7	0·7	0·8	0·7	0·7
Tobacco	0·3	0·3	0·3	0·1	0·1	0·1
Paper and printing	2·4	2·5	2·5	1·2	1·3	1·3
Timber and furniture*	1·3	1·5	1·5	0·2	0·2	0·2
Manufacturing	35·9	35·7	35·2	18·0	17·2	15·4

Sources: See below.

* Capital shares roughly estimated; Feinstein data combine this component with construction.

STATISTICAL SOURCES

Output: C. H. Feinstein, 'Production and Productivity 1920–1962', *London and Cambridge Bulletin*, XLVIII ('*The Times*' *Review of Industry and Technology*, Dec 1963) p. xii (Tables 1 and 2); K. S. Lomax, 'Production and Productivity Movements in the United Kingdom since 1900', *Journal of the Royal Statistical Society*, A122 (1959) 192–3. The sector indexes are weighted by net output in 1938, but the manufacturing components are weighted in a mixed and moving way to produce the manufacturing index.

Employment (man-year equivalents): Agatha L. Chapman, *Wages and Salaries in the United Kingdom 1920–1938* (Cambridge, 1953).

Capital (stocks at beginning of year at first-cost value): C. H. Feinstein, *Domestic Capital Formation in the United Kingdom 1920–1938* (Cambridge, 1965).

The main identifiable problems affect the employment and capital stock data, although this does not mean that the output estimates are really satisfactory—their deficiencies, apart from the weighting question noted above, just cannot be fully assessed at the moment.

The Chapman employment series does not include the self-employed/working proprietor category, which is clearly of considerable (absolute) importance, particularly in agriculture, distribution, and other services. Feinstein, in some calculations of output per man-year changes over the 1924–37 period (1963 paper), claimed to have made a 'very approximate adjustment to include employers and workers on own account' in each sector. Comparing our unadjusted results with his (and adding the Matthews 1964 calculations for discussion below) suggests that the Feinstein adjustments were either small or largely offsetting because the differences could not be smaller without being non-existent.

TABLE 5

United Kingdom: Rates of Change of Output per Man-Year, 1924–37
(*per cent per annum*)

	Dowie	Feinstein	Matthews
Agriculture, forestry and fishing	3·0	3·1	2·5
Mining and quarrying	2·4	2·4	2·3
Manufacturing	2·1	2·0	2·2
Construction	1·5	1·4	1·5
Electricity, gas and water	2·9	2·8	2·8
Transport and communications	1·0	0·9	1·1
Distributive trades	−1·3	−1·3	−0·6
(Insurance, banking and finance)	(−0·4)	(−0·4)	(−0·2)
Other services	−0·6	–	–
G.D.P.	0·9	0·8	1·1

The 1964 Matthews figures, on the other hand, suggest considerable adjustment to the input measures in agriculture and distribution: it is presumably mainly the inclusion of self-employed persons which slows down the deceleration/acceleration in employment and therefore lowers/raises the rate of productivity improvement. Adjustment of this sort is clearly desirable, but we have preferred not to attempt statistical correction on inadequate data; especially since the sub-period focus probably reduces the importance of adjustment somewhat. However, it is clearly important that both the rates of change and structure tables—especially the latter—should be read in the light of these limitations.

The problems with the capital stock estimates are, of course, legion and are fully and frankly treated by Feinstein in his 1965 work. We mention here only the relatively mundane one of industry classification. Feinstein was obliged to use the pre-war trade classification of the Board of Inland Revenue when making his estimates for several industries. This differs considerably from the 1948 Standard Industrial Classification on which the output and employment data are based. Feinstein has set out in his table 13·20 the approximate corresponding S.I.C. classifications for his series and the main transfers can be identified, without there being any possibility of ascertaining their quantitative significance, however. The assumption has usually been made here that the transfers have a less serious effect on the rates of growth calculations than on the structural ones: unless the transferred component is a sizeable fraction of the subdivision *and* has a significantly different rate of change, the transfer will not seriously weaken the calculation. The engineering-vehicles group is the area where more information would be very desirable, and clearly the leather–rubber position is worrying: rubber is joined with leather in the capital data but is part of other manufacturing in the other two cases.

The residual calculations employ the same 70–30 labour–capital income shares as used by Matthews. Individual industries clearly vary from the average, but it takes considerable variation to alter the results significantly unless the rates of change of the two inputs are markedly different.

5   Some Aspects of Post-War Growth in the British Economy in Relation to Historical Experience*

by R. C. O. MATTHEWS

THE purpose of this paper is to present and discuss certain data on movements in output and input in the British economy in the post-war period, viewed in relation to trends over the past hundred years. This work is part of a research project sponsored by the Social Science Research Council of New York on the growth of advanced economies in the post-war period in relation to their historical experience. The part of this project that is concerned with Great Britain is being carried out in Cambridge by C. H. Feinstein, J. Odling-Smee and myself. Our work is still at a relatively early stage, and all the statistics to be quoted in this paper should be regarded as preliminary and subject to revision. Any conclusions to be drawn are still more provisional.

Section I deals with trends in aggregates of output and inputs since 1855. Sections II and III compare the inter-war and post-war periods in more detail, with sectoral breakdowns.

The statistics are derived partly from published sources and partly from our own estimates. Dr Feinstein has done the lion's share of the work in preparing these basic data, while most of the detailed work on the present paper has been done by Mr Odling-Smee.

I

Annual data on G.D.P., employment in man-years, G.D.P. per man-year, capital, and output per unit of input are displayed in Chart 1. Shaded periods are recessions.[1] We shall discuss each of the series in turn. Growth rates over four peacetime sub-periods are summarised in Table 1.

* First published 1964.
[1] For this purpose the dates of recessions are defined according to conventional cycle chronology, rather than according to the behaviour of any one of our series.

TABLE I

Annual Percentage Rates of Growth of Output and Inputs
in the United Kingdom

	Real G.D.P.	Employ-ment in man-years	Capital	G.D.P. per man-year	Growth due to: Residual	Change in capital per man
1856–1899	2·0	0·9	1·3	1·1	0·9	0·2
1899–1913	1·1	1·0	1·8	0·1	−0·2	0·3
1924–1937	2·3	1·2	1·7	1·1	0·9	0·2
1948–1962	2·5	0·6	2·7	1·9	1·3	0·6

Income and income per man-year

The peace-time rate of growth of G.D.P. at constant prices,[1] as shown in Table 1, has been relatively stable over the last hundred years, with the exception of the period 1899–1913, when it was conspicuously lower. There is a slight acceleration of growth between the three periods 1856–99, 1924–37 and 1948–62, but not too much should be made of this, because of the margin of error in the statistics, especially for the earlier years. As is well known, the rate of growth has not in any period come near to the 4 per cent level currently accepted as a target. As may be seen from the chart, the rate of growth has suffered a conspicuous set-back in both war-periods (here defined as 1914–24 and 1938–48 to include post-war read-justment).[2]

In some respect more illuminating is the movement over time of G.D.P. per man-year. This shows some of the same features as G.D.P., such as retardation 1899–1913, but there are also certain differences: the downward shift over the Second World War is less pronounced (because the downward shift in G.D.P. was largely due to the increase in unemployment), and the acceleration in the period since the Second World War is a good deal more pronounced. The picture is much confused by the two wars, both of which led to a fall in pro-ductivity that was not quickly made up. Only very recently has G.D.P. per man-year regained the level to be obtained by extra-polating the inter-war rate of growth over the interval comprised by the Second World War.

[1] The series used here for G.D.P. at constant prices, and also for the capital stock at constant prices, are derived by splicing together separate series for 1855–1900 at 1900 prices, 1900–48 at 1938 prices, and 1948–63 at 1958 prices.
[2] The drop over the Second World War is also partly due to Southern Ireland, which is included up till 1919 and excluded thereafter. This is responsible for a fall of about 5 per cent in G.D.P., but for a rise of about 1½ per cent in G.D.P. per man-year.

Whereas in modern times G.D.P. per man-year has generally
fluctuated with the trade cycle, before 1914 the cyclical movement
of G.D.P. per man-year was irregular. This irregularity, together
with the unusually high level of production and productivity around
1900, makes it possible to read different interpretations into the
record of the earlier period. On the one hand, one can say that there
was a period of stagnation 1900–13, which was prolonged by the

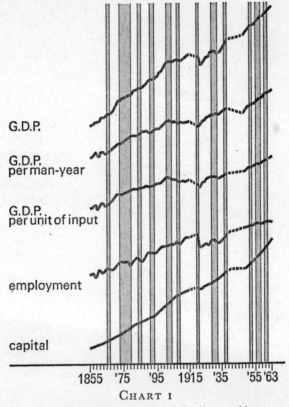

CHART I

Output and Inputs 1855–1963 (log. scale)

effects of the First World War and by the relatively slow growth of
the 1920s. Alternatively, one can argue, as Mr Coppock has done,[1]
that there was retardation already from the 1870s, culminating in
actual cessation of growth 1900–13, but interrupted by an unrepre-
sentative flash-in-the-pan from 1897 to 1902. Both interpretations

[1] D. J. Coppock, 'The Climacteric of the 1890s: a Critical Note', *Manchester
School*, XXIV (1956).

agree in identifying three broad phases in the economic history of the past hundred years: an initial phase of fairly rapid growth, terminating in the 1870s or in 1900 as the case may be; a doldrums period, running from then until the early 1930s; and a concluding period of faster growth, beginning in the 1930s, interrupted by the Second World War, and carrying on up to the present time.

Employment

As may be seen from Table 1, the rate of growth of labour input measured in man-years has been low in the post-war period by the standards of earlier peacetime phases. This has been due mainly to demographic causes; but the pattern of growth shown by the labour force is not identical to that shown by the population.

TABLE 2
Labour Force in the United Kingdom

| | Annual rate of growth since last date | | | | Crude participation Rates | | | 15-64 year-olds as % of total population | Participation rates relative to population aged 15-64 | | |
| | Population | Total | Male | Female | Total | Male | Female | | Total | Male | Female |
		Labour Force									
1861	0·6	0·8	0·7	1·0	45·1	63·6	27·6	60·2	75·0	107·5	45·1
1871	0·9	0·8	0·7	0·9	44·6	62·4	27·8	59·0	75·7	107·7	46·5
1881	1·0	0·8	0·9	0·4	43·3	61·5	26·2	58·9	73·6	105·8	44·0
1891	0·8	1·0	1·0	0·8	44·1	63·0	26·3	60·2	73·3	105·8	43·2
1901	0·9	0·9	1·2	0·4	44·1	64·5	24·9	62·8	70·2	103·7	39·3
1911	0·9	1·0	1·0	1·0	44·6	65·2	25·2	63·6	70·2	103·3	39·3
1921*	0·4	0·5	0·5	0·4		66·3	24·9	65·9			
1921†					44·9	66·6	25·0		68·1	102·3	37·4
1931	0·4	0·6	0·5	0·8	45·4	66·4	26·2	68·2	66·6	98·0	34·9
1938	0·4	1·3	1·2	1·4	48·1	69·7	28·2	69·4	69·4	100·8	40·5
1951	0·4	0·3	0·1	0·7	47·3	66·8	29·2	66·5	71·1	100·5	43·9
1961	0·5	0·6	0·3	1·1	47·8	65·5	31·2	64·9	73·6	99·3	48·9

* Including Southern Ireland.   † Excluding Southern Ireland.

The level of unemployment did not alter much between the opening and closing years of each of the four peacetime phases we have distinguished, so the rate of growth of employment within them was closely similar to that of the labour-force. Decennial data on the labour force are shown in Table 2.[1] It may be seen that the rate of growth of population since the First World War has been about half of what it was previously. Before the First World War, the rate of growth of the labour force did not differ much from that of population. Since then there has been more divergence between

---

[1] 'Labour Force' is here used in the same sense as 'working population' in British official statistics and includes employers and self-employed and also members of the armed forces.

the two. In the inter-war period, although the rate of population growth declined, the rate of growth of the labour force for a while increased. This was due mainly to an increase in the proportion of those of working age in total population. Because of this change in age composition, the full effect of the long-run decline in population growth on the labour supply was not left until after the Second World War. There was also some increase in the inter-war period in the proportion of women of the 15–64 age group who took employment. The continued increase in the participation rate of females is the main reason why in the post-war period the rate of growth of the labour force has been rather higher than that of population.

The slow rate of increase of the labour supply is something which differentiates the post-war period from earlier phases. The change is still more marked if one looks at the supply of male labour. Until the Second World War the rate of growth of supply of male labour was slightly greater than that of female labour. Between 1948 and 1962, on the other hand, the male working population rose by only 0·4 per cent per annum while the female working population rose by 1·3 per cent per annum. As a result, although females comprise only about a third of the total working population, they have contributed nearly two-thirds of the increase in the working population. The release of men from the armed forces, which may be regarded as a once-for-all decline in the importance of an industry requiring male labour, has meant that the relative contribution of women to the increase in civil employment has been less than this, but even so the increase in the number of females in civil employment has been absolutely larger than that of males. The increase in the female participation ratio that has brought about these results reverses the trend of 1871–1931 and has raised the rate to the highest level ever recorded. As is well known, it is mainly due to the increase in the participation rate of married women over 35.[1]

Capital

The concept of capital here used is the gross stock of reproducible fixed assets at constant prices. Capital is thus calculated before

---

[1] The data quoted in the text relate to employment measured in man-years, and take no account of changes in hours. Preliminary estimates of the annual rates of growth of labour input measured in man-hours over our four peacetime periods are as follows: 1856–99, 0·7; 1899–1913, 1·0; 1929–37, 1·4; 1948–62, 0·6. These are not used in the text, partly because more work needs to be done on the data, and partly because of certain doubts about matters of principle, notably about the propriety of adjusting labour input for changes in number of hours worked when a similar adjustment is not made for capital input.

deduction of depreciation but after deduction of estimates of retirements. Inventories, land and mineral wealth, and overseas assets are excluded. The estimates for 1938–63 are taken from the work of G. A. Dean of the Central Statistical Office[1] and correspond to those in the 1964 National Income Blue Book. The estimates for earlier years are from unpublished work by Dr Feinstein.

The growth of the capital stock is, as might be expected, subject to much less short-period fluctuation than the growth of output. Three main points stand out.

(1) The growth of the capital stock in the post-war period has been much faster than ever before. Since the labour force has been growing more slowly than before in the post-war period, the rate of growth of capital per man has outstripped that of previous periods by a still greater extent: capital per man has grown at a rate of 2 per cent a year, as compared with a rate of about ½ per cent in earlier periods. It is likely that some forms of capital accumulation are insufficiently reflected in the data for the earlier years, so that the change may be somewhat overstated, and it must also be remembered that these figures take no account of accumulation of overseas assets, which in some years before 1914 was of the same order of magnitude as gross domestic fixed capital formation. But there can be no doubt that the rate at which domestic assets per man have accumulated in the post-war period is without parallel in the last hundred years.

(2) Net capital formation was brought to a standstill by both wars.

(3) Before 1914 a clear long cycle in the rate of growth of the capital stock is to be observed. This is to be compared with the long cycle found in many statistics of the United States economy but not found in any such clear form in series relating to output in the United Kingdom. Especial interest attaches to the long wave running from 1895 to 1914. From about 1898 to about 1903 the rate of growth of capital was conspicuously above trend. This is associated with the boom in home investment that developed in the late 1890s. It is tempting to relate it to the marked increase in the rate of growth of output per man that occurred in much the same years and which has already been referred to. But the slackening in the rate of growth of the capital stock in the ensuing period, 1904–14, is not sufficient to explain the stagnation of productivity during those years. As will be seen presently, the usual way of taking account of changes in capital input, by the output per unit of input method, does not smooth out the peak around 1900 and the subsequent

[1] G. A. Dean, 'The Stock of Fixed Capital in the United Kingdom in 1961', *Journal of the Royal Statistical Society*, A127 (1964).

stagnation. There is scope for further study and more sophisticated hypotheses relating to this peculiar period.

Capital-output ratio

Chart 2 shows the capital-output ratio at constant prices.[1] The largest movements shown are the fall from 1866–71 and the rise across the First World War, reversed across the Second World War. The first of these is perhaps too ancient and too dubious statistically to be worth very close study. The high capital-output ratio shown for the inter-war period is influenced by the general unemployment and below-capacity working of that time (the capital figures are, of course, not corrected to allow for the degree of utilisation); this consideration is of about the right order of magnitude to account for the higher level of the ratio in the inter-war period compared with the periods before and after.

Excluding the inter-war period and the years before 1870, the capital-output ratio has varied only within a fairly narrow range— roughly from $3\frac{1}{2}$ to $4\frac{1}{4}$, which is hardly larger than the margin of error in the capital stock statistics. The decline across the period of the Second World War is a good deal less pronounced than it has been in the United States, where the capital-output ratio post-war has been about only two-thirds of its 1929 value. And this notwithstanding that there has been a greater change in the level of activity in this country since 1929 than in the United States. The *long-run* downward tendency in the capital-output ratio appears to have been both less continuous and of smaller amplitude in this country. Indeed, at least as far as the period since 1870 is concerned, it cannot be taken as established that there has been such a long-run downward tendency.

If the movements in the capital-output ratio at constant prices are thought to be not large enough to warrant any firm conclusions, still more doubts are engendered by comparing them with data on the capital-output ratio at current prices. These are available only for the three years 1900, 1938 and 1958, which are shown by crosses on Chart 2. It will be seen that whereas the capital-output ratio fell in constant prices between 1938 and 1958, it rose considerably in current prices. This is because capital-goods prices rose relatively to prices in general. The measurement of price changes across the war is inevitably untrustworthy, especially in view of the conceptual

[1] The original series were computed at 1900 prices for 1855–1900, at 1938 prices for 1900–38, and at 1958 prices for 1938–63. The figures for the latter two sub-periods were then spliced on to those for the first sub-period in order to give a continuous series.

and practical difficulties involved in making allowance for improvements in quality of capital goods. But the change recorded is such a large one that it is difficult to attribute it wholly to defects in the statistics.[1]

One way of analysing this type of data is in terms of the tautologies suggested by the Harrod growth model. The rate of growth of the capital stock, K, is equal to the average propensity to save, s, divided by value-capital-output ratio; the rate of growth of total output, Y,

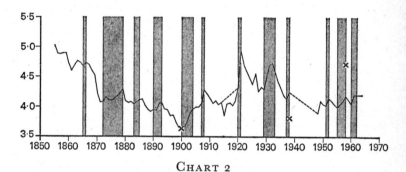

CHART 2

Capital-Output Ratio

— = Capital-output ratio at constant prices.
× = Capital-output ratio at current prices.

is equal to s divided by the incremental capital-output ratio ($ICOR$). Economists in the O.E.C.D. and others who have written comparing the post-war growth experience of different European economies have made much use of this approach. The relevant figures are shown in Table 3. Because of the importance of changes in relative prices of capital goods, this price has been included as a separate item. The figures for s are therefore at current prices and those for the capital-output ratio at constant prices: s is measured net of replacement.

Looking first at the data for capital we note that the rise in the rate of growth of capital in the post-war period compared with earlier is wholly due to the rise in s. The value-capital-output ratio (measured in Table 3 by the reciprocal of the product of the last two columns) has risen, on account of the large rise in capital-goods prices. The rise in $\Delta K/K$ has therefore been rather less than the rise in s. The same applies still more strongly in the case of Y; the

---

[1] It may be noted that the primary data from which the capital stock figures are derived relate in some cases to quantities and in some cases to values, so it is not a clear-cut issue whether the current-price measures or the constant-price measures should be regarded as more reliable.

TABLE 3

Growth Rates, Savings Ratios and Capital-Output Ratios

$$\frac{\Delta K}{K} = \frac{\Delta K p_k}{Y p_y} \times \frac{Y}{K} \times \frac{p_y}{p_k} = s \times \frac{1}{K/Y} \times p$$

$$\frac{\Delta K}{K} (\%) = s (\%) \times \frac{1}{K/Y} \times p \; (1900 = 100)$$

1856–1899	1·3	5·5	0·22	108
1899–1913	1·8	6·6	0·25	111
1924–1937	1·7	6·7	0·20	124
1948–1962	2·7	13·0	0·25	82

$$\frac{\Delta Y}{Y} = \frac{\Delta K p_k}{Y p_y} \times \frac{\Delta Y}{\Delta K} \times \frac{p_y}{p_k} = s \times \frac{1}{ICOR} \times p$$

$$\frac{\Delta Y}{Y} (\%) = s (\%) \times \frac{1}{ICOR} \times p \; (1900 = 100)$$

1856–1899	2·0	5·5	0·34	108
1899–1913	1·1	6·6	0·15	111
1924–1937	2·3	6·7	0·28	124
1948–1962	2·5	13·0	0·24	82

value-incremental-capital-output ratio has risen substantially and the rise in $\Delta Y/Y$ compared with pre-war has come about because the rise in s has been even larger.

All this of course is just a tautological way of arranging the data and no causal significance is necessarily to be inferred. In particular the *ICOR* seems to me to be a concept with little economic significance. But perhaps it is of some interest to note the contrast between these findings and the findings that have come out from comparison of different countries in the post-war period. These have usually shown that although the faster-growing countries have had higher s than slow-growing ones, this difference has been smaller and has contributed less to differences in growth rates than the difference in *ICOR*s.[1] In the historical comparison, on the other hand, as has just been seen, the higher growth is entirely due to s, and the movement in the *ICOR* actually works in the wrong direction. It may be conjectured, therefore, that the reasons why the British economy has grown faster in the post-war period than earlier are unlikely to turn out to be the same as the reasons why other countries have grown faster than Britain in the post-war period—not perhaps a very surprising conclusion.

The uniqueness of the post-war period does stand out from these comparisons. If we look at the last period when $\Delta K/K$ for a while

---

[1] See for example, United Nations Department of Social and Economic Affairs, *World Economic Survey 1959* (New York, 1960) ch.1.

was at a level close to the post-war level, namely in the late 1890s and early 1900s, we find that although *s* was relatively high, a temporarily low K/Y did also contribute significantly to achieving the high $\Delta K/K$ then recorded.

Output per unit of input

This has been calculated by a method that is, broadly speaking, that of Kendrick.[1] An index for total factor input is derived within each sub-period by weighting labour and capital according to their shares in total income in a base year. The indices for the sub-periods are then spliced together, and the resulting series is divided into G.D.P. at constant prices to give output per unit of input.[2] The rate of growth of output per unit of input is the so-called Residual factor in economic growth, measuring that part of the growth in output that is due to causes other than growth in the labour force or capital accumulation.

The limitations of this approach to the analysis of economic growth are well known and need not be repeated here. Not only does its validity depend on certain assumptions implicit in weighting capital and labour according to their shares in income, but also, at best, the 'Residual' is no more than a measure of unknown forces and is not necessarily to be identified with 'technical progress' in the usual sense. My own opinion is that the approach *does* have usefulness, but as a starting-point of research rather than as its conclusion. Inspection of trends in the Residual helps to call attention to the questions most needing examination. Unfortunately in the present paper it is not possible to go much beyond the starting-point.

---

[1] J. W. Kendrick, *Productivity Trends in the United States* (Princeton, for the National Bureau of Economic Research, 1961).

[2] Write F for total factor input, α and $(1 - \alpha)$ for the shares of capital and labour respectively in the base year b, L for labour input, K for capital input, and subscripts for time. Then total factor input in any year t is given by

$$\frac{F_t}{F_b} = (1 - \alpha)\frac{L_t}{L_b}\,\alpha + \frac{K_t}{K_b}$$

This gives measures of F_t for the years within any sub-period. Different base-years and different αs are used for each sub-period, and the results are spliced to give a single series for total factor input. The sub-periods, base-years and αs used are as follows:

Period	Base-year	α
1855–1894	1875	0·40
1894–1914	1906	0·40
1919–1938	1929	0·30
1938–1963	1956	0·26

In general outline, the movement of output per unit of input is similar to that of output per man-year. We find a period of retardation running from about 1900 (or perhaps earlier) until about 1930, followed by more rapid growth. The rate of growth since the Second World War is higher than in any earlier phase, but the difference is rather less marked than in the case of output per man-year because part of the high post-war rate of growth is accounted for by the high rate of capital accumulation. Table 1 shows the parts of the growth in output per man-year attributable in each period to the Residual and to the rise in capital per man respectively. Apart from the anomalous period 1899–1913, the Residual is always responsible for much the greater part of the growth. However the increase in capital per man makes a larger contribution to growth, both absolutely and relatively, in the post-war period than either before 1900 or in the inter-war period.

II

We now compare the two periods 1924–37 and 1948–62 in more detail.

Year-to-year movements in output per unit of input have been calculated for these two periods; but for present purposes we are interested in long-term movements rather than annual fluctuations, so we confine our attention to the rates of growth between the terminal years of the periods. For the inter-war period this does not raise any great problems, since 1924 and 1937 were years with roughly similar levels of activity. (The unemployment percentage was 10·3 in 1924 and 10·8 in 1937.) The years 1948 and 1962 are not quite so similar, for 1962 was a recession year and 1948 can be regarded as still falling within the period of post-war reconstruction. But they are similar in both falling below the trend-line of productivity, and rates of growth between 1948–62 are not very different from those that would be obtained by fitting a trend line or else by taking a peak-to-peak comparison 1951–60.

Growth rates for G.D.P. and its chief sub-divisions are shown in Table 4. 'Production and distribution' is a term used to describe those sectors that are represented in the index of industrial production (manufacturing, mining, construction and utilities), together with agriculture, transport and communications and distribution.

The most striking conclusion that appears is that the higher Residual (rate of growth of output per unit of input) in the post-war period in G.D.P., as compared with inter-war, owes nothing to manufacturing or the other items included in industrial production but derives entirely from the better performance in services and distribution. This point had already been noted[1] in statistics of the rate of growth of output per man, and it stands out still more prominently when account is taken, as here, of capital input. As far as industrial production is concerned, the position is simply stated: output grew at much about the same rate in the two periods, and so did employment, and hence output per man (the rise in

TABLE 4

Annual Growth Rates of Output and Input by Sector

	Output		Employment		Capital		Total input		Residual	
	1924–37	1948–62	1924–37	1948–62	1924–37	1948–62	1924–37	1948–62	1924–37	1948–62
G.D.P.	2·3	2·5	1·2	0·6	1·7	2·7	1·4	1·2	0·9	1·3
Manufacturing	3·3	3·4	1·1	1·1	0·9	3·1	0·9	1·7	2·4	1·7
Industrial production	3·2	3·2	0·9	0·9	1·4	3·4	1·0	1·6	2·2	1·6
Services and distribution	1·6	2·0	2·2	0·7	2·6	2·7	2·3	1·3	0·7	0·7
Production and distribution	2·6	2·9	1·0	0·7	0·9	2·9	1·0	1·3	1·6	1·6

employment in the industrial sector being less rapid than in the economy as a whole inter-war and more rapid post-war). But the rise in the capital stock was much more rapid in the post-war period, especially in manufacturing.[2] Hence there was a faster rate of growth of total input, and the Residual was lower.

Before jumping to the conclusion that this represents a failure in industrial performance post-war, it should be emphasised that these calculations have important limitations. No allowance is made for the degree of utilisation of capital. It is notorious that certain industries, notably the steel industry, were operating well below capacity in 1962. However the contrast between industrial production on the one hand and distribution and services on the other is beyond doubt. Output in distribution and services in the inter-war period rose less rapidly than either employment or capital input, and the result was a substantial negative Residual. In the post-war

[1] C. H. Feinstein, 'Productivity and Production, 1920–62', *London and Cambridge Economic Bulletin* (Dec 1963), and Ch. 1 above.
[2] The data on Capital in Table 4 relate to fixed assets. The inclusion of stocks and work-in-progress does not alter any of the conclusions in the text. The figures for Capital and the Residual for G.D.P. and Manufacturing are then as follows:

	Capital		Residual	
	1924–37	1948–62	1924–37	1948–62
G.D.P.	1·7	2·6	0·9	1·4
Manufacturing	0·9	3·3	2·3	1·6

period the Residual in distribution and services is substantially positive, though still less than in industrial production.

The hypothesis that naturally suggests itself is that in the inter-war period the pressure of unemployment led to a concentration of under-employed labour in services and distribution. The question that then poses itself for the future is whether the gain in produc-tivity in services and distribution since the war is likely to prove a once-for-all gain, due to adaptation to a tighter labour market, or whether this change in the labour market has unleashed forces of progress that will lead to continued advance.

So far the rates of increase in labour and in capital in each of the broad groups, manufacturing, etc., have been computed simply on the basis of the increase in the number of persons em-ployed and in the value (essentially the cost at constant prices) of the capital employed. An alternative procedure is to weight different parts of the labour force and of the capital stock according to differences in their remuneration, on the grounds that higher remuneration reflects higher productivity. Table 5 shows the result of such a calculation, set against the unweighted figures already given. The weighted figures in this table are derived by taking separately the data for each industry specified in Section III below and weighting the increases in labour and capital in those industries by their base-year rate of remuneration.[1] The lower part of the table shows the difference between the weighted growth rates and the corresponding unweighted growth rates given in Table 4.

Where, as in most cases, the weighted index is higher than the unweighted index, it means that there has been a rapider-than-average rise in employment (or capital) in industries where the wage (or the rate of profit) is above average. This can be due to a number of causes, corresponding to different possible causes of the differences in rates of remuneration. Inter-industry differences

[1] Writing L for labour, K for capital, F for total factor input, w for wage, r for the profit rate, denoting individual-industry figures by symbols with the subscript i and aggregative figures by symbols without subscripts, the definitions of the weighted rates of growth are

$$\frac{\Delta L}{L} = \sum \frac{\Delta L_i}{L_i} \cdot \frac{w_i}{w} \cdot \frac{L_i}{L}$$

$$\frac{\Delta K}{K} = \sum \frac{\Delta K_i}{K_i} \cdot \frac{r_i}{r} \cdot \frac{K_i}{K}$$

$$\frac{\Delta F}{F} = \frac{wL}{wL + rK} \cdot \frac{\Delta L}{L} + \frac{rK}{wL + rK} \cdot \frac{\Delta K}{K}$$

For discussion of this approach see B. F. Massell, 'A Disaggregated View of Tech-nical Change', *Journal of Political Economy*, LXIX (1961). Weighted measures of inputs were also used in Kendrick's pioneering study referred to above.

in wages may reflect differences in the quality of the labour force employed, or else they may reflect imperfect mobility of labour of given quality between different industries. In the former case, an excess of the weighted over the unweighted measure of the growth of labour input implies an improvement in the average quality of the labour force; in the latter case it implies a move towards greater efficiency in the allocation of labour between industries. Similarly, differences in the rate of profit may reflect imperfect

TABLE 5

Growth Rates of Weighted Factor Inputs

	Labour		Capital		Factor Input	
	1924–37	*1948–62*	*1924–37*	*1948–62*	*1924–37*	*1948–62*
G.D.P.	1·6	0·9	1·8	3·5	1·7	1·6
Manufacturing	1·5	1·3	1·1	4·0	1·4	2·1
Industrial production	1·5	1·1	1·4	4·4	1·5	2·0
Services and distribution	2·1	1·2	2·5	3·2	2·2	1·8
Production and distribution	1·5	0·9	1·2	4·0	1·4	1·8

Excess of Weighted over Unweighted Growth Rates

	Labour		Capital		Factor Input	
G.D.P.	0·4	0·3	0·1	0·9	0·3	0·4
Manufacturing	0·4	0·2	0·5	0·9	0·5	0·4
Industrial production	0·6	0·2	0·0	1·0	0·5	0·4
Services and distribution	−0·1	0·5	−0·1	0·5	−0·1	0·5
Production and distribution	0·5	0·2	0·3	1·1	0·4	0·5

allowance for quality in the measures used for capital or they may reflect a failure of the system to achieve equimarginal returns; and corresponding alternatives follow in the interpretation of a difference in weighted and unweighted measures of the rate of growth of the capital stock. This difference we shall refer to as the quality-shift change. It is, of course, a statistical measure that has to be understood in the light of the way it is constructed, and it does not claim to be a comprehensive measure of all the benefit derived from changes in the allocation or quality of factor inputs throughout the economy.

Looking first at the figures for labour, we find that in both periods the aggregative figures (G.D.P.) show a sizeable quality-shift change, indicating an improvement in the quality and/or allocation of the labour force. This change is slightly smaller post-war than inter-war. The increasing proportions of females in the labour force in the post-war period has tended to produce a negative quality-shift change, because females earn less than males; the magnitude of the negative quality shift change due to the change in sex-composition in the economy as a whole is —0·1. This is the same as the reduction in the overall quality-shift change in labour between the two periods, and it follows that the magnitude of the quality-shift change due to forces other than changing sex-composition has been the same in the two periods. But this upshot is the net result of opposite movements in services and distribution and in the rest of the economy. The inter-way quality-shift change was actually negative within services and distribution, indicating an above-average rate of increase in the worse-paid sectors. This again is consistent with the notion of labour surplus forcing people into low-productivity employment—not merely into services and distribution generally, but into the worse-paid parts of the services and distribution sector. Outside services and distribution the post-war quality-shift change has been less than inter-war.[1] To that extent some support is given to the commonly-held notion that shifts in industrial structure made a more important contribution to productivity growth inter-war than post-war.

In the case of capital, the picture is rather different. Again we find a negative quality-shift change in services and distribution inter-war but in all sectors the quality-shift change was (algebraically) larger post-war than inter-war. This has to be viewed in relation to the much more rapid overall rate of capital accumulation post-war. The faster the rate of capital accumulation, the more scope there is for increasing the proportion of the capital stock in the sectors with an above-average rate of return. This is evidently what has happened. Relatively to the rate of capital accumulation the quality-shift change in capital inter-war was

---

[1] Changing sex-composition does *not* help to explain this, at least in the case of manufacturing, because in manufacturing, unlike the economy as a whole, the male labour force has increased faster than the female labour force in the post-war period. Changing sex-composition made a *positive* contribution of nearly 0·1 to the post-war quality-shift change within manufacturing. Changing sex-composition does not appear to have made any significant contribution in either direction to the inter-war quality-shift change in manufacturing, though the calculations here are necessarily rough.

somewhat higher than post-war, although, as has been stated, it was lower absolutely.[1]

The net result of the opposite trends in quality-shift change for labour and capital in manufacturing has been that the overall quality-shift change has been fractionally lower post-war than inter-war. It appears that the inter-war period saw a more effective redistribution of labour within manufacturing than the post-war period, but the higher post-war rate of capital accumulation has made possible a larger reallocation of capital within manufacturing. In services and distribution there has been a strong increase in the benefit derived from the quality-shift change, on the side of both capital and labour. The upshot has been that for G.D.P. as a whole, the overall quality-shift has increased slightly.

III

In this section we carry further the comparison of the inter-war and post-war trends by examining individual industries.

The data on rates of growth of output and input are shown in Table 6. As noted above, for the economy as a whole and for broad groups of industries, the movements between the years 1924 and 1937 on the one hand and 1948 and 1962 on the other provide a fair measure of trends within the two periods, despite the imperfect comparability of 1948 and 1962; but for a small number of individual industries, the choice of these terminal years produces an obviously misleading result, mainly because of contractions in output 1960–2. We have dealt with this by using rates of growth between the peak years 1951 and 1960 instead of between 1948 and 1962 in the case of these industries.

We find that each of the four main groups outside industrial production (agriculture, transport, distribution and services) show a higher residual post-war than pre-war, and so contribute to the higher residual found for G.D.P. In the case of services, the capital stock cannot be allocated accurately between sectors, and the output figures are subject to the usual difficulties experienced in measuring this part of G.D.P. The results must therefore be treated with reserve. However the same conventions are adopted for measuring output in both periods, and moreover the higher post-war Residual in services comes about mainly from the lower rate of growth of labour input, which is reasonably free from

[1] The lower rate of growth of the labour force in the post-war period may likewise be held to be partly responsible for the lower quality-shift change in labour. But as far as the industrial sector is concerned, the rate of growth of employment was the same in the two periods, so the fall from 0·6 to 0·2 in the labour quality-shift change under this heading cannot be explained in this way.

statistical ambiguity. Therefore there is no reason to doubt the broad conclusion.

Comparison of the behaviour of other industries produces a confusing picture, and more work is needed to unravel the relationships that may be involved.

We note first that the conclusions to be drawn about the relative performance of different industries on the basis of the Residual conform quite closely, but not perfectly, to the conclusions that would be drawn on the basis of the more familiar concept, rate of growth of productivity per man. This is as expected. Discrepancies arise chiefly in the case of industries where there has been exceptionally rapid capital accumulation, such as chemicals and bricks, pottery and glass. In agriculture the rate of capital accumulation has not been above the average absolutely, but it has taken place at the same time as a rapid reduction in the labour force. Textiles

TABLE 6
Rates of Growth by Industry

	Output 24–37	Output 48–62	Employment 24–37	Employment 48–62	Capital 24–37	Capital 48–62	Factor input 24–37	Factor input 48–62	Residual 24–37	Residual 48–62
Agriculture	1·3	2·6	−1·2	−1·8	−0·1	2·5	−1·0	−0·2	2·3	2·8
Food, drink and tobacco	2·8	2·5	1·4	1·8	0·5	3·9	1·0	2·8	1·8	−0·3
Chemicals	3·1	5·7	1·4	1·5	1·6	6·5	1·5	4·0	1·6	1·7
Iron and steel*	3·0	3·1	0·7	0·7	0·7	4·6	0·7	2·2	2·3	0·9
Electrical engineering*	6·2	6·2	5·1	4·0	2·0	3·8	3·9	3·9	2·3	2·3
Non-electrical engineering*	1·8	2·0	1·0	1·1	0·2	4·0	0·8	1·8	1·0	0·2
Vehicles	6·3	5·6	3·0	1·9	3·0	3·8	3·0	2·2	3·3	3·4
Other metal manufacture*	4·5	2·1	1·8	1·1	1·6	3·2	1·7	1·7	2·8	0·4
Textiles	1·6	0·5	0·8	−1·1	−1·1	−3·1	−0·9	−1·6	2·5	2·1
Clothing	2·1	2·2	0·1	0·2	1·9	1·1	0·3	0·4	1·8	1·8
Bricks, pottery glass	4·6	3·2	2·3	0·8	−0·1	5·4	1·5	2·1	3·1	1·1
Timber and furniture	4·8	2·8	1·5	0·2	2·2	2·8	1·6	0·5	3·2	2·3
Paper and printing	2·8	5·3	1·7	2·3	2·0	2·7	1·8	2·4	1·0	2·9
Other manufactures	4·3	3·1	1·2	1·2	1·6	2·9	1·3	1·6	3·0	1·5
Mining	−0·4	−0·1	−2·7	−1·5	0·4	2·9	−2·0	−1·0	1·6	0·9
Construction	4·6	2·7	3·1	0·9	1·9	9·4	2·9	2·0	1·7	0·7
Gas, electricity, water	5·8	5·5	3·0	1·4	3·6	3·6	3·3	2·5	2·5	3·0
Transport and communications	1·5	2·1	0·6	−0·4	0·2	1·0	0·5	−0·1	1·0	2·2
Distribution	2·0	2·8	2·6	1·7	1·3	4·2	2·0	2·4	0·0	0·8
Total Services	1·5	1·7	1·9	0·3	3·0	2·4	2·2	0·9	−0·7	0·8
Insurance, banking, finance	1·7	3·5	1·9	2·2	–	–	–	–	−0·2†	1·3†
Professional services	1·4	3·3	1·7	3·0	–	–	–	–	−0·3†	0·3†
Miscellaneous services	1·6	0·9	2·2	−0·6	–	–	–	–	−0·6†	1·5†
Government	1·3	−0·8	1·6	−1·8	–	–	–	–	−0·3†	1·0†

* 1951–60, not 1948–62.   † Rate of growth of output per man.

are an exceptional case where a sharp fall in capital stock is recorded because of abnormal scrapping so that total factor input has fallen more rapidly than employment.

Although the two industries with the highest Residual post-war (vehicles and utilities) are both what would popularly be regarded as 'growth' industries, by no means all the industries that are known to have undergone large-scale technical transformations within the post-war period show a high rate of technical progress, as measured by the Residual. The poor showing of iron and steel is notable in this regard.

Previous investigations, notably that of Salter,[1] have shown certain relationships between growth of rates of output and input in different industries. The best known of these findings is that there tends to be a positive correlation between the rate of growth of an industry's output and the site of growth of its productivity per man—sometimes known as 'Verdoorn's Law'.[2] This can be attributed partly to economies of scale, which permit increases in productivity when production rises, and partly to the lowering of price brought about by productivity increases, which stimulate demand and hence output. The following table shows the correlation found in our present data between the two variables mentioned above and also between certain other pairs of variables. The service industries are excluded in calculating these correlations, because of the statistical difficulties noted above.

Some positive correlation is found between $\Delta Q/Q$ and $(\Delta Q/Q - \Delta L/L)$ in both periods, but in the inter-war period the regression coefficient is not significantly different from zero at the 5 per cent level. This result is in some contrast with that of Salter, who for a similar period (1924–35) found a value of r of 0·67.[3] Salter took a much finer breakdown of manufacturing than ours and included only two non-manufacturing industries (coal mining and electricity generation) in his sample of twenty-eight industries. It may be conjectured, therefore, that the Verdoorn relationship holds mainly within manufacturing. On *a priori* grounds this is not altogether surprising—certainly neither of the two possible explanations (scale economies and elastic demand) for the relationship cited above would apply with much force to industries such as construction and distribution.

A natural modification of the Verdoorn hypothesis would be to

---

[1] W. E. G. Salter, *Productivity and Technical Change* (Cambridge, 1960).
[2] P. J. Verdoorn, 'Fattori che regolano lo sviluppo della produttività del lavoro', *L'Industria* (1947).
[3] Salter, *Productivity and Technical Change*, p. 126.

Table 7

Correlation Coefficients (r)

Between	1924–37	1948–62
$\Delta Q/Q$ and $\Delta L/L$	0·85	0·76
$(\Delta Q/Q - \Delta L/L)$ and $\Delta Q/Q$	0·36*	0·61
R and $\Delta Q/Q$	0·59	0·51
R and $\Delta K/K$	0·19*	−0·33*
R, 1924–37 and R 1948–62		0·33*

* Regression coefficient not significantly different from zero at 5% level.

postulate a relationship between $\Delta Q/Q$ and R. Here again, as shown in Table 7, some relationship is found. This time the regression coefficient is significantly different from zero in both periods.

It is sometimes suggested that the share of the product going to capital (which is the weight used in our calculation of total factor input and hence of the Residual) understates capital's importance as the vehicle of technical progress. In so far as this hypothesis would lead one to expect that industries with a high $\Delta K/K$ would show a high R, it is not supported by our data. The correlation found between R and $\Delta K/K$ is of opposite sign in the two periods and statistically significant in neither. We hope at a later stage to test more sophisticated versions of the hypothesis which are based on the 'vintage' principle and require separate valuation of each year's addition to the capital stock, with higher weight being given to the more recent and hence presumably more productive additions.

The correlation between the inter-war and the post-war residuals is low and not statistically significant. Support is therefore lacking for the view that certain industries have a persistently high rate of technical progress and certain other industries a persistently slow one.

The popular concept of a 'progressive' industry is perhaps at least as much concerned with the absolute level of productivity in an industry as with the rate of growth of productivity. In conclusion, therefore, we offer certain measures of comparative productivity between industries in an absolute sense.

Straightforward inter-industry comparisons of the value of output per man are vitiated by the differing capital-intensity of different industries. In order to arrive at figures of value of output per unit of input we therefore define total factor input in an industry (F_i) by the expression

$$F_i = L_i + \frac{r}{w} K_i$$

where L_i and K_i are inputs of labour and capital, measured in man-years and in value respectively, and r and w are the national average rate of profit on capital and wage rate respectively. In the economy as a whole w/r units of K earn the same amount as one man; the above expression therefore gives a measure of total input in equivalent man-years. This may be divided into Q_i, the value of output in the industry, to give the value of output per unit of input. Column I of Table 8 gives figures of output per unit of input so calculated for 1948. These figures are subject to some serious statistical imperfections, in addition to possible conceptual objections, and should be regarded as extremely tentative and subject to revision (to an even greater extent than the other figures given in this paper).[1] What they measure is essentially a weighted

TABLE 8

Value of Output per Unit of Input in 1948 (G.D.P. = 1·00)

	(1) *Labour unweighted*	(2) *Labour weighted*
Manufacturing	1·09	1·15
Food, drink and tobacco	1·63	1·95
Chemicals	1·14	1·14
Iron and steel	1·13	1·00
Electrical engineering	1·17	1·19
Non-electrical engineering	1·00	1·02
Vehicles	1·04	0·92
Other metals	1·13	1·19
Textiles	0·88	1·11
Clothing	0·87	1·19
Bricks, pottery, glass	1·09	1·15
Timber and furniture	1·05	1·12
Paper and printing	1·11	1·07
Other manufacturing	1·12	1·30
Mining and quarrying	1·1	1·0
Construction	1·2	1·1
Gas, Electricity and Water	0·7	0·6
Transport and Communications	1·0	0·9
Distribution	1·1	1·2
Production and distribution	1·1	1·1

[1] The capital data used do not include stocks and work in progress and rK_i/w is calculated from data at 1958 prices instead of at 1948 prices. Land is not included in the measure of capital; for this reason it seemed best not to give a figure for agriculture. A conceptual difficulty is that the present method makes no allowance for the fact that differences in (gross) rates of return on capital may be due partly to differences in the durability of capital. This consideration helps to explain the low level shown for output per unit of input in Gas, Electricity and Water.

average of the extent to which the wage and the profit rate in any industry depart from the national average.

Different wage levels between industries may be the result of differences in the quality of the labour used. If all differences in wages were due to this cause, it would be appropriate to amend the above formula by multiplying L_i by w_i/w, the ratio of the wage in the industry to the national average wage, thus:

$$F_i = \frac{w_i}{w} L_i + \frac{r}{w} K_i$$

Measures of output per unit of input calculated on this alternative basis are shown in column 2 of Table 8. The result provides measures of differences in the rate of return on capital between industries, weighted by the importance of capital in the industry.[1]

In comparing the absolute level of output per unit of input in an industry with its rate of growth over time (the Residual) two opposite hypotheses suggest themselves. Industries that are efficient in an absolute sense at the beginning of a period may be industries that are go-ahead in all respects and therefore have a high Residual. Alternatively, industries may regress towards the mean: those with a low level of output per unit of input at the beginning of the period may have the greatest scope and inducement to improve and hence have the highest Residual. Calculation of the correlation between the absolute level of output per unit of input in 1948 and the Residual 1948–62 gives fairly firm support to the second of these hypotheses. With labour input unweighted by w_i/w the regression equation is $R = 5{\cdot}04 - 3{\cdot}25\ q$, where q is the output per unit of input; r^2 is $0{\cdot}324$. With labour input weighted by w_i/w, the equation is $R = 4{\cdot}16 - 2{\cdot}35\ q$, with $r^2 = 0{\cdot}334$. In both cases the coefficient of q is significantly different from zero at the 5 per cent level.

It would be premature to draw any resounding conclusions from the calculations that have been presented. Enough has been said to make clear that the post-war performance of the British economy in general compares favourably with that achieved in any previous period within the past hundred years. But it is also apparent that the improvement has not been uniform, and that in certain important areas the rate of growth achieved in the inter-war period was higher.

[1] It would of course not do to apply the same procedure as that just described to capital and multiply the second term in the above expression by r_i/r, because then everything cancels out and the value of output per unit of input comes out as equal by definition in all industries.

6   Britain's Growth Performance: The Enigma of the 1950s[*]

by JOHN KNAPP
and KENNETH LOMAX

THE purpose of this article is to insist that the most important single fact about the performance of the British economy since the Second World War is that we do not really know whether it has been good or bad.

We have already briefly questioned the logical and factual basis of the widely-accepted judgement that Britain has clearly been doing badly.[1] We also presented statistical material which conflicts with the explanation most commonly given as the major reason for our supposed failure in the 1950s. We demonstrated that there was no evidence that Britain had been mismanaged into becoming a high-cost source of supply in international trade before 1961, that is, before the supposed most recent improvement in our competitive position.

The diagnosis we have been unwilling to accept has recently been forcefully restated by Mr Angus Maddison in an impressive and comprehensive study.[2] Any expressions of opinion regarding our economic performance coming from Mr Maddison's vantage point at O.E.C.D. must, of course, command great respect. Moreover, Mr Maddison's work is largely free of the crude errors of logic which have characterised many public discussions of our performance in recent years. It also deliberately sets out to view recent developments in the economies of the West in the long-term perspective which, we insist, is appropriate to study of the problems of economic growth.

Since we remain unrepentant sceptics about what appears to be becoming the accepted view of Britain's economic performance, we propose in this article to elaborate the grounds for our attitude in somewhat fuller detail. The issues involved are of considerable importance. For if our performance does not, in fact, reflect mis-

[*] First published 1964.
[1] *The Guardian*, 9 May 1962, and 8 April 1964.
[2] A. Maddison, *Economic Growth in the West* (1964).

management so much as forces of a more persistent and, possibly, intractable character, then our prospects for the future may be less bright than would appear from heeding what most critics say. The earlier this is recognised as a possibility the better. For if the accepted view of our past performance is in fact wrong we will not only find that we have been excessively self-critical in the past but also that we are heading for painful disillusion in the future.

In any event, a different diagnosis is likely to call for a different 'mix' of emphasis on various policies. Our argument is not a quibble over words, nor primarily an attempt to influence the way the history of the recent past is written. It is a plea for more research and thought, for professional and political candour, and for a coolly flexible assessment of our prospects and policies on the part of all concerned. It is not obvious why morale should suffer more from agnosticism in economics than, say, in medicine.

Clarifying some concepts

It is necessary to begin by clarifying our concepts. An elementary point which has been frequently ignored in vociferously conducted public discussion is that slow growth need not entail 'poor' or 'bad' performance. The notion of a poor growth performance lacks all practical meaning and all relevance for policy unless its use is strictly confined to the idea of a performance which falls short of the true growth-potential of an economy. All careful commentators on 'economic league tables' have shown their awareness of this. It is one of the great virtues of Mr Maddison's book that he not only recognises this point but does his best to allow for it in quantitative terms. Slow growth which is unavoidable is merely slow growth and, in a meaningful sense, may in fact represent better performance than faster growth which falls farther short of an even greater growth potential.

It follows that the crucial element in the evaluation of the growth record of any economy must be the assessment of its growth-potential. The reason why we do not know whether the performance of the British economy since the Second World War has been 'good' or 'bad' is that we do not really know how to assess its growth-potential. This, in turn, reflects the fact that economists do not possess any well-tested theory of economic growth.

In this situation, it is in the nature of the case that all attempts to evaluate our recent growth performance through the device of making comparisons—either with our own past growth rates or with the recent growth rates of other countries—are inevitably question-begging in character. For these comparisons have no relevant meaning unless they are taken to assume that the past British or the recent foreign growth rates which are being used as yardsticks for judging our own recent performance were, in fact, attained against a background of equal growth potentials. The trouble is that there is no warrant for any such assumption, and the essence of our argument is to provide evidence for our scepticism on this score.

Our procedure in arguing this way is exactly the same as that of Mr Maddison and of other critics who do, in fact, refuse to allow that our recent performance has been good, in spite of the fact that our growth rate and export increases since the Second World War have compared very favourably with anything we have achieved in the past, for a hundred years or more.

TABLE I

Rates of Growth in the United Kingdom
(percentage per annum)

	Productivity *(output per man)*	Purchasing power *of exports**
	%	%
1870–1913	1·1	2·7
1913–1938	1·5	0·5
1938–1960	1·4	3·4
1950–1960	1·9	4·0
1950–1955	2·0	2·4
1955–1960	1·9	5·6

* Export value index divided by import unit value index.

The critics' dismissal of these facts is based on the view, with which we have much sympathy, that the growth potentials of advanced industrial countries generally must be judged to have increased as compared with past periods. This could be due to the probable effects of the permanent improvements in the techniques of government management of demand brought about by the Keynesian revolution in economic analysis; it could possibly also be a result of an independent world-wide acceleration in scientific and technological advance. It follows that an acceleration in United Kingdom actual growth rates, as compared with our own past experience, is in no way inconsistent with a possible deterioration of our growth performance. For the same reasons, the critics may well also be justified in refusing to accept as evidence of good British performance the fact that the expansion of our exports since the last war has been considerably greater than expected in 1945.

Perspective on Growth Rates in the 1950s

Our quarrel with those who feel in a position to assert that our recent performance has been bad arises from what we regard as the insufficiently critical attitude of these writers towards their own assessment of Britain's growth potential. The critics have, by implication, generally insisted on measuring Britain's potential by the actual performance of other industrial countries during the 1950s. In doing so, they appear to have ignored much relevant evidence which suggests that this procedure may well overstate our own potential by a wide margin.

TABLE 2

Rates of Growth in United Kingdom and Other Industrial Countries, 1950–60, 1950–5 and 1955–60
(percentages per annum)

	Productivity (output per man)			Purchasing power of exports		
	1950–60	1950–5	1955–60	1950–60	1950–5	1955–60
	%	%	%	%	%	%
Germany (F.R.)	5·3	6·2	4·4	19·7	24·2	15·3
Italy	4·1	4·4	3·9	11·6	6·0	17·4
France	4·0	4·2	3·7	7·7	7·5	7·8
Switzerland	3·8	4·4	3·1	6·0	5·7	6·3
Netherlands	3·7	4·2	3·2	9·8	11·3	8·4
Norway	3·2	3·2	3·3	6·5	6·7	6·4
Sweden	2·7	2·8	2·6	6·6	5·3	7·9
Belgium	2·5	2·5	2·4	7·8	8·7	7·0
Denmark	2·3	0·6	3·9	–	–	–
U.S.A.	2·1	2·8	1·4	5·8	5·7	6·0
Canada	2·0	2·8	1·1	4·9	6·6	3·2
U.K.	1·9	2·0	1·9	4·0	2·4	5·6

In our view, international 'league tables' such as Table 2, based on the decade of the 1950s, are likely to yield grossly derogatory estimates of British performance and to exaggerate accordingly the possible future gains to be achieved from the pursuit of new policies on our part.

Overstatement of our growth potential on this basis is liable to arise for three distinct reasons. First, insufficient allowance for delayed recovery of productivity and exports after the Second World War in Continental countries. Second, insufficient allowance for the different rates of recovery in Continental countries, compared with Britain, from the adverse effects on productivity of the First World War and of the inter-war years. Third, insufficient allowance for the long-established secular tendency for the growth of British productivity and exports to lag behind the average of the corresponding growth rates of other industrial countries.

We must consider the nature and possible importance of each

of these sources of error separately, in estimating our growth potential. For while some—though in our view insufficient—allowance has indeed been made for some of the above factors by the more careful critics, the relevance of others may be questioned, and conceivably with justice. In particular, while some critics of our performance have tried to allow for the element of distortion introduced into the 'league tables' by the geographically unequal phasing, in point of time, of recovery after the Second World War, Mr Maddison has been alone in attempting to make explicit allowance for the possible effects of delayed recovery from the multiple disturbances of the inter-war period on comparative performances in the 1950s. Moreover, although he does present long-run statistical data for the comparatively undisturbed run of decades 1870–1913 (for which, incidentally, all workers in this field are heavily in his debt), even Mr Maddison fails to consider at any length whether the history of that period might not have significance for the assessment of recent British performance and our future prospects.

Altogether, it looks as if the valid idea that pre-1938 standards for judging growth potentials should no longer apply, has, by and large, been transposed into a tacit and dubious assumption to the effect that the pre-1938 pattern of events may be taken to have had no significant and systematic influence on the actual course of events in the 1950s. Perhaps this attitude reflects, at least in part, the influence of an apparently world-wide trend in social psychology, which expresses itself in an ardent desire to get away from the past. However much we may sympathise with the radicalism implicit in this attitude, it is clear that the wishful thinking it entails cannot be made to serve as a substitute for reasoned argument. In the following paragraphs we present some preliminary evidence which suggests that the widely implied assumption that, for the purposes of international 'league tables', we all started much the same in 1953 or 1955 is likely to be untenable.

When did recovery from the Second World War end?

We need not dwell at any length on the fallacious character of comparisons of our growth rates in the 1950s with those of other countries which make no reference at all to unequal recovery from the effects of the Second World War. Such comparisons were, for example, frequently made in the course of the discussions on Britain's application to join the Common Market and they will almost certainly recur, explicitly or implicitly, in the October

1964 election campaign in this country. These comparisons ignore such facts as that in Germany output per head of population was, in 1950, 13 per cent *below* its 1938 level, while it was 13 per cent *above* that level in the United Kingdom, or that in 1950 the purchasing power of German exports was only 44 per cent of their 1938 value, while in the United Kingdom it was 142 per cent of that value.

A much more important source of distorted views on our performance among serious students of the British economy has been the well-nigh universal acceptance of the assumption that by 1953 or, at most, by 1955 the delayed effects of differential recovery from the Second World War, particularly in Europe, may be taken to have worked themselves out. The basis of this assumption appears to have been the fact that, by the mid-1950s, productivity (that is, output per man) in Germany and other war-damaged European countries had risen to levels as far, or even farther, above their 1938 levels as had been achieved by the mid-1950s in the United Kingdom.

TABLE 3

Productivity and Purchasing Power of Exports per Person Employed
(1938 = 100)

	Productivity (output per man)				Purchasing power of exports per person employed			
	1950	1953	1955	1960	1950	1953	1955	1960
Germany (F.R.)	101·4	121·7	136·8	169·5	42·9	84·1	111·1	207·9
U.K.	111·0	117·4	122·5	134·5	131·9	133·7	141·9	183·0
Averages for the ⎱ (Unweighted)	120·2	133·4	141·3	162·9	112·1	131·4	151·4	214·7
12 industrial countries* ⎰ (Weighted)	119·5	133·3	141·3	160·1	111·9	129·4	142·5	201·0

* Belgium, Canada, Denmark, France, Germany, Italy, Netherlands, Norway, Sweden, Switzerland, U.K., U.S.A.

As Table 3 shows, one of the shortcomings of this judgement was that it failed to make a distinction between recovery in productivity and recovery in international trade. The measurement relevant for completion of recovery in international trade after the Second World War corresponding to the above-mentioned criterion for recovery of production is that of exports *per person employed*. It is clear from the table that exports from Germany—which is, of course, one of the world's premier trading countries—had, in contrast to production, failed to reach even their pre-war level in these terms by 1953, and had not reached a level at which post-war recovery can be regarded as complete until the end of the 1950s. We would expect a similar record for Japan—another major war-damaged industrial exporter.

This failure of perspective has had important consequences. For the logic of the argument so frequently presented to the public has been that the failure of British productivity to increase roughly in step with the rise in productivity in other industrial countries after 1955 and our failure to maintain something like our 1955 share in world exports of manufactures[1] should both be taken as interrelated causes of and also consequences and symptoms of a 'bad' performance. The 'failure' of exports, by way of causing balance of payments crises, stop–go policies, uncertainty and insufficient investment, is said to have reacted adversely on our growth rates in productivity. At the same time, low growth rates of productivity, it is argued, have undermined our competitive position, given the absence of an effective incomes policy and given our strong reluctance to contemplate another devaluation of sterling after 1949. This, in turn, is supposed to have given rise to further declines in the relative rate of growth of our exports.

Now, since the management of demand and policy in regard to exchange rates can both be regarded as wholly within the responsibility of government, and since ability to secure agreement to an effective incomes policy can also be looked upon as a test of the ability of government to provide necessary leadership, the role of policy was, if the above diagnosis is correct, of crucial importance in giving rise to the lagging performance of the British economy, at any rate after 1955.

This staple view is strongly expressed by Mr Maddison, as well as by Dr S. J. Wells in his recent volume on British export performance.[2] Indeed, Mr Maddison believes that the growth momentum of modern Western industrial economics is everywhere primarily a reflection of the success or otherwise of their governmental policies. It is, at any rate, clear that the actual performance of the British economy can, on this view, be legitimately described as having been bad in the 1950s, and it would follow that we have been operating below our potential to an extent indicated, by and large, by the average of other industrial countries after 1955.

We ourselves feel unable to accept these interpretations as they stand, and suggest that altogether different hypotheses might be much more relevant and certainly require to be tested before a verdict can be given on these issues. We believe, for one thing, that

---

[1] Our share was 21 per cent in 1953, 19·3 per cent in 1955, falling to 15·9 per cent in 1960, 15·1 per cent in 1962 and 14·9 per cent in 1963.

[2] S. J. Wells, *British Export Performance—A comparative Study* (1964).

the continued fall in our share of exports of manufactures after 1955 was probably to be expected in view of the incomplete recovery, among others, of Germany's exports per head in that year, as well as on the basis of longer-term considerations to be discussed presently. The continuing lagging tendency of our productivity in the 1950s might well also be related partly to the consequences of an erroneous standard of dating full recovery from the Second World War and partly to longer-run forces, rather than to the effects of post-war government policy, as we shall suggest in the following paragraphs.

TABLE 4

Growth Rates in Productivity (Output per Man) Since 1938
(percentages per annum)

	1938 -50	1938 -55	1938 -60	1950 -60	1955 -60
	%	%	%	%	%
Germany (F.R.)	0·1	1·9	2·4	5·3	4·4
Italy	0·4	1·6	2·1	4·1	3·9
France	1·3	2·1	2·5	4·0	3·7
Switzerland	1·0	2·0	2·2	3·8	3·1
Netherlands	0·6	1·6	2·0	3·7	3·2
Norway	1·6	2·0	2·3	3·2	3·3
Sweden	2·5	2·6	2·6	2·7	2·6
Belgium	1·5	1·8	2·0	2·5	2·4
Denmark	1·7	1·4	2·0	2·3	3·9
U.S.A.	2·2	2·4	2·2	2·1	1·4
Canada	4·1	3·4	3·1	2·0	1·1
U.K.	0·9	1·2	1·4	1·9	1·9
Unweighted average of all excluding the U.K.	1·5	2·1	2·3	3·2	3·0
Unweighted average of the 5 fast growers in the 1950s (*)	0·7	1·8	2·2	4·2	3·7
Unweighted average of the 6 slow growers in the 1950s (†)	2·3	2·3	2·4	2·5	2·5
Weighted average of all excluding the U.K.	1·4	2·1	2·3	3·2	2·6
Weighted average of the 5 fast growers in the 1950s	0·6	1·9	2·3	4·4	3·9
Weighted average of the 6 slow growers in the 1950s	2·3	2·4	2·3	2·2	1·6

(*) Germany, Italy, France, Switzerland, Netherlands.
(†) Norway, Sweden, Belgium, Denmark, U.S.A., Canada.

Table 4 places the different productivity increases observed in the 1950s into a slightly longer perspective. The countries listed in the table are arranged in order of their productivity increases during the 1950s.

It will be seen that when growth rates are taken over the whole period 1938–60, rather than over the decade 1950–60, the higher growth rates of the so-called 'dynamic' countries listed at the top of the table in the 1950s disappear completely. The 'fast growers' of the 1950s had grown no faster than the 'slow growers' of that decade (excluding the United Kingdom) between 1938 and 1960. The most 'dynamic' country over the longer period has, in fact, been Canada, which grew more and more sluggishly as the 1950s wore on. But the growth rate of productivity in the United Kingdom alone was markedly lower than that of all other countries in the table between 1938 and 1960, as well as in the 1950s.

Now, the general criterion adopted by the critics of Britain's performance for dating full recovery from the effects of the Second World War was, as we have seen, equal increase in productivity as compared with 1938. But since the fast growers of the 1950s were *still lagging significantly behind* the slow growers of the 1950s (except for the United Kingdom) as late as 1955 (cf. column 2 of Table 4) it follows that the proper dating of full recovery from the war should, on the critics' own criterion and on a general view, be the same for productivity as for exports: it should, that is, be taken to be the end of the 1950s or early 1960s and not 1953 or 1955. Use of the singularly sluggish British growth rate of productivity as one's overall benchmark in this connection is potentially misleading as well as egocentric. For it begs and biases the principal question which is at issue for ourselves: namely, whether the British growth rate of productivity can or cannot be expected to be as high as that of other countries.

The foregoing must not be taken as an assertion on our part that 1938 is a suitable base year for any significant international 'league table' (whether one includes or excludes Britain). That would amount to asserting that we know that between 1938 and 1960 all these countries (including or excluding Britain) should have been expected to raise their productivity in step with one another. There is nothing in tested economic theory to suggest any such thing. There is consequently no reliable basis for such assumptions, whatever the base year taken for one's league table. However, by the same token of our general ignorance, we have no reliable reason either to think that many or most countries do not have roughly the same potential for raising their productivity over longish periods.

All we have been concerned to establish so far is that there is in any case evidence which suggests that, on their own criteria, the choice, by the critics of our performance, of 1953 or 1955 as the base year for their league tables is likely to bias assessments of growth performance in favour of the fast-growing countries of the 1950s, both as against the slow growers of the 1950s, in general, and as against the British performance in particular. This much can, we assert, be said with confidence, even if the range of our observations is carried back no farther than 1938.

Delayed recovery from the inter-war period

Our next five tables can be used to suggest that much of the apparent 'dynamism' of the fast-growing countries of the 1950s might be merely a reflection of delayed recovery from comparatively retarded growth rates over the seventy-year period preceding 1938. They also suggest that the growth potential of the British economy may be lower than that of most other industrial countries. This, if true, would imply that our recent growth performance may have been quite good.

TABLE 5

Levels of Output per Man-Hour (1960) and Growth Rates in Productivity (Output per Man) 1870–1960

	1960 level of output per man-hour (European relative prices)	Growth rates in output per man (percentages per annum)						
		1870 –1913	1913 –38	1938 –50	1950 –60	1870 –1938	1870 –1950	1870 –1960
		%	%	%	%	%	%	%
U.S.A.	100	1·9	1·2	2·2	2·1	1·7	1·8	1·8
Canada	82	1·6	0·1	4·1	2·0	1·1	1·5	1·6
Norway	47	1·4	1·9	1·6	3·2	1·6	1·6	1·7
Belgium	46	1·6	0·9	1·5	2·5	1·3	1·4	1·5
Sweden	43	2·2	1·0	2·5	2·7	1·8	1·9	2·0
Denmark	40	2·1	0·4	1·7	2·3	1·6	1·6	1·7
Germany (F.R.)	39	1·6	0·8	0·1	5·3	1·3	1·1	1·6
France	38	1·4	0·9	1·3	4·0	1·2	1·2	1·5
Netherlands*	38	0·7	0·9	0·6	3·7	0·8	0·8	1·2
U.K.	38	1·1	1·5	0·9	1·9	1·2	1·2	1·3
Switzerland†	36	1·1	1·8	1·0	3·8	1·5	1·4	1·7
Italy	27	0·8	1·5	0·4	4·1	1·1	1·0	1·3
Unweighted average of all excluding the U.K.		1·5	1·0	1·5	3·2	1·4	1·4	1·6
Unweighted average of the 5 fast growers in the 1950s		1·1	1·2	0·7	4·2	1·2	1·1	1·5
Unweighted average of the 6 slow growers in the 1950s		1·8	0·9	2·3	2·5	1·5	1·6	1·7
Weighted average of all excluding the U.K.		1·4	1·1	1·4	3·2	1·3	1·3	1·6
Weighted average of the 5 fast growers in the 1950s		1·2	1·1	0·6	4·4	1·2	1·1	1·5
Weighted average of the 6 slow growers in the 1950s		1·9	1·1	2·3	2·2	1·6	1·7	1·8

* Netherlands: for 1870 read 1900.   † Switzerland: for 1870 read 1890.

Table 5 places the experience of the 1950s into what we regard as an adequately long time perspective. In this table all countries for which Mr Maddison has provided data are listed in order of the *levels* of man-hour productivity they had reached by 1960.

It will be noticed that the six countries which had the *highest levels* of man-hour productivity in 1960 were the six *slowest growing* countries in the 1950s (apart from the United Kingdom); while the six countries having the *lowest levels* of man-hour productivity in 1960 are the five fastest growing countries in the 1950s, together with the United Kingdom. The table also shows that, except for Switzerland, the five fastest growing countries of the 1950s have been slow-growing countries over long periods previously, while the six slowest growing countries in the 1950s (apart from the United Kingdom) have, except perhaps for Belgium, been the 'dynamic' countries over the long run. The United Kingdom was alone in displaying *consistently* low growth rates, both over long periods and also during the 1950s. The one period during which United Kingdom productivity grew faster than productivity in most other countries was 1913–38, when the aftermath of the First World War, followed by depression, resulted in drastic reductions in rates of productivity growth in the majority of industrial countries. Even then, the United Kingdom growth rate could not be described as high.

In considering the possible bearing of the pre-1938 pattern of events on the relative 'dynamism' of different countries in the 1950s we must clearly make a distinction between the 1913–38 period and the preceding 1870–1913 period. The 1913–38 data reflect the effects of severe and multiple disturbances, while the 1870–1913 period was an age of relatively smooth and 'normal' development in a predominantly *laissez-faire* setting.

Mr Maddison has made an attempt to measure the influence of the recovery element due to the elimination of the prolonged unemployment of the inter-war period on different rates of productivity growth in the 1950s. His method turns on using measurements of movements out of agriculture during the 1950s as (admittedly) crude indicators of the variations in backlogs of accumulated under-utilisation of labour in different countries. This yields the following estimates of relative productivity growths due to delayed recovery from the inter-war period (Table 6).

Although Mr Maddison claims that the recovery elements measured in the above way have been of some importance in explaining part of the differences in various national rates of growth during the 1950s, he nevertheless has to conclude that these effects have been, on the basis of these figures, generally minor.

We do not agree with Mr Maddison's judgement in this matter.

Our own view is that the bulk of the bonus in productivity growth due to absorption of resources under-utilised in the inter-war period may be expected to have taken place *at different times* in the slow-growing and the fast-growing countries of the 1950s, owing mainly to the differential course of wartime and immediate post-war developments in these two groups of countries.

TABLE 6

The Impact of Disguised Agricultural Unemployment on Productivity 1950–60

	Actual annual average percentage increase in output per man-hour	*Annual average percentage increase in output per man-hour due to absorption of accumulated disguised unemployment 1950–60*	*Col.* (i) *minus Col.* (ii)
	(i)	(ii)	
	%	%	
U.S.A.	2·4	0·4	2·0
Canada	2·5	0·7	1·8
Norway	3·9	0·7	3·2
Belgium	2·5	0·3	2·2
Sweden	—	—	—
Denmark	2·9	0·5	2·4
Germany (F.R.)	6·0	0·8	5·2
France	3·9	0·8	3·1
Netherlands	3·7	0·1	3·6
U.K.	2·0	0·1	1·9
Switzerland	—	—	—
Italy	4·1	0·6	3·5

Source: Maddison, *Economic Growth in the West*, p. 61.

Table 7 shows that, while in most countries output grew by about 40–70 per cent during the twenty-five years of the 1913–38 period, in the next twelve-year period, during and just after the Second World War, the growth of output became very uneven. In the slow-growing group of countries of the 1950s (other than the United Kingdom)—which in fact consists of the North American and Scandinavian countries plus Belgium—all countries except Belgium achieved a marked acceleration of the rate of growth of their output in 1938–50 in the face of wartime conditions. By contrast, the Continental countries of Europe, which were the fast growers of the 1950s, suffered significant reductions in the

TABLE 7

Productivity Increases 1950–60 and Percentage Increases in Output 1938–50
and 1913–38

	Annual average percentage increases in productivity (output per man) 1950–60	Percentage increase in output 1938–50	Annual average percentage increase in output 1938–50	Percentage increase in output 1913–38	Annual average percentage increase in output 1913–38
U.S.A.	2·1	79·4	5·0	63·3	2·0
Canada	2·0	93·9	5·7	43·7	1·5
Norway	3·2	31·1	2·3	102·8	2·9
Belgium	2·5	19·7	1·5	22·0	0·8
Sweden	2·7	45·5	3·2	54·6	1·8
Denmark	2·3	34·6	2·5	60·5	1·9
Germany (F.R.)	5·3	4·9	0·4	49·9	1·6
France	4·0	19·1	1·5	9·4	0·4
Netherlands	3·7	27·3	2·0	70·3	2·2
U.K.	1·9	19·8	1·5	58·3	1·9
Switzerland	3·8	26·1	2·0	62·6	2·0
Italy	4·1	5·2	0·4	53·8	1·7

average growth rates of their output, with the solitary exception
of previously stagnant France.

Now, it seems to us plausible to suppose that in the countries in
which output grew markedly during the war and immediate post-
war years a much higher proportion of the productivity bonus
deriving from under-employment in the inter-war years would
already have been reaped by 1950 than in the countries in which
output grew slowly. In *both* groups of countries, the disappearance
of cyclical unemployment inherited from 1913–38 can be expected
to have occurred within a year or two of the emergence of wartime
conditions. But the gathering in of the longer-term productivity
bonuses derived from the stepping up of investment, technical advance, and movement to higher productivity occupations, which
had been frustrated during the depression years, must be expected
to have been well spread out over time. It seems reasonable to
suppose that the harvest time for these bonuses was in fact related
to the varying extent to which countries had been able to make
resources available for investments of a kind which could be put to
productive use, both during the war and subsequently.

Physical wartime damage and other disorganisation due to war
and its aftermath must obviously have affected the figures for the
different countries shown in Table 7. We are nevertheless prepared,
until further research is done, to regard the figures in this table
as rough approximate indicators of wartime and immediate post-
war extensions of productive capacity. If this assumption is valid,

it then follows that the average age of productive equipment had been lowered more, by 1950, in those countries in which output grew a great deal in the 1938–50 period than in those where output grew less. Consequently, the productivity bonuses potentially available to the latter group of countries during the subsequent 1950–60 period would have been relatively larger and—given the continuation of high world-wide levels of activity during the 1950s, together with a not unfavourable structure of exchange rates—the inducement to invest in them would also, other things being equal, be relatively large. When we add to these considerations the fact that the supply of modern equipment *provided by way of foreign aid* to the principal fast-growing countries of the 1950s was vastly greater than the extent to which it was either requested by or made available to the others, it appears reasonable to think that a very significant part of the differences in productivity increases during the 1950s might well have been due to delayed modernisation of equipment in the fast-growing countries.

It may, of course, turn out to be difficult to distinguish between the part played by delayed modernisation attributable to different rates of recovery from sluggishness in growth during 1913–38 and those played by both earlier (1870–1913) and later (1938–50) differences in experience. Until the relevant research is done, however, there is some reason to think the impact of delayed recovery from 1913 to 1938 may have been of much greater and clearer-cut importance in explaining the general pattern of differences in rates of productivity growth in the 1950s than Mr Maddison's statistics and arguments allow.

Table 8 (page 115) shows that the differences in productivity growth between fast- and slow-growing countries in the 1950s were not associated with marked differences in their rates of investment so much as with differences in the increases in output obtained from their investment efforts (the last two columns—the lower the ratio the greater the increment of output obtained from given investment). This table fits in well with the theory of differences in timing of modernisation suggested above but less well with Mr Maddison's view, which places greater emphasis on high investment or 'investment-dynamism' induced by high and steady increasing demand.

Our own line of reasoning does also appear to go some way towards accounting for the lag of British productivity growth behind Conti-

nental European countries during the 1950s. Going by the measures
shown in Table 7, the wartime and immediate post-war expansion
of capacity appear to have been markedly less, by 1950, in Germany
and Italy than in the United Kingdom. Similarly, in France and
Belgium the growth in output during 1913–38 was much less than
in the United Kingdom. The backlogs of potential bonuses from
modernisation to be reaped during the 1950s may therefore be

TABLE 8

Productivity Increases, Investment Ratios, and Incremental
Capital-Output Ratios, 1950–60

	Annual average percentage increase in productivity (output per man) 1950–60	*Ratio of gross domestic investment to G.N.P. at current prices averaged over 1950–60*	*Investment-output ratio* averaged over 1950–60*	*Fixed non-residential-investment-output ratio averaged over 1950–60*
	%	%		
U.S.A.	2·1	19·1	5·8	4·1
Canada	2·0	24·8	6·4	4·8
Norway	3·2	26·4	7·5	6·2
Belgium	2·5	16·5	5·7	4·0
Sweden	2·7	21·3	6·5	4·6
Denmark	2·3	18·1	5·5	4·2
Germany (F.R.)	5·3	24·0	3·2	2·1
France	4·0	19·1	4·3	3·1
Netherlands	3·7	24·2	5·0	3·6
U.K.	1·9	15·4	5·9	4·3
Switzerland	3·8	—	—	—
Italy	4·1	20·8	3·5	2·6

Source: Maddison, *Economic Growth in the West*, pp. 76–81.

*Average ratio of total gross domestic investment to G.N.P. at current prices
divided by the rate of growth of output in real terms.

supposed to have been greater in these four countries than in the
United Kingdom.

In addition, Table 5 (on page 110) shows that in the United
States, Canada, Sweden, Denmark and the Netherlands *productivity*
growth did lag significantly behind that in the United Kingdom
between 1913 and 1938, even when the actual growth in output
did not. If we take this to reflect a further source of varying backlogs of modernisation to be made good, it might help to explain
the fact that the United Kingdom was unable, during the 1950s, to
match the mostly rather moderate degree of 'dynamism' of these
last five countries either, in spite of the fact that their output-

capacity presumably grew by more during 1938–50 than did that of the United Kingdom. On this reasoning, we would then be left only with the superior Swiss and Norwegian performances during the 1950s as entirely untouched by the factors we are invoking.

TABLE 9

Growth Rates in Productivity in Selected Countries (Output per Man)
(Percentages per annum)

	1870 –1913	1913 –38	1938 –50	1950 –60	1938 –60	1870 –1938	1870 –1950	1870 –1960
	%	%	%	%	%	%	%	%
E.E.C.								
Germany (F.R.)	1·6	0·8	0·1	5·3	2·4	1·3	1·1	1·6
Italy	0·8	1·5	0·4	4·1	2·1	1·1	1·0	1·3
France	1·4	0·9	1·3	4·0	2·5	1·2	1·2	1·5
Netherlands*	0·7	0·9	0·6	3·7	2·0	0·8	0·8	1·2
Belgium	1·6	0·9	1·5	2·5	2·0	1·3	1·4	1·5
Unweighted average	1·2	1·0	0·8	3·9	2·2	1·1	1·1	1·4
Weighted average	1·3	1·0	0·6	4·3	2·3	1·2	1·1	1·5
E.F.T.A. (excluding U.K.)								
Switzerland†	1·1	1·8	1·0	3·8	2·2	1·5	1·4	1·7
Norway	1·4	1·9	1·6	3·2	2·3	1·6	1·6	1·7
Sweden	2·2	1·0	2·5	2·7	2·6	1·8	1·9	2·0
Denmark	2·1	0·4	1·7	2·3	2·0	1·6	1·6	1·7
Unweighted average	1·7	1·3	1·7	3·0	2·3	1·6	1·6	1·8
Weighted average	1·8	1·2	1·8	3·0	2·3	1·6	1·7	1·8
N. America								
U.S.A.	1·9	1·2	2·2	2·1	2·2	1·7	1·8	1·8
Canada	1·6	0·1	4·1	2·0	3·1	1·1	1·5	1·6
Unweighted average	1·8	0·7	3·2	2·1	2·7	1·4	1·7	1·7
Weighted average	1·9	1·1	2·4	2·1	2·3	1·7	1·8	1·8
United Kingdom	1·1	1·5	0·9	1·9	1·4	1·2	1·2	1·3

* Netherlands: for 1870 read 1900.
† Switzerland: for 1870 read 1890.

Long-term trends in productivity

The most serious source of possible error in judging the comparative economic performances of different countries during the 1950s may well result from failure to allow for long-run influences.

In Table 9 the data in Table 5 are rearranged so as to bring out the regional patterns of long-run growth rates. Two features stand out. First, the Common Market countries—which include most of the star performers of the 1950s—have lagged behind both the Scandinavian countries and North America in all previous periods distinguished in the table. As a result, the long-run growth rates of the E.E.C. countries remain below those of Scandinavia and North America, and it is by no means clear which of the countries of the Western world should be regarded as being the truly 'dynamic' ones. It is at any rate possible that a part of the high growth rates of the E.E.C. countries during the 1950s reflects long-run recovery elements of a kind which are due to catching-up on differences in pre-1913 developments. (Mr Maddison himself is quite ready to contemplate this kind of thing as a possibility.)

A second feature of Tables 5 and 9 is that they clearly show the United Kingdom to have been a peculiarly slow-growing country over a long period. We suggest that the nature of the unknown determinants of this fact must be regarded as having a crucial

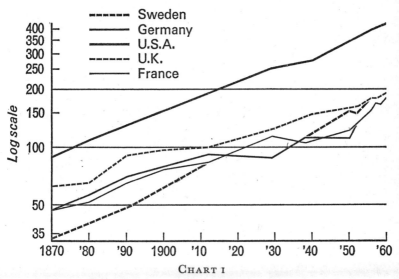

CHART I

Productivity: Output per man (U.K. 1913 = 100)

significance for judging British economic policy and performance during the 1950s, as well as for assessing the prospects of an improved performance in the future (see Chart 1).

Putting the matter brutally and, perhaps, too simply, the question here is how far our past relative sluggishness is intractable, being a symptom of what Professor H. G. Johnson has called the 'economic senescence' of an old and inherently conservative industrial power in a fast-changing world, and how far it merely reflects the easy-going inertia of social and economic habits acquired during a past age of effortless superiority, which may yield to a new set of responses under the influence of fresh challenges and ideas. Unfortunately, there is nothing in existing economic knowledge that enables one to give a confident verdict about this, one way or the other. The example of Italy is frequently quoted in order to refute the view that the past low growth rates of a country must be expected to continue into the future. Mr Maddison asserts without detailed demonstration that, basically, the scope for increasing productivity is now much the same in most countries of Western Europe. An ominous pointer towards a less encouraging possibility is that the disadvantage of an early start may be both real and intractable.[1]

Belgium and the Netherlands were, it seems, together with the United Kingdom, the countries of highest productivity in Europe in the 1870s. They are, like Britain, old-established industrial powers. They led Europe in the eighteenth century. They have shared the bottom places in the *long-run* league table with the United Kingdom and Italy. As for Italy herself, she led Europe towards her (quite recently shed) superiority in modern times during the renaissance, but has started her 'miracle of the 1950s' from the bottom position among European industrial countries. However, all this can hardly be counted as more than speculation, given our present lack of tested knowledge about the underlying determinants and mechanisms of growth in capitalist economies. Given this ignorance, there can, we submit, be no warrant for Mr Maddison's explicitly stated assumption that 'the scope for better performance in the Western Industrial World is greatest in the slower-growing countries'.

The 1950s: A critique of an alternative view

We have so far suggested that much, and possibly all, of the relatively slow growth of productivity in the British economy during the 1950s might conceivably be accounted for by a variety of short-term, medium-term and long-term factors, independently of any mistakes in British policy. The nature of the factors we have invoked was such that they could have lowered the growth potential of the British economy relatively to that of other countries, in some cases temporarily, in others persistently. In pressing these hypotheses as deserving of attention and investigation we have gone against the trend of recent fashion in comment on the British economy in two ways.

First, we have refused to assume that a lagging British perfor-

[1] For a highly suggestive recent argument to this effect by an industrial economist, the reader is referred to an article on 'Real issues in the steel debate' by Mr Georg Tugendhat in *The Guardian*, 25 June 1964.

mance, after 1955 at any rate, must necessarily imply both poor performance and poor policy on the part of the United Kingdom authorities and, secondly, we have been led to our alternative hypotheses by the consideration of suggestive patterns in data viewed from a longish historical perspective.

We now propose to use this same twofold strategy in order to suggest that there is, so far, no *prima facie* evidence to support the influential and widely-held view that Britain's lagging performance in productivity, exports and domestic investment since, say, 1955 is very largely attributable to mistaken government policies in its management of demand, wages and the foreign exchange rate. By the same token, however, we question that there is evidence to support the optimism of those who suppose that the key to closing the gap between the dynamism of Britain and other countries is likely to be found in our being able to operate a successful incomes policy sooner and more easily than others. We cannot here attempt an exhaustive critique and conclusive refutation of the views we are questioning. Our present purpose is merely to marshal the

TABLE 10

Average Annual Lags in British Growth Rates*
(Percentages per annum)

	1870 to 1913	*1913 to 1938*	*1938 to 1960*	*1938 to 1950*	*1950 to 1960*	*1950 to 1955*	*1955 to 1960*	*1960 to 1966*
	%	%	%	%	%	%	%	%
(1) Wages rates in national currencies	−0·3	−1·4	−2·2	−2·7	−0·7	−0·4	−0·8	−0·6
(2) Labour costs per unit of output (in national currencies)	0·3	−1·2	−1·9	−2·5	0·9	1·7	0·2	−0·5
(3) Labour costs per unit of output in dollars	0·3	−0·3	−1·9	−4·9	1·4	1·6	0·8	−0·5
(4) Export prices in dollars	0·4	1·4	−0·4	−1·6	1·1	1·6	0·6	—
(5) Purchasing power of exports	−0·7	−1·4	−0·8	0·7	−4·8	−6·1	−2·8	—
(6) Productivity (output per man)	−0·7	0·5	−1·0	−0·6	−1·6	−1·9	−1·1	−0·8
(7) Competitive performance	−1·9†	−2·9	−0·3	3·0	−4·8	−6·0	−3·25	—

* The lags are derived from the ratio $\dfrac{100 + a}{100 + b}$ where a = annual average British rate of increase and b = annual average rate of increase for France, Germany, Sweden and the U.S. (weighted, except for productivity, by national shares of world exports).

† 1899–1913.

readily available data in a preliminary way in order to define some of the grounds which underlie our scepticism.

Table 10 is a revised version of that previously published in *The Guardian* of 8 April 1964. The revisions are based on data given, since that article was written, in Mr Maddison's book, while the 1960–8 predictions are derived from assumptions given by the U.S. Council of Economic Advisers and from O.E.C.D. target rates of growth for Europe, as shown in the Brookings Institution's publication *The United States Balance of Payments in 1968*. The lags in 'competitive performance' are defined as the annual compound rates of change in our exports which would have taken place as a result of changes in our share of individual foreign markets, if it had not been for changes in the total volume or area and commodity composition of world trade.

Let us recall the line of argument we wish to scrutinise. It states, in essence, that an inefficient and self-defeating stabilisation policy— 'stop–go'—has been operated during the 1950s in dealing with balance-of-payments problems. Investment was discouraged by the process of repeatedly applying restrictive monetary measures to damp down demand. The policy also failed to halt inflation, which depended on wage increases secured through the strong bargaining position of the trade unions in conditions of full employment. The discouragement of investment, the argument goes on, slowed down productivity growth and, together with continuing cost-inflation, undermined Britain's competitive position, so that future balance-of-payments difficulties were generated by each attempt to deal with an ever-recurring trouble. Given the reluctance to devalue sterling, it is claimed that the lagging performance of the economy was an inevitable result.

The first thing to note about Table 10 is that, although our money wages rose less rapidly than those of our competitors in spite of our domestic inflation, the figures do confirm the existence, during the 1950s, of an association between rising British costs per unit of output, lagging productivity, and lagging exports in relation to other countries. These facts are not in dispute. Moreover, it is quite acceptable to believe that if our labour costs had risen less in the 1950s our export performance would have been better than it was. What matters, however, is the widely-held view that we were becoming a high-cost source of supplies, and that the rise in our cost-structure was indirectly responsible for the bulk of our lagging performance in regard to productivity and exports after 1955. We submit that

Table 10 not only fails to support these views, but goes a considerable way towards refuting them.

First, consider the suggestion that we were becoming a high-cost source of supplies. Rows 2 and 3 of Table 10 and Chart 2 show that the relatively fast increase in our costs in the 1950s did no more than retrace a *part* of what was, in effect, a double devaluation of the British cost-structure relatively to our competitors between 1938 and 1950. The fact that the negative entries in rows 2 and 3 in the 1938–60 column are the same means that during the 1950s the

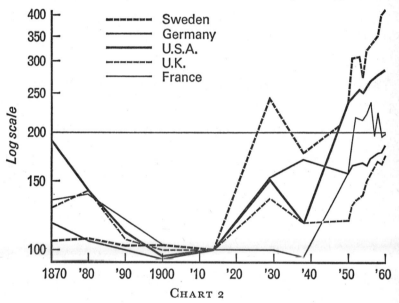

CHART 2

Labour Costs per Unit of Output in Terms of Dollars
$(1913 = 100)$

entire cost advantage gained by Britain in the 1949 devaluation had been lost again—not through wage increases, but as a result mainly of lagging productivity and partly of further devaluations on the part of France. But this still left a British labour-cost structure in 1960 which was 51 per cent lower relatively to our competitors' costs than it had been in 1938. Table 10 and Chart 2 both show Britain to have become relatively an increasingly low-cost source of supplies since 1913.

Secondly, we have already given a variety of possible reasons for our view that temporary recovery factors, on the one hand, and deep-seated historically-caused factors, on the other, may well have been responsible for our productivity lags in the 1950s. There is nothing in Table 10 to suggest that increases in our relative cost structure operating indirectly by way of stop–go policies have been a major independent influence. Indeed, the figures in the 1960–8 column actually predict a course of events for the 1960s during which British productivity, while growing faster than in the 1950s, would continue to lag behind our competitors *by rather more* than at any time between 1870 and 1938, even though our labour costs are projected as likely to be *falling* relatively to other countries.

Finally, row 7 of Table 10 confirms our own dating of the exhaustion of post-war recovery factors in international trade and helps to refute the view that our falling share of world exports after 1955 has been primarily the result of our rising relative cost-structure in the 1950s. If by 1955 the international trade pattern had in some sense returned to 'normal' and if relative cost movements subsequently dominated it, one would expect that our continuing relative cost increases after 1955 would have given rise to a rate of deterioration in our 'competitive performance', measured year by year, which would have, first, fallen to some minimum in 1955 or 1956 and then subsequently increased. Instead, we find that the 1957–8 deterioration (January–September) was −2·61 per cent, and the 1958–9 deterioration −1·88 per cent, less that is, than the 1955–60 average and less than the pre-1938 historical norm. Moreover, during the whole 1938–60 period, which is free of short-term 'recovery' elements, our 'competitive performance' was extremely good by historical standards.

CONCLUSION

To regard the analysis of this article as furnishing grounds either for complacency or, for that matter, for defeatism would be to misunderstand its meaning completely.

What we have said cannot give grounds for complacency in regard to the past because we cannot be sure, at this stage, that we have been doing well. In order to establish that, it would be necessary to show conclusively, not only that the effects of short-term mismanagement of the British economy during the 1950s have not been serious, but also that government policy had, during that decade, done as much as was possible and practicable at the time to halt or reverse the operation of the complex set of underlying economic and social forces which have given rise to the persistent long-term lags in British growth rates behind our industrial rivals. To demonstrate that good long-term management was in fact achieved or, indeed, that it was not, is hardly possible at present. For in order to be in a position to do this one would have to possess a tested body of knowledge concerning the long-term determinants of growth in capitalist economies—and this knowledge is not available. The fact that this is so and our own insistence that the ill effects of short-term mismanagement may well have been much exaggerated do not together really add up to a justification for complacency in regard to our recent performance. They merely indicate a need to suspend judgement for the present.

As for the future, our analysis leads, on balance, to essentially less complacent conclusions than does the argument of those who claim to be able to assert that we have been doing badly. This is because we insist on recognition of the possibility—ignored by the critics of our recent performance—that our persistently-lagging long-run performance may be, at least partly, intractable. Paradoxically, we must all fervently hope that our recent performance has, in fact, been very bad. Our own position is that this can only be a hope and cannot be either known or counted upon at present.

It is certainly a sobering thought that if recent government submissions to O.E.C.D. of planned prospective growth rates for 1960–8 are projected twenty to twenty-five years ahead, Britain would find herself operating by 1980 or 1985 at a productivity level 25 to 30 per cent below that of her principal European rivals.

Defeatism in regard to our prospects must, however, be as unwarranted as complacency would be. By the same token of our underlying ignorance of the factors and mechanisms involved, we cannot rule out the possibility that our performance will cease to lag in the future. The most hopeful portent visible at present in this connection is the existence of a widespread desire, on all sides, for a 'modernisation' of the economy and for related changes in our institutions and ways of doing things. Although their diagnosis may have been quite wrong, the vociferous critics of our recent performance have in fact made a valuable contribution here, by helping to create a general climate of dissatisfaction with the way we have been going on. This is, presumably, a necessary condition for needed radical reforms. The danger is that, by their emphasis on short-term mismanagement, the critics may have made the problems which lie ahead of this country appear too easy.

Our point is not just that better management of demand, of the external position, or even of incomes appears on the face of it to be an easier task than modernisation of our various institutions and practices. There is also the fundamental difficulty that, while we have a comparatively well-developed body of tested modern economic knowledge concerning the essentially short-term matters on which the critics have concentrated, we are, by contrast, very much in the dark about the long-run problems involved in the economics of modernisation. In this, as with the other major contemporary questions in respect of which economic statesmanship is now everywhere called for—the competition of economic systems, policy towards under-developed countries and the formation of larger international economic units—tested economic knowledge is, for the present, mostly just not available. This means, perhaps, that at this juncture our politicians should be offered more sympathy than they commonly get from economists. In return, they might in future do more than they traditionally have done in this country to promote research in the social sciences, both inside and outside the government machine.

7 The Growth of Services in the Economy[*]

I. Their Stabilising Influence

by C. W. McMAHON
and G. D. N. WORSWICK

In forty years the number of Americans engaged in producing commodities has barely changed. The entire increase in the work-force has gone into what can broadly be called services of all kinds: there are many more taxi-drivers, salesmen, bankers, barbers, doctors, teachers, insurance agents and restaurateurs for example; and, as will surprise no one, many, many more people employed by government. Total employment in all 'service' industries has in fact risen by some 130 per cent in the past forty years, while the numbers employed in manufacturing, mining, construction and agriculture are only about 3 per cent up.

These developments have not gone unnoticed,[1] and a number of things have commonly been said about them. It is often alleged that this trend is common to all advanced industrialised countries, because productivity rises much faster in the goods industries than in the service industries. Moreover, an increase in the proportion of total workers engaged in producing services (more than half the American labour force is now so engaged) is often said to have some very important effects on the economy as a whole. Because of the alleged lower productivity in services referred to above, a shift of labour from goods to services will tend to slow down the growth of the economy and (on certain plausible assumptions about wage increases) will tend to push up prices. On the other hand it is said that service industries are less subject to cyclical fluctuations, so that a higher proportion of service workers should render an economy more 'depression-proof'.[2]

In this article we shall look at what can be said about the growth

---

[*] First published 1960.
[1] See for example an interesting article by Edwin L. Dale, 'America's Drift from the Factory', in The Banker (June 1957).
[2] See Dale in The Banker (June 1957).

of employment in service industries in this country and discuss the reasons and evidence for believing that they help to stabilise the economy. In the next article we shall consider the more complicated questions of whether service productivity does grow more slowly than productivity in goods industries, and what effects any difference in rates of productivity growth are likely to have on employment trends, prices and the growth of the economy as a whole.

The trends in employment

Professor Simon Kuznets has investigated the long-term trends in employment for a large number of countries.[1] His comparisons of the distribution of the labour force, both in individual countries at two points of time (in most cases about fifty years apart) and between various countries at different stages of development at the same point of time, suggest that the tendency for the proportion of the labour force producing services to rise as the country advances is almost universal. But the main factor in this trend is the universal decline in the numbers engaged in agriculture. Now agriculture is in many respects *sui generis*. Granted that in most countries there is a steady movement of workers off the land and into the cities, the more interesting question is whether more of them go into services or into the non-agricultural goods industries, i.e. manufacturing, mining and construction (which we can call 'industrial production', or just 'industry', for short).[2] To this question Kuznets's broad approach gives a much less conclusive answer. His figures suggest that service employment generally tends to rise faster than industrial employment; but the tendency may not be universal, nor, where it occurs, very striking.

In the United States, the omission of agriculture greatly reduces the sharpness of the contrast which we presented at the beginning, though the trend towards services is still strongly shown; over the forty years service employment rose by 130 per cent while industrial employment rose only by 55 per cent.

What do the figures show for this country? In trying to answer this question we are immediately faced with two difficulties which barely arise in the American case. First, the impact of the war on

---

[1] See Simon Kuznets, *Economic Growth* (Illinois, 1959) lecture III.

[2] Industrial production in the United Kingdom is normally understood also to include the public utilities—gas, electricity and water. We have classed them as services, on the grounds that they share most of the qualities by virtue of which services are thought to act as stabilisers (see pages 131–4). But the numbers involved are too small to make any significant difference to the broad trends, whichever group they are included in.

the distribution of employment was very much greater in this country than in the United States and lasted much longer. The numbers engaged in distribution, for example, were reduced by as much as one-third below their pre-war level by 1944, and even by 1948 were still nearly 20 per cent below; whereas in the United States employment in distribution fell by only 3 per cent from 1941 to 1943 and had reached a new peak by 1945. We cannot say with any certainty when distribution employment in this country regained its pre-war level; and this is our second difficulty. We have no single consistent series of figures spanning both the pre- and post-war periods.

Chart 1 shows the movements in service and industrial employment from 1920 to 1938. At first sight there may appear to be no

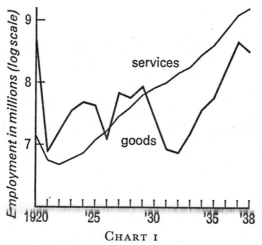

CHART 1

Goods and Service Employment in the
United Kingdom, 1920–38

Source: Agatha L. Chapman, *Wages and Salaries in the United Kingdom, 1920–38* (Cambridge, 1953).

Notes: Goods industries are taken as manufacturing, mining and construction. Services are taken as including all other employment except agriculture, fishing and forestry, and the armed forces. The figures refer to employees, and thus exclude employers and the self-employed.

difference in trend between the two series. But the very high level of industrial employment in 1920 was freakish and artificial: it was part of the aftermath of the First World War and, as can be seen, was followed immediately by a very sharp drop. It is clear that industrial employment over the whole period fluctuated very widely and we shall obviously have to compare roughly similar years to see anything of any underlying trend. Perhaps 1923 and 1937 are as fair to compare as any: and between them employment in services rose rather more than twice as fast as employment in industry (33 per cent compared with 15 per cent) becoming larger in absolute size about the middle of the period—at the beginning of the depression.

From 1937 on, however, it is very difficult to see any underlying trend. By 1948 it appears that, on a basis roughly comparable with the pre-war figures, service employment may have been about

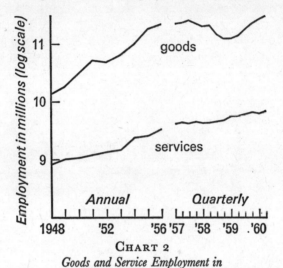

CHART 2
*Goods and Service Employment in
Great Britain, 1948–60*

Source: National Institute of Economic and Social Research

Notes: Goods and service industries are defined as in Chart 1. The figures refer to employees (as in Chart 1) but exclude men over 65 and women over 60. They refer to Great Britain, whereas Chart I refers to the United Kingdom as a whole. Quarterly figures are seasonally adjusted.

equal to 1938 while industrial employment was probably some 20 per cent higher. Chart 2 shows developments from 1948 to the middle of 1960 on a somewhat different coverage. Here the only conclusion that seems to emerge is the opposite of the view we are investigating. From 1948 to mid-1960 industrial employment rose by nearly 14 per cent while service employment rose by only 10 per cent. Even if we postulate a post-war aftermath of nearly ten years during which shortage of manpower, persistence of controls and the emphasis on exports hindered the resurgence of the service industries, we still find only that from 1954 to mid-1960 service employment rose by 5 per cent; industrial employment by 4 per cent. This is not the stuff of which trends are made.

However, there is more to be said. There have been some very different trends within the service sector. Employment in both distribution and the financial services (banking, insurance, etc.) has been rising more than twice as fast as employment in industrial production since 1950; but the effect of this has been masked by declines elsewhere. Employment in transport and communications, which accounts for about one-sixth of total service employment, has actually been falling throughout most of the post-war period; and those dazzled by Parkinsonian fireworks may be surprised to learn that employment in the civil service has fallen by over 10 per cent in the last twelve years. It may be objected that in establishing a trend it is not a very scientific procedure simply to omit those elements which move in the opposite direction. There are, after all, groups within the industrial sector which have also declined over the period (e.g. mining). But the decline in transport and communication employment highlights an important shortcoming in the overall figures we have been using as a measure of relative trends in employment in producing goods and producing services.

The bulk of the fall in transport employment has occurred in road and rail passenger transport: obviously the fact that in the last ten years the number of private passenger cars on the roads has much more than doubled is relevant to this. Further, the numbers employed in 'goods transport by road' have not risen at all since 1950; but the number of goods vehicles with current licences has gone up by nearly one-third. The explanation of this apparent oddity can be seen in the very large rise in 'C' licences (which permit the vehicle to be used only for the carriage of goods in the holder's own business) while the increase in the number of 'A' licences (for carriage of goods for hire or reward) has been relatively small. In other words, there has certainly been a rise in the volume of both passenger and goods transport, and in the numbers of people providing this, but the work is increasingly being done by people not included in the transport industries. On the one hand more passenger transport is being handled by unpaid individuals driving their own cars; on the other, more goods are being transported by truck and van drivers working for a company which is primarily engaged in doing something else—e.g. manufacturing or building. (Some of the 'C' licences will be for, say, delivery vans for retail stores and, to the extent that they are, the *total* service employment will not be understated by the figures—the numbers in the distribution industries will be swelled to the extent that those in transport are reduced; but much of the shift must have been to the industrial sector.)

The hidden element

With this example before us it is easy to think of a number of other
ways in which the people providing services are increasingly to be
found outside the category of service industries. The fall in the
number of domestic servants (over 30 per cent in the last ten years
alone) has not been accompanied by a fall of anything like the same
proportions in the amount of domestic service done. To a large
extent there has simply been a shift towards using the unpaid labour
of housewives—unsung by both poets and statisticians. The supermarket and the cafeteria reduce the amount of service provided by
the paid staff (and hence the numbers necessary) while increasing
that done by the shopper or eater himself. More washing is done
at home and less by paid launderers as more washing machines are
bought. And so on. The only comparable movement of industrial
production into the home is the do-it-yourself movement. It is hard
to get any idea of how much this has reduced the work of the
building trades (particularly in view of the growing volume of
'you-did-it-yourself—we'll-fix-it' jobs by the professionals). But it
must be very much smaller than the corresponding movements on
the service side.

More important, however, than the shift towards the unpaid
personal sector is the trend towards providing more services within
the so-called industrial sector. It is not only a question of a shift by
manufacturers and builders from using common carriers to running
their own fleets of trucks or vans, or, to take another example, the
growth of works canteens. There is the growth of almost entirely
new service industries within industry—e.g. the research and
development and economic and statistical divisions of a company.
Finally, and most important of all, there is the disproportionate
growth of that section of those employed by goods industries which
has always existed, which has always been necessary to the production
of the goods but which is nevertheless truly providing a service—the
executives, the sales, accounts, advertising and legal divisions of a
firm, the clerical workers and typists, the foremen and overseers,
etc.

It is impossible to get a precise indication for this country of how
much more, within the goods industries themselves, service employment (interpreted in its widest sense) has increased than true goods-
producers employment. But some general idea can be obtained.
The United States figures for manufacturing employment separate
out 'production workers' from the rest. (Even this category does not

represent 'pure' producers—it includes various types of overseers, watchmen, etc.—but it is a good approximation.) The figures show that over the past forty years the number of 'non-production' workers in manufacturing almost doubled, while production workers rose by only 45 per cent. Moreover, the paths of the two groups are diverging at an increasing rate: since the war, the non-production workers have risen by two-thirds while the number of production workers has barely changed. For the United Kingdom we have only the division into wage and salary earners. This under-states the position because many wage earners—e.g. clerks—strictly produce services not goods. But even so the trend is quite striking: in 1959 manufacturing industry employed the same number of wage-earners as it had done in 1950, while the number of salary earners-had risen by one-third.

There is one more point which is worth bearing in mind, though we have no means of assessing its significance. As automation spreads through industry the work of more and more of the production workers themselves will come to resemble service- rather than goods-production. This brings the whole matter perilously close to one of definitions, but without trying to draw any clear (and artificial) distinctions we might all agree that the work of a man using even a very complicated lathe is closer to, say, a blacksmith than to some-one watching the dials, co-ordinating the activities and maintaining ('servicing') a relatively self-sufficient machine.

Thus, in this country there is not discernible at least since before the war, any clear trend in the relative shares in the labour force of the services and industrial goods sectors (as defined by the statis-ticians) as there is in some other countries—notably in the United States. Nevertheless there is a good deal of evidence that the number of people engaged in producing services (wherever they appear in the official figures—or whether they appear at all) is here, as elsewhere, rising a good deal faster than the number engaged in producing goods. A slightly different way of putting it is to say that the pro-portion of workers who are in some sense 'overhead' is increasing. Putting it like that leads us naturally into the reasons often given for believing that a higher proportion of service workers will tend to make the economy more 'depression-proof'.

Services as stabilisers

There are perhaps four main reasons for believing that in recessions employment in services is likely to fall less than employment in goods-industries. First, many services are offered in large 'lumps'. The air-hostess, the girl at the counter, the doctor and the civil servant must be at their posts whether the plane, shop, surgery or in-tray is full or empty. If the fall in demand for their services is both large and (very important) is not expected to be soon reversed, then of course fewer planes can be flown, shops can close down, and the number of civil servants can be reduced. (Civil servants are not, in the ordinary way, dismissed, but intake can be varied in relation to retirements.) But these adjustments cannot be made quickly or precisely. Even where the fluctuations in demand are predictable and the provision of the services varied accordingly, the adjustment is far from exact: there are part-time helpers in the shops at Christmas but one still has to wait longer then to be served than at other times during the year.

It is this general characteristic which the employment of 'non-production' workers in the goods industries themselves shares with employment in the service industries. Even if all the sales figures are 10 per cent smaller, the firm is likely to need just as many people to add them up and interpret them; just as many typists for correspondence with suppliers; just as many people on the sales side—or perhaps even more if an attempt is to be made to recapture a market. On the other hand, it is a relatively simple matter, at least in principle, to hire and fire production workers (or vary their hours of employment) in accordance with fluctuations in the demand for cars, shirts, houses or whatever the product is.

The second reason for expecting employment in services to be relatively stable is that demand for many of them probably fluctuates less than incomes. Some services are 'contractual' or semi-contractual. You cannot adjust the family budget to harder times by taking a boy away from a fee-paying school for a term, or by skipping an insurance premium, or by using less of your house to economise on rent for a month or two. Some services are in the nature of a relatively fixed charge applied to other activities. As long as you continue to work at your job, or your wife to do the shopping, you may both have to continue to pay a fixed sum in fares. And, though your wife may economise at the butcher's and the grocer's, she may not be able to cut down on the unseen transport and distribution costs she is paying for if she shifts from butter to margarine or from sirloin to stewing steak. Finally, in Britain today a great number of services are provided free by the government—education and health are the most obvious examples, but the police, the judiciary, the armed services and the civil service are equally providing their output for us, the consumers, free of charge. (Of course we pay for them—in taxes—in the sense that we pay the wages and salaries of those who provide the services; but we do not pay for them in the sense that we can decide to buy a little less law-enforcement this year than last because we have installed a burglar alarm; or, on the strength perhaps of an excellent White Paper on the balance of payments, a little more of the output of the overseas finance division of the Treasury.) Since they are not sold on any market, the demand for these government services is unlikely to be reduced by reductions in incomes.

These two reasons for expecting service employment to be relatively stable are those most commonly stressed and probably the most important ones. They can be summed up in the economist's language in terms of elasticities: the supply of services is likely to be relatively inelastic in response to changes in the demand for them; and the demand for services is likely to be relatively inelastic to changes in income. But there are at least two other reasons, less often stressed and involving some conceptual complications, for believing that service employment is likely to be relatively stable.

The first of these is that the types of demand which may be said to initiate general fluctuations in the economy, and which themselves fluctuate most violently, are precisely those that affect goods production to a greater degree than service production. Thus it is usual to think of exports, investment and government expenditure as in some sense 'initiating' or 'autonomous' variables, and movements in consumers' expenditure as basically depending on the movements of the other items.[1] Now input-output analysis of data derived from the United Kingdom Censuses of Production shows that at any rate in 1954 the services components of gross fixed investment and exports were only 17 and 28 per cent respectively, while the goods industries components were 65 and 51 per cent respectively (the balance in each case being imports). The services component of total government expenditure is high (63 per cent) but the services component of the items within government expenditure which are most likely to fluctuate sharply is probably much lower. Thus defence expenditure is in principle the item most likely to change significantly and

---

[1] Of these, only government expenditure can strictly be called autonomous. Our exports depend to some extent at least on our imports which in turn are influenced by consumption; and any theory of fluctuations of national income has to take into account the way in which investment is influenced by changes in incomes and consumption as well as the influences in the opposite direction. But there are factors in investment and exports—such as technological advances at home and the pace of economic development abroad—which may be truly autonomous from our point of view; and in any case it is perhaps a reasonable first approximation to think of these types of demand as having primary responsibility for initiating fluctuations.

autonomously (a fall in defence expenditure was one of the main factors in the 1953/4 recession in the United States) and the services component of defence expenditure is probably close to that of fixed investment. On the other hand, in consumers' expenditure (changes in which tend to be induced and much less violent) the services component is higher than the goods component: 35 per cent compared with 25 per cent in 1954, the balance being supplied by agriculture and imports. (Only about 25 per cent of consumers' expenditure is on services as such, but all the goods they buy have of course a service cost—e.g. retailing and transport costs—built into them.) Thus we might expect expenditure on services to fluctuate less than expenditure on goods, since the main fluctuations in demand arise in those sectors where the services component is relatively small.

The last of our four reasons concerns stocks or inventories. It is a basic characteristic of services that you cannot stockpile them. You cannot have a year's haircuts in January or cope with a busy day ahead by taking tomorrow's bus ride today.[1] This distinction between services and most goods works two ways as far as stability is concerned. The ability to run stocks up and down enables goods-producing industries to ride out small, day-to-day or month-to-month fluctuations in demand for their products—especially when they can be predicted. Thus within limits this characteristic acts as a stabilising influence similar to the inelasticity of supply that we have suggested characterises many service industries. But if for any reason there should be an unexpected fall in demand, or a fall greater than is usually experienced, or one that looks likely to last longer than usual, then changes in the level of stocks can be a destabilising influence. When industry sees its stocks of goods rising because demand for them has fallen it may react by cutting back output sharply, throwing people out of work and thus further reducing demand and increasing stocks. In actual fact the rate of stockbuilding is by far the most volatile element in any advanced economy and accounts arithmetically in most recessions for the largest share of both decline and the subsequent recovery (this is not to say, of course, that such movements can be regarded as the main *causal* factor in recessions). In so far as service industries cannot give rise to the violent stock changes, they may be said to be more stable elements in the economy than goods industries.

---

[1] This distinction is not quite clear-cut; the services which are 'built-in' to a commodity when it is bought may perhaps be said to be stockpiled when the commodity is. Thus when a firm orders more raw materials it is in a sense stocking up on delivery charge as well as on the material itself. But for services bought for themselves the distinction from most goods seems to hold.

Cross currents

Thus, for any or all of these reasons, one may fairly plausibly argue that the service sector of the economy exercises a stabilising influence on the economy and hence, perhaps, that a relative increase in the numbers employed in this sector will make an economy more stable than before. However, the case as outlined above has been over-stated. The demand for a number of services purchased by individuals would appear likely to vary quite sharply with changes in incomes. When economic activity fell in a town and unemployment rose would we not expect to see fewer people at the cinema, more wives ironing shirts instead of sending them to the laundry, fewer people taking taxis and eating out, domestic servants being dismissed, and many women ceasing to have their hair waved or set? Moreover, though for many individual hairdressers or taxi-drivers this might simply mean more time spent being paid for waiting about, for some establishments it would probably mean the difference between staying in and going out of business altogether. Casualties among restaurants and beauty parlours might well be very high in a recession of any severity. Thus, though the supply elasticity may be small for any individual service establishment, it is likely to be much larger for the industry or trade as a whole.

Looking at the distinction the other way round we should also expect to find great differences in behaviour as between various goods-producing industries. Thus demand for cars and washing machines may fall off sharply when incomes fall, but what about demand for food? As one might expect, demand for food as a whole is fairly unresponsive to changes in income though there may be quite large shifts between different types of food. The same is true, whether one would expect it or not, of demand for cigarettes, for example. On the supply side, it has long been observed that a manufacturing firm tends to lay off fewer workers than is proportionate to the fall in demand for its products. This tendency has moreover increased greatly in recent years.[1] An important reason for it is of course the growth in the relative numbers of 'overhead' or 'non-production' workers to which we have already referred. We regarded this not as contradicting the general thesis that a growing share of the work force is engaged on producing services, but as an aspect of this growth. However, even among production-workers, lay-offs may be less than in proportion to a reduction in demand, for many reasons,

[1] See A. J. Brown, 'Inflation and the British Economy', *Economic Journal*, LXVIII (1958).

e.g. contracts with unions and a desire to maintain good labour relations, long-run scarcity of skilled workers which makes a firm willing to lose money on its key people for a while rather than risk being short of them in the succeeding boom, and so on.

Thus the issue is not clear-cut. We need, as always, strong support from figures before we can make a confident statement. To this evidence we now turn.

A glance back at the charts on pages 127 and 128 shows immediately that, whatever conclusions we may come to about long-term trends, service employment in this country has for the past forty years been very much less sensitive to fluctuations than has industrial employment. In the inter-war period, indeed, service employment fell only in 1921 and 1922, rising strongly thereafter, apparently entirely unaffected by the great depression. The post-war figures, though much less striking, also show no decline in service employment, while industrial employment faltered in 1952 and fell significantly in 1958. Figures for distribution and a number of other individual service industries taken separately would show a sharper contrast.

Within manufacturing the movements of employment of wage- and salary-earners shows a similar contrast—a contrast moreover that has become sharper since the war. Between 1921 and 1938 the number of salary-earners fell only once—by 10 per cent between 1929 and 1931. The number of wage-earners fell three times: in 1926 ($3\frac{1}{2}$ per cent), 1929–31 (15 per cent) and 1938 ($2\frac{1}{2}$ per cent). Since the war the number of salary-earners has risen steadily while the number of wage-earners has fallen twice: in 1952 ($1\frac{1}{2}$ per cent) and from 1955 to 1958 ($4\frac{1}{2}$ per cent).

American statistics give the same picture. Although service employment did decline in the United States between 1929 and 1932, that was the only significant fall in the last forty years, while industrial employment has dropped no less than nine times. Again, in each of three recessions since the war, employment of production workers in manufacturing has dropped by 9–10 per cent while the number of 'non-production' manufacturing workers fell by less than 2 per cent.

CONCLUSION

The evidence for our thesis thus looks strong. But it is nevertheless not conclusive. The continued increases (or very small falls) of service employment of various kinds during recessions that produce relatively sharp drops in the numbers of goods-producers may indicate the stabilising effect not of service employment itself but of an underlying long-term shift towards a higher demand by the community for services. (While a once largely vegetarian community were in the process of abandoning their beliefs, we might see a relatively steady rise in meat consumption despite sharp fluctuations in incomes and prices; but when everyone had become a potential meat-eater, in principle, price and income changes might at last be reflected in quite sharp changes in the consumption of meat.) An assessment of this factor leads us into a number of conceptual difficulties, some of which we hope to discuss in a later article.

What can be said with some degree of firmness on the basis of this article is perhaps as follows. The proportion of the labour force engaged in producing services (widely interpreted) has grown steadily in both this country and in the United States—though the trend has been stronger and more easily seen in the United States. A number of theoretical reasons can be adduced for believing that service employment is more stable than goods employment. And finally, the record of the past forty years in both this country and the United States shows that in recession or depression service employment has in fact been much less subject than goods employment to decline.

8 The Growth of Services in the Economy*

II. Do They Slow Down Overall Expansion?

by C. W. McMAHON
and G. D. N. WORSWICK

In the previous article we examined the proposition that the proportion of the labour force engaged in producing services (as opposed to goods) was steadily increasing. We found that for the United States this was incontrovertibly true. For the United Kingdom there appeared to be no marked difference in long-run employment trends between goods industries and service industries as a whole, but we suggested a number of ways in which true service employment was growing outside the service industries as such—both within the goods industries and outside the market sector altogether. We then suggested a number of reasons for believing that a relative growth in service employment—whether reflected in the statistics or not—is a stabilising influence in the economy. In this article we want to examine the view that it is also a brake on the growth of the economy as a whole, and an inflationary influence.

Since in the previous article we found no clear evidence of a shift in employment from goods-producing to service-producing, it might seem perverse to look for any slowing down of growth from this source. But since in many socio-economic trends, the recent past in the United States provides a suggestive pointer to the near future in the United Kingdom, the fact of the shift to service employment in the United States may retain an interest for us. In any case the fact that about half our labour force has been and is now engaged in producing services makes any stagnating or inflationary effects of such employment important: the more so if these effects were also present among the growing numbers of 'service' workers in the goods industries themselves, though in fact we cannot submit this aspect of things to any empirical test.

The basis for the view that we are examining is the alleged fact that productivity (i.e. output per worker) rises more slowly, if at all, in services than in goods-production. Hence, it is said, a shift in employment from the fast-rising to the slow-rising sector of the economy slows down the overall rate of growth.

* First published 1961.

The logic of this argument is not as simple as it looks. There is, for example, a hidden assumption about relative *levels*, as distinct from rates of increase, of productivity in the different sectors. It is also implicitly assumed that any shifts in *proportions* are unconnected with the growth of total employment. These are, unfortunately, not the only, or even the most intractable, of the conceptual difficulties. But let us for the moment put such difficulties aside and deploy the statistical facts.

The statistics of productivity growth

Productivity—output per worker—what do we mean? Surely that is simple enough: a matter of tons of coal per miner, cars per automobile worker, yards of cloth per weaver and so on. But what about big sectors of the economy? We cannot add x tons of coal to y cars to z yards of cloth and divide by p miners $+ q$ automobile workers $+ r$ weavers. Well—possibly with the $(p+q+r)$—they are all 'workers', are they not? But certainly not the $(x+y+z)$, as they stand in tons, and units, and yards. However, here comes the economic statistician with his measuring rod of money. Let us measure the economic 'volume' of goods by their money value—or, more precisely, in order to avoid counting the same thing twice—by the 'value added' in the industry concerned. Thus if the manufacturer spends $5d$ on yarn and fuel and other materials, to produce cloth which he sells for $1s$, the value added in weaving is $7d$. (There are problems about how to handle the use of durable plant and equipment— depreciation—which need not detain us.) Now we *can* add money values to get an apparently meaningful total economic volume of output. If we are comparing two separate years when prices are rising we can do this in two ways. We can either compare the actual 'value added', or as it is sometimes put, 'the contribution to gross domestic product', in terms of money, in each year; or we can compare the value added in the first year with what it would have been in the second year had prices not risen, i.e. correct for price changes.

This we have done for various groups of industries in Table 1, dividing the totals by the number of persons engaged in each sector. If prices are rising the current money totals will rise faster than the constant price totals, and in the third column we provide the implicit[1] price increase of each sector (in the order in which they

---

[1] For example, in Transport and Communications productivity measured at current prices increased by 90 per cent and at constant prices by 27 per cent. The implicit price increase is thus 50 per cent since $\frac{190}{127} \times 100 = 150$.

appear in column 2). The industries are labelled *g* or *s* according to the goods/services distinction made in our previous article. Perhaps the most striking point to emerge from the table is that although there are considerable differences in the relative placings of industries between the two columns, it is hard to see how, in either column, goods and service industries could be more thoroughly intermingled. An average rise in productivity for service industries as a whole, as contrasted with goods industries, cannot be calculated for the constant price figures. For the current price figures the increase in goods productivity over the ten years emerges as 82 per cent (78 per cent if agriculture is included) while that in service productivity

TABLE 1

Percentage increases between 1949 and 1959 in the contribution to gross domestic product per person engaged

(1) *At current prices*		(2) *At constant prices*		(3) *Implicit price increases*
s Gas, electricity water	122	s Gas, electricity, water	49	49
s Public administration and defence	112	g Agriculture	46	2
s Transport and communications	90	s Transport and communications	27	50
g Construction	83	g Manufacturing	26	44
g Manufacturing	82	s Miscellaneous services	24	46
s Insurance, banking and finance	80			
Total gross domestic product	79	Total gross domestic product	20	49
g Mining and quarrying	77	s Insurance, banking and finance	19	51
s Professional and miscellaneous services	64	g Construction	16	58
g Agriculture	50	s Distribution	10	32
s Distribution	45	s Public administration and defence	6	101
		g Mining and quarrying	4	71
		s Professional services	2	46

Sources: H.M.S.O., *National Income and Expenditure 1960*; H.M.S.O., *Annual Abstract of Statistics 1960*.

is 75 per cent (72 per cent if gas, electricity and water are excluded). This difference may be thought to provide some slight grounds for the view that goods productivity rises faster than service productivity; but it is hardly striking, taken by itself, and becomes even less convincing in view of the wide spread between industries within both goods and service averages. We would also draw attention to the widely different rankings of productivity increase given by the two measures to particular sectors. We shall comment on this below.

An immediate objection to drawing *any* conclusion from our figures is that the period is too short. A longer period would, of course, be desirable, but pre-war U.K. figures for gross domestic product do not seem reliable enough to use. To start earlier than 1949 in the post-war period would put us back into post-war readjustments; indeed, since the distributive trades, for example, were very severely curtailed during the war we may still have some once-for-all re-adjustments occurring within our period. 1959—just coming out of recession—is not ideal, either, but we have no later figures.

If we take the best post-war period for the American economy, on the other hand, the divergence in the rates of growth of the two sectors is quite marked, though figures are available only in current prices and in terms of employees (as contrasted with 'total persons engaged' in the U.K. figures in Table 1). Between 1947 and 1957 value added per employee rose by 73 per cent in the non-agricultural goods industries and by 54 per cent in the service industries. Over the longer run the difference in rate is striking. Between 1929 and 1957, current value added per employee rose by 220 per cent in goods industries but by only 130 per cent in services.

Thus the U.S.A. figures tend to support the idea of slower growth of productivity in services than in goods, but the U.K. figures are much less definite. The conclusion that the growth of services would constitute a brake on the overall growth of the economy does not, however, follow immediately.

In the first place, as we pointed out at the beginning, differential *rates* of increase are not sufficient to warrant the conclusion. If the average *level* of value added per person in services is higher than in goods, then a shift of employment to services would *raise* the overall growth rate until the (faster rising) goods productivity overtook services productivity. Table 2 shows that in the U.K. value added per person in services has been and still is considerably higher than in goods:[1] the gap has narrowed only slightly in ten years.

This was also the case until relatively recently in the United States. But about five years ago the gap was finally closed and now

[1] But see page 156 for a correction of this.

TABLE 2

Value added per person engaged by industries in 1949 and 1959

1949	£	1959	£
s Insurance, banking and finance	655	s Gas, electricity, water	1,450
s Gas, electricity, water	654	s Insurance, banking and finance	1,175
s Distribution	583	s Transport and communications	962
g Agriculture	542	s Distribution	844
s Transport and communications	505	s Professional and miscellaneous services	821
s Professional and miscellaneous services	501	g Agriculture	810
g Mining and quarrying	453	g Mining and quarrying	803
g Manufacturing	439	g Manufacturing	800
g Construction	420	g Construction	767
s Public administration and defence	313	s Public administration and defence	662
Total services	492		860
Total goods	449		797

Sources: H.M.S.O., *National Income and Expenditure 1960*; H.M.S.O., *Annual Abstract of Statistics 1960*.

value added per employee is higher—as well as rising faster—in goods than in services.

Secondly, when total employment is rising it is important to determine whether the rise in services should be regarded as a 'shift from goods' or as an addition to the total labour force of people who would otherwise not be employed at all. In the latter case, whatever the relative rates of growth, these extra workers could hardly be slowing things down. Whether the well-known rise in 'participation' which occurs in booms is biased towards services would be difficult to establish. However a similar point may have a real influence in another way. If demand for goods is sluggish over a long period, causing unemployment for unskilled workers, an increasing number of them may seek low-paid and part-time jobs in service industries, e.g. catering, hotels, laundries, local authority rubbish collection, and so on. A recent study of the American economy makes a good deal of this 'services as a sponge for labour' point and argues that it has been important there in the last six or eight years.[1] To the extent that this interpretation is

[1] U.S. Congress, Joint Economic Committee; Staff Report, *Employment, Growth and Price Levels* (Dec 1959) ch. 3.

correct, developments in services would be more an effect than a cause of stagnation.

Some practical difficulties

It might have been easier for our—and our readers'—peace of mind if we had stopped short here with a few words—suitably cautious and vague—to the effect that there might be something in the thesis, at any rate for the United States. But our consciences prick us and we feel obliged from now on to undermine the rather flimsy structure we have managed to put up.

Let us look first at the denominator of the output per person ratio. In Table 1 we took 'persons' to include all engaged in the industries concerned, whether employer, employee or self-employed. This is perhaps the most meaningful figure when considering broad shifts in employment. For other purposes, e.g. analysing inflation, it might be more appropriate to estimate productivity per employee. The choice of method is important: whereas the proportion of employers and self-employed in the goods industries is small and stable (around 1 per cent), it is as high as 15 or 20 per cent in some of the service industries, e.g. distribution and miscellaneous services. Moreover this ratio has fallen significantly over the last ten years. If we made our comparison on an output per *employee* basis we should therefore slightly increase the goods–service difference calculated above.

Even if employees only are taken, we should remember that workers are not homogeneous: they are men and women, young and old, skilled and unskilled, full- and part-time, in changing proportions. To lump them all together may be too crude. Again, output per man-year is less satisfactory in studying trends than output per man-hour—though in the particular case of United Kingdom 1949/1959 this is not likely to matter. We have no figures for various services, but average hours worked in the goods industries showed little change.

However, these troubles with the denominator, whether 'persons' or 'employees', though tiresome, are quite minor when we compare them with the difficulties involved in the concepts of 'output' and 'productivity'.

The concepts of output and productivity

We have already seen that it is necessary to work in terms of value added rather than physical output when absolute levels of productivity are being compared or when we want to speak of the changes in the overall productivity of a large sector of the economy. But the reader may feel that such value comparisons are a great deal less satisfactory than comparisons of changes in measurable physical output or output per head. Could we not produce figures for productivity changes of this kind at least for individual goods and service industries? And if we did, would they not be sure to show that these 'real' increases in productivity tended to be much higher in goods than in service industries? One thinks of productivity increases as stemming from mechanisation, mass production and automation, and are not these particularly associated with manufacturing? One's first impulse might be to say that in services they do not and cannot occur. Take the barber. Electric clippers may not pinch as the old hand-operated ones did, and the air may now be thick with smells our fathers' nostrils never knew: but if we find our hair being cut more quickly than once it was, this must alas, be because there is less to cut. Nor is this simply a contingent fact of history. It is inherent in the nature of the work: there can never be a Henry Ford for the hairdressers.

In answer to a 'common sense' argument along these lines, we may point out in passing that barbers are far from typical of the service sector as a whole. Think of the revolutions effected in communications by the telephone, in distribution by the cash register and the supermarket, in banking and insurance by pooling risks. But the main point to be made is that the concept of simple, unambiguous physical productivity changes and comparisons is by no means as simple as it sounds.

In particular, it is often extremely difficult to decide just what the physical unit of output of a given worker or firm is—let alone measure changes in it. It is simple enough with nails or tons of coal; but not so easy in the case of say, a firm making large and complicated turbine engines, each one made to order to unique specifications. Moreover, what is important in the present context is that this difficulty usually becomes particularly acute when we turn to services. We could think of the barber's output in terms of haircuts, but in most cases it is more complicated than this.

Take transport, a relatively straightforward example. We should probably be inclined to measure the output of a bus company's employees in terms of passenger-miles. But then should we not also try to take account of the number of routes and the frequency of buses? A company that ran one full bus into the market town every morning would be providing the same number of passenger-miles as one that ran two, an hour apart, and each only half-full. Yet we should say that the second company gave more service.

With other services the problems get more difficult and the measures of productivity increasingly arbitrary. A shop assistant's output is measured in terms of the volume of turnover he handles, weighted by the retail margins on each item. Changes in the output per head of bank clerks are represented by changes in the numbers of cheques cashed. The output of teachers is made to depend inversely on the pupil–teacher ratio; of dustmen, on the population of the United Kingdom. The output of cemetery staff depends on the number of deaths plus a constant for upkeep of the cemetery; of undertakers, on deaths alone. The contribution of bookmakers and pools firms is assessed in terms of net losses suffered by bettors, deflated by the consumer price index: thus even if they take more away from you this year than they did last, they still will not be able to pride themselves on increased output, if prices have risen by a greater proportion.[1] Clearly some heroic assumptions are being made. But this reflects on the nature of the task, not on the imagination or ingenuity of the statisticians who are attempting it. It is not easy to suggest better indicators than those which are officially chosen; and it should be pointed out that some of the more bizarre of these refer to very small groups. Whatever we assumed about the productivity of grave-diggers, it would be unlikely that the trends for the economy or for the service sector as a whole would be much affected.

However, there is a large section of the service industries which presents a new and bigger problem; not only do they have no easily identifiable physical product, but their output—the services they provide—is free. Take the policeman. One would be hard put to it to 'quantify' his output. (Ultimately it might be something like the number of crimes which did not occur in relation to the number that did—but such statistics are hard to come by.) But one cannot here fall back satisfactorily on our second measure either: we do not pay him by results. His timely presence may save the Crown Jewels one week, while in the next he may be called on for nothing more than an explanation of how to get to Westminster Abbey. His pay packet each week is the same. That, indeed, is all the money we ever pay him. Hence it is on this that the statistician must seize to value his output.

The same applies to almost all government officials, members of the armed forces, parsons and others. It is the best that can be done, no doubt, but of course it utterly prohibits the unfortunate police-

[1] For further details on the estimation of real product by industries see H.M.S.O. *National Income Statistics: Sources and Methods* (1956) ch. iii and app. vi. (A revised edition of *Sources and Methods* was published in 1968.)

man or parson from ever increasing his productivity unless he gets a rise (and even then, in a comparison with another industry where price changes had been corrected for, this would be 'deflated' away). Hence the very small rise in productivity (measured in constant prices) that Table 1 showed for 'public administration and defence' while the rise measured in current prices was very large. But this is a large group. We should hardly be surprised to find some tendency for 'productivity' to lag in the service sector as a whole when a substantial part of it is immutably condemned—however hard they work or efficient they become, whatever ingenious new methods they employ—to virtual constancy of output per man.

Changes in quality and price

Another way of saying that for a given industry we are satisfied that productivity or output has increased but can find no way of measuring this, is to say simply that the quality of the goods or service has risen. Quality changes are of course ubiquitous and make nonsense of the simple notion that changes in output consist of changes in the number of homogeneous standard units produced. They give rise to plenty of uncertainty in estimation of goods productivity. Today's car is very different from that of twenty years ago: even if the annual number of cars produced per worker were no greater now than then, we might well want to maintain that productivity in the industry had risen. But because the unit of output tends to be vaguer in services, more of the changes in service output have to be considered as qualitative. How does one go about measuring the improvement in the quality of medical services as medical science advances? In the service 'transportation across the Atlantic', what is the difference between a jet and an ordinary flight? The list is obviously endless.

The assessment of quality changes is essential to the assessment of price changes, and price changes give rise to a lot of difficulty in the concept of productivity. There is a strong impulse to say that, if productivity changes are to be measured in terms of value not of physical changes, then at any rate price changes must be corrected for. But of course, unless one is dealing with changes in the output of standardised physically identifiable goods or services, one's decision about how much of an increase in the value of an output is due to a price rise will depend on what one decides about quality changes. If we are now paying more for something but are getting 'more for our money', we might say that there had not been any increase in its price. But there are pitfalls here.

Suppose we were previously offered vanilla ice-cream alone and are now offered the additional choice of strawberry ice-cream for a penny extra, there are no grounds for saying that the price of ice-cream has changed. But should vanilla ice-cream now be withdrawn entirely from the market, if we want ice-cream we must pay more for it than we used to do. There will be purists who find coloured ices vulgar—for whom, that is, there has not been a rise in quality at all: rather a deterioration. But there is a larger question than the relativity of tastes and hence of quality evaluations (though this is big and important). Even if we all admit the strawberry ice-cream to be superior we may not all or always wish to spend the extra on it. Unfortunately, in practice, most of the quality improvements that occur are of this latter, take-it-or-leave-it kind. The simple, cheap old product is no longer available side-by-side with the better, dearer one. In such a situation, has a 'real' price rise occurred or has it not? If we decide it has (and our decision must be to some extent arbitrary) we shall perhaps correct for it, and the result will be that our figures show no productivity increase among the ice-cream workers. If not, there may be a rise.[1]

But even when the price increase is clear and unambiguous, when there has been no change in the physical product but more is being charged for it, will 'correcting' for the price rise always and necessarily give us a better insight into the 'real' productivity rise? No. The most fundamental argument against the view that changes in physical output are the best measures of productivity changes is that we are not necessarily interested in such changes in physical output at all. They may be meaningless—or even of negative significance. We do not normally measure the output of a steel-mill in terms of slag, a chemical factory in terms of effluent, a timber-mill in terms of sawdust. But if someone discovers a use for the waste material and is prepared to pay for it—e.g. to turn sawdust into board by compressing it—then changes in its output become meaningful. We call it a by-product and take it into account when assessing the total output of the firm.

This point can be put in another way. Suppose that between one period and another the number of bricks produced per brickmaker is unchanged but the price of bricks goes up by 10 per cent. Thus, in current prices, the value added, or the 'productivity', of the brickmakers, has risen. Common sense would suggest 'correcting' for the price increase, and saying that true productivity, i.e. in

---

[1] Where quality improvements are undetected or arbitrarily ignored, price indices will show increases that are too high. There is no doubt that, as a result of this, retail price indices in advanced countries usually overstate the degree of inflation though it is usually impossible to say by how much.

constant prices, had not risen. On the other hand if, over the same period, the amount of cement produced per cement-maker rose by 10 per cent while the price of cement was unchanged, we should certainly say that productivity in cement had risen by 10 per cent. But suppose that in the first year the value of bricks produced equalled the value of cement produced. Then it would also equal it in the second year. The levels of output per head in the two industries would remain the same (assuming employment constant), while common sense is telling us that the productivity in cement had risen, while in bricks it had not.

The point is, of course, that relative price changes are not simply distortions, hiding pure, 'real' changes beneath. For some purposes we may want to 'correct' for them but for others we may not. Relative prices are indicators in some way of relative valuations by the economy and, since we are interested only in 'economic' productivity, they are important.

This brings us to our final conclusion—more nihilistic, unfortunately, than all that has gone before, destructive though that may have seemed. To talk of slowing down or speeding up the rate of growth of the economy as a whole because of relative shifts to slower growing industries involves such ambiguities as to be virtually meaningless. It is not merely that, in the United Kingdom at least, such figures as there are do not seem to show the expected productivity differences; it is not merely that the argument involves hidden assumptions at least one of which is not valid; it is not merely that the measurement of productivity is such an impossible business that what the figures indicate may be wildly at variance with what we know but cannot quantify. Over and above all there is the fundamental point that in some sense we produce what we want. If we happened to want in increasing volume something that the statistics show we can produce in increasing volume per head, then our economy would indeed grow fast. But if our tastes turn towards items where growth in measurable productivity is slow (and the economist's battered old concept of diminishing marginal utility would suggest that this will always be likely), then our economy *may* appear to grow more slowly. But what sort of a measure of growth of output and welfare is it that pillories us for our tastes?

CONCLUSION

The reader who has followed us so far may nevertheless have felt a mounting irritation. Surely we all know, and who better than economists, that Britain's growth of productivity lags behind others and that something must be done to speed things up. What is the point of all these niceties which seem to cast doubt on the very idea of productivity? The whole thing is academic and irresponsible.

Naturally we should not agree with this. In setting out to examine the thesis concerning the influence of the alleged growth of services we started by deploying the available statistical facts. We went on to point out that there are a good many unknowns and ambiguities in the data themselves. There is, however, a genuine danger that people will come to believe that in this kind of problem 'lack of statistics' is all that is at stake. This is not so. There is present a risk of a fundamental conceptual confusion between 'statistical' output and productivity and the economic concept of quantity. Where we are concerned with micro-economics, e.g. comparison of two coal mines, or changes in boot and shoe output over short periods, it may be safe, as a first approximation, to identify the two. Again, when we compare rates of growth of total gross national product per worker between different countries, it may be that the distortions and ambiguities are of the same order of magnitude for all, so that the comparisons have some point (though it might be sensible in making international comparisons to remove at least the public administration sector in each case). But when the comparisons are made between industries or sectors of the economy over a relatively long period of time, the likelihood of a divergence between 'statistical' and 'economic' productivity becomes very large and to ignore this is to run the risk of serious misconceptions in policy making.

Consider the widespread doctrine 'no wage increases without productivity increases'. Applied to the whole economy this has, at first sight, a sturdy common sense. But if we apply it to separate sectors and, in addition, confuse, for example, physical and economic productivity, we may get some very strange results. Our politician, parson or civil servant might never have a rise, while workers in goods industries with high rates of increase of physical output per man would enjoy ever rising incomes. In fact, as we have hinted above, this could not last because it confuses what is physically possible by way of output with what we actually want. Somehow or other through the mechanism of relative wage and price changes (and occasionally unemployment), things will get sorted out. (We noticed in Table 1 that the Public Administration and Defence sectors did in fact get a very big rise in pay between 1949 and 1959.) But the particular way in which things sort themselves out can still be important. Thus, if the pace of money wage increases is set by the rate of increase in physical productivity in just those goods sectors where physical productivity (*a*) can be measured and (*b*) grows fastest, the prices of these goods may simply remain the same. But if the wage increases are transferred to the other sectors where physical productivity does not rise, prices in such sectors will have to rise to cover costs—and so the overall level of prices rises. Hence the adjustment which must ultimately be made 'somehow or other' would in this instance be made through the mechanism of continuous inflation.

Whether, and to what extent, this kind of thing has in fact been occurring in recent years is an open question, but we believe there is sufficient in the argument to justify the closest scrutiny of any theories and policies based on propositions about 'productivity'.

9 Goods and Services Once Again*

by G. D. N. WORSWICK and C. G. FANE

INTRODUCTION

SIX years ago, two articles were published in the *District Bank Review* on the subject of the growth of services in the economy.[1] The background of these articles was the notion that in advanced economies, as real income per head rises, so the share of services, as distinct from goods, in the national output rises. This, it was thought, would have two consequences: first it would increase the stability of economies; secondly, it would tend to slow down the overall rate of growth of the economy, on the alleged grounds that the level, and the rate of growth, of productivity is lower in services than in goods. The two articles examined this thesis in the light of facts available up to the year 1959, mainly for the United Kingdom but with some data for the United States.

The introduction of the Selective Employment Tax, which was designed to fall on employment in services but not on employment in goods, makes it worth while returning to these original articles and bringing them up to date in the light of six more years of post-war experience. In any case, a re-examination is desirable, since the important reclassification of U.K. manpower statistics in 1958, as well as revisions in National Income estimates, lead us to come up with a somewhat different picture for the year 1959 than that which was originally presented.

The present article is primarily concerned with bringing the facts up to date, but we shall re-examine certain conclusions, some of which must be modified in the light of the new data.

THE DISTINCTION BETWEEN GOODS AND SERVICES

The point of emphasising the distinction between goods and services is that intuitively we have the idea that in the nature of things

---

* First published 1967.

[1] C. W. McMahon and G. D. N. Worswick, 'The Growth of Services in the Economy', *District Bank Review*, Dec 1960 and Mar 1961, and Chs. 7 & 8 above.

increases of output per unit of input (especially labour) are somewhat easier to achieve for the former than for the latter. It is easier
to visualise the application of science and technology to the manufacture of material things than to the provision of immaterial
services. The idea of mass production of soap comes more naturally
than the concept of mass production of hair-cuts.

We shall have something to say about these ideas at the end of this
article. Meanwhile, before looking at the statistics, we wish to
draw attention to two points. The first is that the statistics for

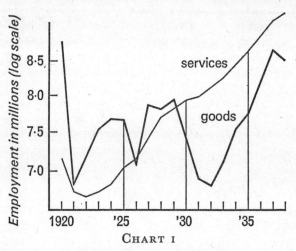

CHART I

Goods and Service Employment in the
United Kingdom, 1920–38

Source: Agatha L. Chapman, *Wages and Salaries in the United Kingdom, 1920–38*
(Cambridge, 1953).
Goods: Manufacturing, mining and construction.
Services: All other employment except agriculture, forestry and fishing and the
armed forces.
The figures refer to employees only and thus exclude employers and the self-
employed.

employment or for output which are available for illustrating this
problem are statistics for industrial groups, and one has to decide
whether to label a particular industrial group 'goods' or 'services'.
Thus, one classifies manufacturing as goods but distributive trades
or transport as services. However, goods are used in the process of
providing services, and services are used in the manufacture of
goods. The final consumer thinks of having a service performed
when having his hair cut, but the inputs going into that hair-cut,
while consisting mainly of the personal labour of the hairdresser,

also include the depreciation of the scissors (capital) and the use of materials, if he has a shampoo. Vice versa, in factories producing refrigerators there are people engaged in design work, typing, and so forth. If a letter is typed by a person employed by the manufacturing enterprise, that work is counted as part of manufacturing, but if the typing were sent out to an agency, then in the statistics the typing would count as a service. In short, there is a goods/service distinction within enterprises and within industries just as there is between industrial groups. There is some reason to think that the nature of modern production is such as to raise the proportion of service activities within enterprises as against the activities one thinks of as the processing of goods. Thus, the available statistics will be giving only a very blurred picture of the situation we are really after.

The second major consideration is that our intuition may mislead us. It has been argued, for example, that one of the most fruitful areas of application of computers is precisely in the service sector, in accounting, banking, and so forth. Again, there has been a revolution in the distributive trades with the growth of self-service shops and supermarkets. Thus, the commonly held view that services are, of their nature, an area where productivity increases are hard to come by, may need substantial qualification.

THE NEW DATA

I. *Employment trends*

Charts 1 and 2 show the trends in employment in goods and services in the United Kingdom for the inter-war and post-war years respectively. Chart 3 shows the corresponding data for the United States during the period 1940–64.

First, to consider the stability question: all three charts illustrate the greater stability of service employment than goods employment. What appears to happen is that in periods of 'go' goods employment rises considerably faster than service employment, but that during 'stops' goods employment actually falls, whereas service employment continues to rise, albeit at a slightly reduced rate.

Secondly, the hypothesis that employment in services expands faster than employment in goods needs to be considered. The U.S. data certainly support this: between 1940 and 1964 service employment in the United States grew at an average rate of 2·8 per cent per annum, goods employment at an average of 2·0 per cent. The difference is even more marked if we consider only the later part of the period—as Chart 3 shows. The hypothesis is also clearly supported by the United Kingdom data for the inter-war period. Choosing 1923 and 1937 as reasonably comparable years we observe an increase in service employment of 33 per cent over the period, which is more than twice the increase of 15 per cent in goods employment during the same period. However, from 1937 onward it is difficult to see any clear trend: in the years 1937–48 there was a big expansion of goods employment relative to service employment, but in the period 1948–64 the two sectors have grown at almost the same overall rate.

The White Paper[1] introducing the Selective Employment Tax drew attention to the quite remarkable absorption of most of the

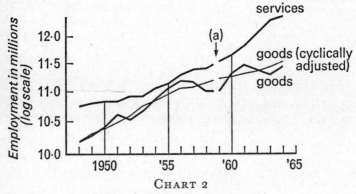

CHART 2

Goods and Service Employment in the
United Kingdom, 1948–64

Source: *Annual Abstract of Statistics* (see Appendix).
Goods: Mining and quarrying, manufacturing and construction.
Services: Gas, etc., public administration, insurance, etc., professional and miscellaneous services and distribution.
(a) Post-1959 data are based on the S.I.C. 1958; pre-1959 data are obtained by linking (see Appendix).

increase in manpower since 1960 into the services sector, with only a small net gain to manufacturing. Chart 2 puts this contrast into a somewhat broader setting. It is misleading to extrapolate the trend over a fairly short period without adjusting for normal cyclical fluctuations. Since 1960 there have been two 'stops' and one 'go'. It was, therefore, to be expected that service employment would grow much faster than goods employment during such a period. However, while we think that the White Paper gives an exaggerated picture of the trend in the relative growth of services, the fact re-

[1] Cmnd 2986 (1966).

mains that in the later post-war period there has been an acceleration of the growth of employment in services relative to the growth
of employment in the goods sector: over the whole cycle 1959–64
service employment grew about twice as fast as goods employment
—7¾ per cent compared with 3¾ per cent.

The definitions of the two sectors are necessarily somewhat
arbitrary. We have excluded agriculture on the ground that it is

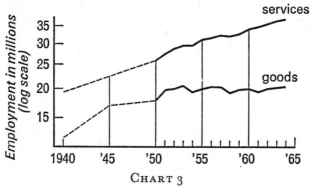

CHART 3

*Goods and Service Employment in the
United States 1940–64*

Source: *Annual Abstract of the U.S. 1965*, Table 305.
Goods: Mining, contract construction and manufacturing.
Services: Transportation and public utilities, wholesale and retail trade, government,
finance, etc., and services and miscellaneous.

sui generis. Some economists would wish to include agriculture in
the goods sector. Had this been done the figures would have provided more clear-cut support for the 'differential-growth-of-em-
ployment' thesis, since employment in agriculture has been falling
steadily in both the United States and the United Kingdom
throughout the period to which our data refer.

II.   *Value-added data and price data*

We have computed the average value added per man at current
prices in various industries in the United States and the United
Kingdom for several post-war years. The average annual percentage rates of change of value added per man at current prices and at
constant prices have also been calculated. These results together
with the implied price changes are presented in Tables 1, 2 and 3.
The sources and methods which have been used in arriving
at these figures are given in the Appendix. A discussion of the

implications of the results appears later. Here we may note the following points:

(i) As regards levels of productivity, the March 1961 article made service productivity in the United Kingdom, as measured by value added per person, some 8–10 per cent higher than goods productivity in both 1949 and 1959. We now find a somewhat different picture. Using the Standard Industrial Classification of 1948, we still make service productivity higher than goods productivity in 1949, by about 5 per cent, but in 1959 productivity in services was fractionally lower—1 per cent—than in goods. Using the 1958 S.I.C. brings 1959 service productivity more distinctly below goods productivity—nearly 4 per cent—but by 1964, while service productivity is still lower, the gap is narrower.

The level of service productivity in the United States was rather higher than productivity in goods both in 1950 and in 1963, 7 per cent and 3 per cent respectively if agriculture is excluded from

TABLE I

U.K. Value Added per Man in Current Pounds

1949 (S.I.C. 1948)			1959 (S.I.C. 1948)		1959 (S.I.C. 1958)		1964 (S.I.C. 1958)	
s	Gas, etc.	663	Gas, etc.	1496	Gas, etc.	1496	Gas, etc.	2238
s	Insrnce, banks	654	Insrnce, banks	1134	Insrnce, banks	1134	Transport	1480
s	Distrib. trades	558	Transport	994	Transport	992	Insrnce, banks	1467
	Agriculture	551	Manufacturing	843	Manufacturing	861	Construction	1151
s	Transport	519	Mining	819	Mining	817	Manufacturing	1117
g	Mining	470	Agriculture	816	Agriculture	815	Mining	1108
g	Manufacturing	467	Distrib. trades	811	Construction	801	Agriculture	1080
s	Various services	449	Construction	800	Distrib. trades	789	Distrib. trades	982
g	Construction	411	Various services	731	Various services	723	Pub. admin.	962
s	Pub. admin.	332	Pub. admin.	685	Pub. admin.	687	Various services	957
	Goods (less agric.)	459		836		849		1122
	Goods (plus agric.)	468½		833		846		1119
	Services	478		828		815½		1096
	Total	473		830		830½		1108

s denotes services; *g* denotes goods.

goods. In the case of the United States the inclusion of agriculture in goods, or its exclusion, makes a deal of difference to the totals, because measured productivity in agriculture is very much lower than in the other sectors. This is not so in the United Kingdom.

For comparing *levels* of productivity in different industries there is, of course, only one possible common measure—the money value of output per person. When comparing *rates of change* through time we have two measures: the change in money value added per person, as with levels, but we now have also indices of change

TABLE 2

Percentage Increases in Output per Man in U.K.: Average Rates per Annum over Given Period

	1949 to 1959						1959 to 1964					
	At current prices		At constant prices		Implicit price change		At current prices		At constant prices		Implicit price change	
s	Gas, etc.	8.5	Gas, etc.	4.0	Gas, etc.	4.4	Gas, etc.	6.5	Agriculture	8.4	Agriculture	−0.6
s	Pub. admin.	8.0	Agriculture	3.6	Transport	0.3	Transport	4.3	Gas, etc.	8.3	Gas, etc.	3.9
g	Construction	6.9	Transport	2.5	Construction	4.1	Construction	4.2	Mining	7.5	Mining	1.9
s	Transport	6.7	Manufacturing	2.3	Pub. admin.	3.7	Pub. admin.	3.3	Transport	7.0	Transport	3.9
g	Manufacturing	6.1	Ins., Banks	1.9	Mining	3.7	Mining	2.0	Manufacturing	6.3	Manufacturing	2.0
g	Mining	5.7	Construction	1.6	Agriculture	5.2	Agriculture	1.6	Construction	5.8	Construction	5.4
s	Ins., banks	5.7	Distrib. trades	1.3	Various services	2.5	Various services	1.4	Pub. admin.	5.8	Pub. admin.	5.3
s	Various services	5.0	Various services	1.0	Manufacturing	4.0	Manufacturing	1.0	Distrib. trades	5.3	Distrib. trades	2.9
s	Agriculture	4.0	Pub. admin.	0.6	Ins., banks	7.4	Ins., banks	1.0	Ins., banks	5.3	Ins., banks	4.1
s	Distrib. trades	3.8	Mining	0.4	Distrib. trades	5.3	Distrib. trades	0.6	Various services	4.3	Various services	5.1
	Goods (less agric.)	6.2		2.1		4.0		3.2		5.8		2.5
	Goods (plus agric.)	5.9		2.2		3.7		3.4		5.8		2.3
	Services	5.6		1.6		4.0		1.8		6.1		4.2
	Total	5.8		1.9		3.8		2.7		5.9		3.1

s denotes services; *g* denotes goods.

TABLE 3

U.S. PRODUCTIVITY DATA

Value Added per Man in Current Dollars   Average Percentage Increases per Annum 1950–63

	Value Added per Man in Current Dollars				Average Percentage Increases per Annum 1950–63				
	1950		1963		Value added per man at current prices		Value added per man at constant prices		Implicit price change
	Finance, etc.	15,780	Finance, etc.	25,110	Mining	5·7	Mining	4·9	0·8
g	Mining	9,110	Mining	18,750	Public utilities	5·1	Agriculture	4·5	−0·4
g	Wholesale & retail	5,760	Public utilities	10,140	Govt. & govt. enterprise	4·7	Public utilities	4·4	0·7
	Services & comms.	5,630	Services & comms.	9,520	Manufacturing	4·4	Manufacturing	2·3	2·1
g	Contract construction	5,420	Manufacturing	9,450	Services & comms.	4·1	Finance, etc.	1·0	2·6
g	Manufacturing	5,370	Contract construction	9,050	Contract construction }	4·0	Services & comms.	0·9	3·1
s	Public utilities	5,280	Wholesale & retail	8,720	Agriculture		Wholesale & retail	0·8	2·4
s	Govt. & govt. enterprise	3,920	Govt. & govt. enterprise	7,090	Finance, etc.	3·9	Contract construction }	0·0	4·0
	Agriculture	2,140	Agriculture	3,570	Wholesale & retail	3·2	Govt. & govt. enterprise		4·7
	Goods (less agric.)	5,560		9,670		4·4		2·0	2·3
	Goods (inc. agric.)	4,470		8,215		5·0		3·0	1·9
	Services	5,970		9,940		4·0		1·2	2·7
	Total	5,140		9,200		4·6		2·2	2·4

s denotes services;   *g* denotes goods.

in *real* output (there are of course, conceptual difficulties in compiling such indices, as well as practical problems of measurement, which are more serious in some sectors than in others).

(ii) Real productivity, *as measured*, has increased faster in the goods sector than in the service sector. This is true of the United States and the United Kingdom in both the periods we have studied.

(iii) The above result does not only hold true for broad inter-sector comparisons, it is also the case that *measured* real productivity rises faster in the majority of goods industries than in the majority of service industries.

(iv) The growth rates of value added per man at current prices are similar for the two sectors. Also, there is no tendency for the individual industries with the fastest rates of increase of value added per man at current prices to be goods industries rather than service industries.

(v) There is a rough inverse correlation, at the level of the ten broad industry groups, between the rates of increase of measured real productivity and measured price increases.

(vi) Table 4 shows percentage price rises for consumer goods and services in eight industrial countries during the period 1960–5. Just as Tables 2 and 3 show that measured price increases have been larger in the service sector than in the goods sector for both the United States and the United Kingdom in the post-war period,

TABLE 4

Price Indices in 1965 (1960 = 100) for Consumer Goods and Consumer Services. Selected O.E.C.D. Countries

	All goods less food	All services less rent	Total All goods and services	Goods and services less food
Canada	100·7	116·8	108·4	107·3
U.S.	103·2	113·1	106·6	106·5
Japan	125·7	137·4	135·2	130·8
France	111·6	126·3	120·3	117·4
Germany	111·0	119·0	114·9	116·0
Italy	120·2	137·9	127·1	128·9
Netherlands	111·0	120·0	119·0	116·0
U.K.	112·7	126·3	119·0	118·6

O.E.C.D., Consumer Price Indices (Nov 1966).

so Table 4 shows that in all the eight countries for which figures are readily available the prices of consumer services have risen faster than the prices of consumer goods.

INTERPRETATION OF THE NEW DATA

There are difficulties confronting the National Accounts statistician in providing good measures of monetary aggregates, e.g. consumption, exports, or the value of output of a particular industry. He has to worry whether the returns he receives are accurate, whether their coverage is complete, and so forth. The figures for many countries, especially the less developed ones, may be suspect on these practical grounds alone. But the conceptual headaches begin when the statistician tries to decompose the change in a money aggregate into a 'volume' component and a price component. The problem is quite general; for convenience, let us illustrate with respect to the output of an industry. For single commodities this may look fairly straightforward. If we are told that the value of output of bricks has gone up from 100 to 132 and that the number of bricks produced has gone up from 100 to 120, we are inclined to say 'increase in volume 20 per cent and increase in price 10 per cent'. But even here there could be snags. Chief among them is whether the quality of the bricks is still the same. Economic volume is often approximated by physical volume, but it is not identical; any over- or under-statement of quality improvement will mean a corresponding over- or under-statement of the economic volume change and a corresponding under- or over-statement of the price change.

Very often we have a situation in which we have usable output indicators for some but not all items in an industry group, and price indicators for some but not all items (the items for which we have output indicators being not necessarily the same as those for which we have price data). In such a case, the statistician can use two approaches; he can make an output index from the data he has got and hope that it will be representative of the whole group: by dividing into the value change he derives an implicit price change. And he can start at the other end: by making a price index from the data he has got, he can derive an implicit volume change. If the two approaches lead to much the same price volume breakdown, one can proceed with some confidence. If they do not, one can, of course, split the difference, but this is a pragmatic device, to be used with great caution.

But what do we do when there is no plausible, direct measure of output? One line would be not to make the attempt to secure a price/volume breakdown in such cases. But National Accounts statisticians do not like leaving empty spaces lying about all over their tables; it is messy, and people like to have totals as a frame of reference for the parts. In such cases what the statistician very often does is to use an input indicator, e.g. employment, as a proxy for output. This is not wholly arbitrary. If something has to be done to fill the empty space, this may be the best device to use. But obviously if employment is used as a proxy for output, when the latter has no direct measure, we should not be altogether surprised, when we go to the Tables and divide the output indicator by employment, if we find that the real productivity of labour in such cases has not changed! Now it is precisely in the services sector that direct measures of output are the hardest to come by and the statisticians are driven to make do with proxies. There is a strong presumption that in most National Accounts statistics the growth in the volume of services is understated, and the corresponding, implicit price deflators over-stated. This question has been very fully discussed in an excellent article by A. T. P. Hill and J. McGibbon in the first issue of the *Review of Income and Wealth*.[1] 'It must be accepted, therefore,' they say, 'that in most countries statistics on growth of output per person in a wide range of services are totally devoid of economic or any other significance.'

The fact that National Accounts statistics probably understate the 'true' growth of productivity in services needs to be borne in mind when drawing conclusions from those statistics. Unfortunately, we do not know the degree of the under-statement. The question whether over the past twenty years, say, the 'true' productivity of teachers or judges has increased, and by how much, has only to be asked for it to be realised that any convincing answer could hardly be given by a single statistic, but would have to be based upon a very detailed study of the educational or judiciary system; and we might well doubt whether such an inquiry, however exhaustive, would yield us any very precise measure.

Yet even if we could get direct measures of 'true' productivity in services, and even if we found that such measures showed a slower rate of increase than that of goods productivity, it would still not follow that this fact (combined with the fact that the level of productivity in services was lower than in goods) was sufficient to justify new policies, e.g. alterations of the tax structure, designed to shift resources from the service sector in which productivity

[1] Yale University Press (March 1966).

grows slowly to the goods sector where productivity grows faster, simply in order to raise the average rate of growth of the economy.

One objection, incidentally, to this type of argument is that, in its more naïve forms, the point is ignored that in such shifts of resources it is the marginal productivities which are relevant, and these need not be the same as the average productivities, which are what the statistics usually provide. But we do not wish to pursue this point here.

The point we wish to make is this: in constructing indices of real output we start off from physical measurements, e.g. tons of steel, yards of cloth, number of cars, ton-miles of freight, number of telegrams, and the like. To combine these physical series into indices of output, we have to put values on the physical units of the various sectors, and these relative values are not constant, but changing. When we come to consider the best use of national resources, we cannot ignore such changes in valuation.

We noticed in Table 4 that in 1960–5 in eight countries for which there are easily accessible figures, the prices of consumer services rose faster than the prices of consumer goods. This is not new, but the continuation of a phenomenon observed pretty widely in advanced countries at least since 1953.[1] It is possible, for the reasons already mentioned, that some of these price increases for services may be over-stated, with an exactly corresponding under-statement of the rise in the real output of the services concerned. But even if these figures are taken at their face value as true indicators, there could be a simple and rational explanation for them. Consider the extreme case in which we assume that increases in true productivity occur in goods but cannot occur in services. In this case there is a sense in which any increase in real income or real output for the whole economy can only originate from an increase in productivity in goods. But this does not mean that we would necessarily wish to take out the fruits of such an increase in real income entirely in the goods where the productivity increase originated. We may prefer to take out some or all of the gain in terms of more services. This would mean a relative shift in employment from goods to services, and, for reasons discussed at greater length in the article just quoted, might well mean a change in the relative prices of goods and services in order to bring about the desired shift. Thus, while it is arithmetically correct to say that such an economy could grow faster if people would consume only goods and not services, it would not be a very sensible policy

[1] See G. D. N. Worswick, 'Services and Inflation', *Manchester Statistical Society* (1962).

recommendation if the people happened to want more services more keenly than they wanted more goods.

We do not wish to be misunderstood. In the first place, although it might be more difficult to measure productivity in services than in goods, this does not mean that one should abandon the attempt to get increases in productivity in services. There have in fact been some quite striking changes in recent decades in the distributive trades, banking, and so on; nor need one abandon all efforts to improve productivity in the civil service, armed forces, or the House of Commons, merely because there do not exist simple statistical indicators of such productivity. Secondly, while we are thoroughly sceptical of arguments for taxing services which are based on statistics on comparative rates of increase in productivity for broad sectors of the economy, this does not mean that there are not arguments for taxing services. On the contrary, historically indirect taxation in Britain has fallen almost exclusively on goods and not on services. General welfare economic theory gives us a strong presumption that this discrimination is undesirable and that its reduction or elimination will probably be a good thing.

APPENDIX

Classification of U.K. Industries

There was a substantial reclassification of U.K. manpower in 1959. We have, therefore, provided two estimates of average value added per man in that year, one based on the Standard Industrial Classification 1948, the other based on the S.I.C. 1958. The most important difference is that 700,000 men (whose average value added was relatively low) were listed under manufacturing in the S.I.C. 1948 but under distribution and various services in the S.I.C. 1958. The reclassification thus raised the average value added per man in manufacturing but lowered it in distribution and various services (see Table 1).

Sources and Explanations

TABLE I

Employment data—*Annual Abstract of Statistics*.
Value-added data (S.I.C. 1958) in 1959 and 1964—*1966 Blue Book*.

Value added data (S.I.C. 1948). The *1958 Blue Book* was the last one to use the S.I.C. 1948. To estimate value added in 1949 we have therefore started with the estimates from this *Blue Book* and tried to estimate the size of subsequent revisions (excluding, of course, that part of the published revision which we estimate to have been caused by the reclassification). This necessarily means that the margin of error is large.

To obtain value-added figures for 1959 on the S.I.C. 1948 we used figures from the *1966 Blue Book* (based on the S.I.C. 1958) and applied a rough correction for the reclassification. Again there is a large margin of error.

'Various services': Output is defined as the aggregate of the *Blue Book*'s 'Public health and educational services' and 'Other services'. Employment is the aggregate of the *Annual Abstract*'s 'Professional services' and 'Miscellaneous services'.

TABLE 2

Percentage changes in output per man at current prices are derived from the data of Table 1.

Percentage changes in output per man at constant prices are derived by combining the employment data from the *Annual Abstract of Statistics 1965*, with the *Blue Book* index numbers of output at constant factor cost (*1966 Blue Book*, Table 14).

The implicit price changes are derived as a quotient from percentage in output per man at current prices and at constant prices. The entries in the column 'implicit price change' refer to the corresponding industries in the column 'percentage change in output per man at constant prices'.

TABLE 3

Source: *Statistical Abstract of the U.S. 1965.*

(1) Employment data:
   Non-agricultural employment: Table 305.
   Agricultural employment: Table 327 (column for 'total').
(2) Output data:
   G.N.P. in current and constant 1954 dollars: Table 450. Output per man in 'services and communications' was taken as output in services plus output in communications divided by employment in 'services and miscellaneous'.

'Implicit price changes': derived and set out as in Table 2.

CHART 2

The employment data for 1959–64 are based on the S.I.C. 1958. The published data for 1948–59 are based on the S.I.C. 1948. To obtain the series shown in this Chart we have joined the earlier series on to the current ones by chain linking.

The cyclically adjusted series is a five-year moving average for the years 1950–62 inclusive. For the years 1948, 1949, 1963 and 1964 the actual figures have been adjusted, the particular adjustment depending on the stage of the cycle.

10 The Management of the British Economy*

by F. W. PAISH

THE continual argument about the management of the British economy since the war has been confused by widespread misunderstanding, both about the effects of government measures and about the way in which the economy in fact behaves. The publication of Mr J. C. R. Dow's book[1] should serve to remove much, if not of the confusion, at any rate of the excuse for it. It is the fruit of many years of research, mainly at the National Institute of Economic and Social Research, and is by far the best documented and argued work which has appeared in this field. It will undoubtedly become a leading textbook in applied economics.

Dow's main purpose is to discuss the way in which successive governments have attempted to regulate the general level of demand in the economy. He therefore does not deal, except incidentally, with other possible objectives of government economic policy, such as a more equal distribution of incomes or of wealth. In considering the effects of policy, however, he is obliged to devote much space to the discussion of a wide range of interrelations within the economic system, which throws a great deal of light on the way in which the economy actually seems to work.

The book is not an easy one to summarise. This is partly because of the way in which it is arranged. It is divided into four parts. In the first, we get a rapid factual survey of the economic and financial history of the United Kingdom, first under Labour and then under Conservative chancellors. The second part is devoted to a detailed analysis of the various measures taken, and the third part to a discussion of the general behaviour of the economy. Not until part IV do we hear Dow's own conclusions, though some indications of these appear here and there on the way. Under this arrangement the same general subject may be discussed two, three, or even four times at different levels and from different aspects, and to obtain a complete idea of Dow's views on any particular question it is necessary to collate passages from different, and often widely separated, sections of the book. An additional

* First published 1965.

[1] J. C. R. Dow, *The Management of the British Economy 1945–60* (1964).

difficulty is that much, not only of the information but also of the argument, is presented in the form of small-scale diagrams and charts, and that even where information is presented in tabular form the figures are often highly processed, making them difficult to check without laborious reconstruction from the original data.

In view of these difficulties, no attempt will be made in this review article to follow Dow through the whole of his work. Instead, a limited number of questions will be selected for discussion and followed through the different sections of the book, often by assembling elements separated by many pages of other matter.

The cyclical pattern of the economy

The best place to start the discussion seems to be with the cyclical pattern of changes in demand; for without a picture of this it is impossible to form any clear judgements about the appropriateness of the timing of government measures. The most convenient measure of the pressure of demand at any given time is an index showing how fully the resources of the economy are employed. To construct such an index we need three pieces of information. The first is an index of production; the second is an index of the growth of capacity to produce, or what the Treasury, in their *Economic Report for 1963*, call 'productive potential'; and, thirdly, we need to be able to relate the two indices on some particular date, from which we can then proceed to measure their relative variations.

Dow's index of the growth of productive potential (which he calls productive capacity) is shown in a small-scale diagram on p. 115 of his book. This is transcribed (within the limits of accuracy possible) in the second column of Table 1. Dow relates his index to that of gross domestic product (apparently measured from the output side by making it equal to gross domestic product whenever the number of unemployed is equal to the number of unfilled vacancies; for intervening dates he makes it differ from the output index by twice the difference between the percentage of unemployment and the percentage of vacancies. In Table 1, Dow's index is compared both with the index of gross domestic product and with two other indices of productive potential, one published by myself in 1962[1] and one by W. A. H. Godley and J. R. Shepherd in their article on 'Long-term Growth and Short-term Policy' in the August 1964 issue of the *National Institute Economic Review*. The National Institute index is made equal to that of gross domestic product on dates

[1] F. W. Paish, *Studies in an Inflationary Economy* (1962) ch. 17, p. 333.

when unemployment stood at 1½ per cent, and mine when it stood at 1 per cent in the last quarter of 1955, the lowest level recorded since the war. To facilitate comparison, all three indices and the index of output are shown, in the last four columns of Table 1, on a common base of 100 for the last quarter of 1955.

TABLE I

Indexes of Productive Potential and Gross Domestic Product

	Index of gross domestic product (1958 = 100)	Indices of productive potential (own bases)			Index of gross domestic product	Indices of productive potential (common bases)		
		Dow ('full employ-ment' output)	National Institute (1½% un-employ-ment output)	Paish (1% un-employ-ment output)		Dow	National Institute	Paish
						Oct.–Dec. 1955 = 100		
1946	75·6	70·7			76·3	73·5		
1947	76·3	74·0			77·0	77·0		
1948	79·8	77·3		81·8	80·5	80·4		82·6
1949	82·6	80·6		83·8	83·4	83·8		84·6
1950	85·7	83·4		85·9	86·5	86·7		86·8
1951	87·6	85·8	85·1	88·0	88·4	89·2	89·0	88·9
1952	87·0	88·1	87·5	90·3	87·8	91·6	91·4	92·2
1953	90·5	90·5	89·8	92·5	91·4	94·1	93·8	93·4
1954	94·3	92·9	92·2	94·8	95·1	96·5	96·2	95·7
1955	97·5	95·2	94·7	97·8	98·5	99·0	98·9	98·8
1956	98·4	97·5	97·4	100·8	99·3	101·4	101·6	101·8
1957	100·1	100·0	100·0	103·9	101·0	103·9	104·3	105·0
1958	100·0	102·8	102·8	107·0	100·9	106·8	107·3	108·2
1959	104·5	107·5	105·6	110·4	105·4	111·7	110·2	111·5
1960	110·0	112·2	108·4	112·7	111·0	116·6	113·1	113·8
1961	112·0		111·6	116·0	113·1		116·4	117·2
1962	113·5		115·2	119·6	114·6		120·1	120·8
1963	117·2		119·0	123·4	118·3		124·2	124·6
1964	(123·6)		122·8		(124·8)		128·2	

It will be seen that all three indices of productive potential move very similarly in the years between 1951 and 1958. From 1958 to 1960, however, Dow's index rises much more sharply than either of the other two. This seems to be partly because he fails to allow for the effects of a sharp reduction in the average length of the working week. Where the indices differ, that of the National Institute, which has been prepared with the aid of much more refined statistical methods than either of the other two, is to be preferred. For the period before 1951, which the National Institute index does not cover, Dow's index may well be nearer the mark than mine. While since 1951 it is reasonable to assume that the critical factor limiting the growth of output has been labour, it is likely that before 1951 supplies of materials, and especially of semi-finished products, were also limiting factors, and that as these shortages were progressively removed output was able to grow at a rate which could not be maintained once the shortages had disappeared.

The margin of potential and unemployment

If we can assume that the economy was quite fully employed in the last quarter of 1955, and accept the National Institute's index of productive potential for the years from 1951 onwards, we can calculate the average percentage of potential utilised, and with it the unused margin of potential, in each year. If we further assume

TABLE 2

Unused Margins of Productive Potential and Labour

	Productive potential		Labour		
	Percentage employed	Unused margin	Percentage employed	Unused margin	Unused margin × 4½
1951	99·3	0·7	98·8	0·2	1·0
1952	96·1	3·9	98·0	1·0	4·5
1953	97·4	2·6	98·4	0·6	2·9
1954	98·9	1·1	98·7	0·3	1·5
1955	99·6	0·4	98·9	0·1	0·4
1956	97·7	2·3	98·8	0·2	0·8
1957	96·8	3·2	98·6	0·4	1·9
1958	94·1	5·9	97·9	1·1	5·0
1959	95·6	4·4	97·8	1·2	5·3
1960	98·1	1·9	98·4	0·6	2·9
1961	97·1	2·9	98·5	0·5	2·3
1962	95·4	4·6	98·0	1·0	4·6
1963	95·3	4·7	97·5	1·5	6·7
1964	(97·3)	(2·7)	98·4	0·6	2·9

that an average of 1 per cent unemployment in Great Britain (equivalent to about 0·7 per cent in the midlands and south, where two-thirds of the working population live) is an irreducible peacetime minimum, we can also calculate the unused margin of manpower.

The comparison of the two series in Table 2 shows that the unused margin of potential fluctuates much more widely than the unused margin of manpower. Dow's method of estimation requires that fluctuations in the margin of unused potential should be about four times as large as those in unemployment, but he does not explain why the difference should be of just this size. Godley and Shepherd, however, explain at some length why each 1 per cent rise or fall in output above or below productive trend is accompanied by a rise or fall of just over 0·5 per cent in the number employed, and why a rise or fall of 250,000 in the number employed is accompanied by a fall or rise of about 100,000 in the number of unemployed. A combination of the two relationships shows that a rise or fall of 1 per cent in output above or below productive trend is accompanied by a fall or rise in unemployment of just over 0·2 per cent, giving a ratio of about 4½ to 1. To facilitate comparison between the unused margins of potential and manpower, we therefore multiply the unused margin of manpower by 4½. The result is shown in the last column of Table 2.

It will be seen that changes in unemployment tend not only to be much smaller than changes in the margin of potential, but also to lag behind them, both on the upswing and on the downswing of the cycle. The lags are particularly marked in 1955–7, when unemployment rose much more slowly than the margin of potential; in 1958–9, when it continued to rise after the margin of potential had begun to fall; and in 1960–1, when it continued to fall after the margin of potential had begun to rise. Godley and Shepherd attribute this lag largely to delay by employers in adjusting the size of the labour force to changes in the amount of work to be done.

The margin of potential and the rise in incomes

Before accepting an index of the unused margin of productive potential as a reliable frame of reference against which to judge the timing of government measures, we must test it against the most reliable measure of the pressure of demand: the rate of rise of money incomes. Such a comparison between a static and a dynamic concept is similar to that between the age-structure of a population and its rate of increase or decrease. In Table 3 the average margin of productive potential in each year is compared with the annual rates of increase of a number of the components of national money income and of its total.

It is clear from Table 3 that changes in the unused margins of productive potential and manpower are accompanied or closely followed by opposite changes in the rates of rise of money incomes. Dow estimates that each 1 per cent rise or fall in the level of unemployment is associated with a fall or rise of about 3 per cent in the annual rate of increase in wage rates. Since, as we have seen, the ratio of changes in the margin of productive potential to changes in unemployment is about 4½ to 1, this would imply that a change of 1½ per cent in the margin of productive potential would be associated with a change of about 1 per cent in the rate of increase of wage rates. Further, since, on the average, fluctuations in weekly earnings and national money income are considerably larger than those in wage rates, this would seem to imply that each rise of 1 per cent in the proportion of productive potential employed is accompanied by a rise of nearly 1 per cent a year in money incomes.

TABLE 3

Margin of Productive Potential and Rates of Growth of Output and Incomes

	Margin of productive potential	Margin of manpower	Output		Money incomes			
					Percentage increase over previous year			
			Productive potential	Gross domestic product	Wage rates		Weekly earnings	Gross company trading profits	Net national money income
					Weekly	Hourly			
	%	%							
1951	0·7	0·2	(2·6)	2·3	9·1	9·1	9·3	16·8	10·0
1952	3·9	1·0	2·7	−0·7	8·3	8·3	8·0	−12·2	7·6
1953	2·6	0·6	2·6	4·0	4·3	4·3	6·8	6·1	7·7
1954	1·1	0·3	2·7	4·2	4·1	4·2	7·4	11·5	5·8
1955	0·4	0·1	2·7	3·5	6·7	6·7	9·2	12·3	6·0
1956	2·3	0·2	2·8	0·9	7·4	7·4	7·0	1·6	8·8
1957	3·2	0·4	2·7	1·7	5·0	5·1	4·5	5·3	5·7
1958	5·9	1·1	2·8	−0·1	3·3	3·5	3·3	−3·0	4·3
1959	4·4	1·2	2·8	4·5	2·6	2·7	5·0	10·9	5·1
1960	1·9	0·6	2·6	3·2	2·0	3·4	8·4	12·8	6·7
1961	2·9	0·5	2·9	1·8	4·0	6·2	5·6	−2·8	6·8
1962	4·6	1·0	3·2	1·3	2·8	3·7	2·8	1·5	4·1
1963	4·7	1·5	3·4	3·3	2·8	2·9	4·2	8·0	5·6
1964	(2·7)	0·6	3·2	(5·5)	5·0	5·4	(7·9)		

We still have one step to take before we can use the unused margin of productive potential as a frame of reference for judging government policies. This is to determine at what point the rate of rise of money incomes begins to be too rapid, and therefore what margin of potential represents à level of demand which is neither inadequate nor excessive. The highest rate of rise of money incomes which is consistent with the absence of inflation is that which can be achieved without its exceeding the rate of rise of real income.

Of the three constituents which determine the level of real national income—the output of goods and services, the international terms of trade and the net foreign investment income—output, in the long run, is by far the most important. In most periods, therefore, we can determine the point at which the rate of rise of money incomes becomes excessive by comparing it with the rate of rise of output. But if output is rising at a rate greater than can be permanently maintained (i.e. faster than the rate of rise of productive potential), money incomes, though rising no faster than output, are rising at a rate faster than can be permanently maintained without generating excess demand. In such conditions, therefore, the balance between the rate of rise of incomes and the rate of rise of output is temporary and unstable; it occurs only during the upswing of the business cycle and breaks down into excess demand as soon as the margin of productive potential approaches exhaustion. To achieve a stable equilibrium, we must therefore ensure not only that incomes are rising only as fast as output, but also that output is rising only as fast as productive potential—that is to say, at present rates of growth, by rather less than $3\frac{1}{2}$ per cent a year.

Reference to Table 3 shows that there has been no year since 1951 (and in fact since the war) in which national money income has risen by less than 4 per cent, the lowest being 4·3 per cent from 1957 to 1958, when the margin of potential rose from 3·2 to 5·9 per cent, and 4·1 per cent from 1961 to 1962, when the margin of potential rose from 2·9 to 4·6 per cent. A rough inspection therefore suggests that the margin of potential needed to prevent an excessively rapid rise of money incomes is over 5 per cent, equivalent to an unemployment percentage of over 2 per cent.

Unemployment and the rise of prices

Confirmation of this impression is provided by some very interesting calculations by Dow, based on earlier research by L. A. Dicks-Mireaux. These are shown in diagram form on p. 362, and are transcribed, as accurately as the small-scale chart permits, in Table 4. In this, the actual rise in prices (of final expenditure at factor cost) from 1947 to 1959 is compared with what it is estimated that it would have been if the level of unemployment, instead of fluctuating widely about an average of $1\frac{1}{2}$ per cent, had been held steady at (a) $1\frac{3}{4}$ per cent and (b) $2\frac{1}{4}$ per cent. It is assumed that, with unemployment steady, output per head would have risen steadily instead of fluctuating cyclically.

It will be seen that, after the end of the rise in import prices in 1951, with $2\frac{1}{4}$ per cent unemployment (the equivalent to a margin of unused productive potential of about $5\frac{1}{2}$ per cent) prices up to 1959 remain roughly stable. With $1\frac{3}{4}$ per cent unemployment (corresponding to a margin of potential of about $3\frac{1}{2}$ per cent) the

rise in prices averages 1½ per cent a year, while with the actual
level fluctuating about 1¼ per cent unemployment (equivalent to
about 2¼ per cent of potential) the rise in prices averaged about
2¼ per cent a year.

Dow chooses a level of 1¾ per cent unemployment because this
corresponds to his concept of zero excess demand for labour,
with unemployment equal to unfilled vacancies. This concept
appears to have a strong resemblance to my own of a margin of

TABLE 4

Reconstruction of Price Trends to Show Effect of Lower Pressure of Demand
(index of factor cost of final expenditure, 1947 = 100)

	Actual course of prices (Unemployment average 1½%)	Estimated course of prices at levels of unemployment of	
		1¾%	2¼%
1947	100	100	100
1948	107	104	103
1949	110	106	104
1950	112	108	105
1951	126	120	115
1952	135	126	119
1953	135	125	117
1954	137	127	116
1955	141	130	115
1956	147	135	118
1957	151	138	119
1958	156	140	120
1959	157	140	117

unemployment which would be just high enough to prevent price
increases (apart from those caused by higher import prices) with
a purely competitive labour market.[1] The figure of 1¾ per cent is,
however, in my view probably too low. I should put it nearer
2 per cent.

While Dow recognises that the evidence of his 'artificial history'
for the consistency between a 2¼ per cent level of unemployment
and price stability is not conclusive, he attaches sufficient weight
to it to commit himself to the view that 'if unemployment were
kept at 2 to 2½ per cent, instead of the post-war average of 1½ per

[1] F. W. Paish, *Policy for Incomes?* (1964) p. 30.

cent, this would probably make a major difference to the rate of rise in prices'.

The level of demand and growth

Before finally accepting the maintenance of a somewhat larger margin of productive potential as an objective of policy, there is one further argument to be considered. This is that, even if a somewhat lower level of demand is necessary to prevent inflation, such a policy would slow down the rate of growth, and that a measure of inflation must therefore be accepted. Dow does not agree with this view. He holds that 'if the pressure of demand had been somewhat lower, and the margin of unused capacity somewhat larger, than in most of the post-war years, there could have been steady expansion of expenditure, output and output per head as rapid as that which in fact occurred' (p. 361). He therefore considers that 'the pursuit of faster growth requires action aimed directly at accelerating the growth of capacity. A faster expansion of demand without such action seems likely to lead to an insupportable degree of excess demand' (p. 403).

On this question I myself would go further than Dow, and would support a policy of providing a somewhat larger margin of unused potential as a means not only of checking inflation and reducing the magnitude of cyclical fluctuations, but also of promoting faster growth. Without a margin of unused potential there can be no effective competition; without effective competition it is impossible to ensure the elimination of inefficient managements; and the surest way of slowing down the rate of growth is to conserve inefficiency.

From his long and careful investigation of the way in which the system works, Dow draws the following conclusions for government policy:

> Fiscal and monetary policy should: (I) aim to produce a steady growth of demand in line with the growth of capacity: this seems desirable partly because 'stop/go' policies probably upset the process of growth; partly because such policies would produce periods of excess demand, which would speed up the rise in prices. (II) aim to keep demand at a point which left a rather greater margin of spare capacity than on average in the past. This seems desirable because a wages policy on its own seems unlikely to be sufficiently effective, at least at first; and greater price stability seems desirable, partly for its own sake, but largely as a means of getting the growth of exports to pay for the import needed for faster growth (p. 404).

The balance of payments

It will be observed that, in his prescription for policy, Dow makes no reference to the balance of payments, except to say that greater price stability would facilitate the growth of exports. This relegation of the balance-of-payments problem to the position of a side-effect of the pressure of internal demand is no doubt the reason why, apart from some purely descriptive references in part I, and a discussion of the accuracy of balance-of-payments forecasts in chapter V, he devotes only about a dozen pages to the subject, right at the end of the book. Here he again emphasises the distinction, invariably blurred in popular discussion, between cyclical and secular movements. The cyclical effects of changes in the level of internal demand are seen mainly in imports. There may well be cyclical effects also on exports, but these are frequently concealed, as in 1952 and 1958, by the larger effects of developments in the outside world. In the longer run, a cyclical excess of demand is likely to result in a permanent rise in the level of costs, and if this is greater than in other countries the ability to compete in export markets may be permanently impaired. Thus, while the cyclical effects of excess demand are shown mainly in imports, the long-term effects are shown mainly in exports.

Table 5 shows, with the margin of productive potential, annual percentage changes in the volumes of imports and exports of goods and services, and annual values, at constant prices, of the balance of payments on income account and of the physical increase in stocks and work-in-progress. Table 5 also shows the totals of the balance of payments and of stock changes, which, apart from errors and omissions, are together equal to the difference between saving and domestic fixed investment and are in themselves quite a good index of the secular trend in the pressure of internal demand.

As will be seen from Table 5, the four years (1951, 1955, 1960 and 1964) in which sharp rises in imports led to substantial adverse balances of payments were also years of high stock accumulation. The rise in stocks occurs not in the early stages of the upswing of the cycle, but in the second or, as in 1955, even in the third year of the rise. Table 5 also indicates a long-term deterioration in exports, since the rise in volume was smaller in 1962–4 than it had been in 1958–60, and smaller again than in 1953–5, although the margin of unused potential became progressively larger. The rate of rise in imports, on the other hand, shows little change from one cycle to the next.

Although, for purposes of analysis, it may well be justified to regard changes in the balance of payments as mere side-effects of changes in the level of internal demand, in discussions of government policy they surely deserve a more central position. In place of the policy objectives set up by Dow, governments hitherto seem to have reacted mainly to two types of stimulus: an adverse balance

TABLE 5

Balance of Payments and Increase in Stocks

	Margin of productive potential	Imports of goods and services	Exports of goods and services	Balance of payments on current a/c	Physical increase in stocks	Balance of payments plus stock increase
	%	annual percentage increase at 1958 prices		£ mn. at 1958 prices*		
1951	0·7	+ 7·0	−1·0	−308	+615	+307
1952	3·9	− 6·9	−1·9	+169	+ 65	+234
1953	2·6	+ 6·9	+4·2	+154	+135	+289
1954	1·1	+ 3·8	+5·8	+123	+ 54	+177
1955	0·4	+ 8·5	+5·9	−157	+313	+156
1956	2·3	+ 0·5	+4·3	+205	+243	+448
1957	3·2	+ 2·7	+2·5	+208	+242	+450
1958	5·9	+ 1·1	−1·7	+345	+100	+445
1959	4·4	+ 6·4	+2·8	+153	+174	+327
1960	1·9	+11·1	+5·6	−254	+592	+338
1961	2·9	− 0·2	+2·9	− 1	+319	+318
1962	4·6	+ 1·3	+1·6	+113	+101	+214
1963	4·7	+ 4·0	+4·3	+109	+147	+256
1964 (est.)	2·7	+ 9·0	+1·5	−350	+470	+120

* Average of import and export prices for balance-of-payments figures.

of payments, especially when reinforced by pressure on sterling, as a stimulus to restrict demand; and a rise in unemployment, as a stimulus to expand it. Since both these developments normally lag well behind changes in the margin of unused potential, it is natural that government action tends always to be taken too late.

The instruments of government policy

For their contra-cyclical measures, the various governments since the war have relied on four types of instrument: physical controls, control of public-sector fixed investment, fiscal policy and monetary policy (including financial controls). With the release of resources from the war effort, the wartime physical controls became increasingly difficult to make effective, although control of private-sector housing remained very important up to 1951, and its relaxation in 1952 was the main reason for the housing boom of 1952–4. Import controls were also important in the early post-war years, and Dow attributes about half the drop in imports from 1951 to 1952 to their reimposition. Since 1952 physical controls have not played an important part.

Control of public-sector investment, which before the war was often advocated as the main contra-cyclical instrument, has also proved ineffective. This has been largely because of the long time-lag between the time when policy is changed and the time when its effects are seen in a change in the actual use of resources. Thus, an expansion of public-sector investment decided on during a recession is likely to become effective (as in 1964) as an aggravation of an excessive increase in demand a couple of years later, while the effects of a policy of restriction may well be seen (as in 1958) as aggravating a subsequent recession. The occasions when public-investment policy has acted contra-cyclically (as in 1955) seem to have been the accidental results of changes in general policy rather than of contra-cyclical design. Until it becomes possible to make allowance for so long a time-lag, and perhaps to inaugurate measures to expand public investment while at the same time taking action to restrict consumption, attempts to use public investment as a contra-cyclical weapon are likely to do more harm than good.

Fiscal policy

Since 1951, effective contra-cyclical policy has depended mainly on fiscal and monetary measures. Contra-cyclical fiscal measures have consisted almost entirely of changes in taxation (or in subsidies and other transfer payments which, as Dow points out, can be regarded as negative taxes). Changes in government current expenditure on goods and services are so difficult to make, and have to be planned so far in advance, that they are of little practical use as contra-cyclical measures. Not all tax changes, however, are equally effective. Measures designed to encourage or discourage private-sector fixed investment, even if effective, operate with so long a time-lag that, like government investment policy, they run the risk of aggravating, rather than reducing, cyclical fluctuations. The only tax changes likely to act as contra-cyclical measures are those designed to affect personal consumption within the next few months, and Dow publishes (pp. 198–9) an extremely interesting table showing his estimates of the impact of tax changes on personal consumption for each year from 1945 to 1960. His conclusions are summarised in Table 6, together with rough estimates on the same lines for 1961–4.

TABLE 6

Taxation and Monetary Changes, 1945–64

		Margin of productive potential	Tax changes		Monetary changes		Ratio of net bank deposits to net national income	Yield on 2½% Consols
			Est. effect on total yield	Est. impact on consumption (£ mn.)	Increase over previous year in			
					Clearing bank advances	Net clearing bank deposits		
		%					%	
1945			−385	+242	+ 2	+13	53·5	2·92
1946			−146	+ 87	+16	+ 8	61·3	2·60
1947	Apr.		+ 54	− 8⎫	+25	+11	63·5	2·76
1947	Nov.		+197	−120⎭				
1948			+ 49	+ 42	+19	+ 5	59·4	3·21
1949			− 92	+ 38	+ 9	+ 1	56·7	3·30
1950			− 1	+ 37	+11	+ 1	54·2	3·54
1951		0·7	+387	− 84	+14	+ 2	50·2	3·78
1952		3·9	− 67	+176	+ 1	− 1	46·1	4·23
1953		2·6	−412	+128	− 6	+ 3	43·9	4·08
1954		1·1	− 10	+ 3	+ 4	+ 4	43·0	3·75
1955	Apr.	⎱0·4	⎧−155	+ 90⎫	+12	− 1	40·2	4·17
1955	Oct.	⎰	⎩+113	− 59⎭				
1956		2·3	− 2	+ 10	− 6	− 3	35·9	4·73
1957		3·2	−131	+ 70	+ 3	+ 2	34·6	4·98
1958		5·9	−108	+ 52	+ 3	+ 3	34·2	4·98
1959		4·4	−359	+215	+31	+ 5	34·2	4·82
1960		1·9	+ 71	− 4	+24	+ 4	33·3	5·42
1961		2·9	+193	−123	+ 7	+ 3	32·0	6·16
1962		4·6	− 10	+ 8	+ 2	+ 3	31·6	6·00
1963		4·7	−269	+228	+14	+ 5	31·4	5·59
1964		(2·7)	+103	− 80	+12	+ 7	31·3	6·03

To obtain his estimates of the effect of tax changes on personal consumption, Dow first eliminates all changes in company taxation. He then evaluates the remainder on a scale, ranging from 100 per cent of the change in income tax at reduced rates and allowances to 80 per cent of changes in taxes on personal expenditure, 67 per cent of changes in the standard rates of income tax or surtax, 50 per cent of changes in taxes on dividends and trading incomes, and 10 per cent of changes in taxes on capital. The effect of his evaluation is greatly to modify the impression given by the crude tax changes. Thus, the immediately disinflationary effects of the apparently drastic budget of 1951 are seen to be quite moderate, while the expansionary effects of the modest total tax reductions in 1952 are seen to be considerably greater than those of the much larger aggregate tax reductions of 1953.

Over the whole period, the net effects of budgetary changes are shown as having been substantially expansionary. The main expansionary budgets have been concentrated into four short periods: 1945–6, 1952–3, 1959 and 1963. In the intervening periods budgetary net effects have either been slightly restrictive, as in 1947–51 and 1960–2, or slightly expansionary, as in 1954–8. Dow points out that the net tax reductions cannot be justified on the ground that they were needed to offset the impact of rising incomes on a progressive structure of direct taxation, for this was largely or wholly offset by their opposite effects on the very large amount of specific indirect taxation.

Apart from the quite unjustifiable tax reductions of April 1955, which were largely reversed in the October budget of the same year, the major tax reductions since 1947 have all taken place in years in which the level of unemployment was, or had recently been, unusually high—2·0 per cent in 1952, 2·1 per cent in 1958 and 2·2 per cent in 1959, and 2·5 per cent in 1963. The main restrictive budgets of November 1947, April 1951, October 1955, April 1961 and April 1964, were in years in which the balance of payments on current account was, or had recently been, highly adverse—minus £351 millions in 1947, minus £322 millions in 1951, minus £157 millions in 1955, minus £258 millions in 1960, and probably about minus £370 millions in 1964. Government policy thus seems to be an automatic reflex to unemployment on the one side and balance-of-payments trouble on the other—both of which lag very much as indicators of an inadequate or excessive level of internal demand.

The effects of fiscal policy

The annual percentage changes in various types of national expenditure, set out in Table 7, confirm the impression that the main contra-cyclical effects of fiscal policy must be looked for in personal consumption, which accounts for about two-thirds of all expenditure. Although in most years the combination of fiscal and monetary measures makes it impossible to attribute effects with certainty, it seems reasonable to conclude that the tax reductions of 1952–3 contributed greatly to the rise in consumption of 1953–5, those of 1959 to the rise of 1959–60, and those of 1963 to the rise of 1963–4. The effects of the relatively smaller tax increases of 1951, 1955 and 1961 were more strongly supplemented by monetary measures, but they presumably contributed to the checks to the rise of consumption in 1951–2, 1956 and 1961–2.

Dow considers that changes in company taxation probably had a substantial effect on industrial and commercial fixed investment, though only after a considerable time-lag. He doubts whether changes in initial and investment allowances had any greater effect than other fiscal changes resulting in similar alterations in the amount of tax paid.

TABLE 7

Growth in Expenditure at 1958 Prices

	Margin of productive potential	Gross domestic product	Public sector		Private sector		
							Percentage change from previous year
			Current expenditure on goods and services	Gross fixed investment		Personal consumption	Gross fixed investment	
	%			Housing	Other		Housing	Other
1951	0·7	+2·3	+7·8	− 2·4	+13·0	−1·4	− 1·5	− 7·1
1952	3·9	−0·7	+9·9	+13·1	+ 4·5	−0·5	−55·5	−10·3
1953	2·6	+4·0	+2·7	+19·6	+ 8·1	+4·5	+71·4	+ 2·9
1954	1·1	+4·2	−0·5	− 7·9	+ 3·2	+4·1	+34·3	+17·2
1955	0·4	+3·5	−3·1	−20·5	+ 1·9	+4·0	+10·9	+15·2
1956	2·3	+0·9	−0·5	− 9·5	+ 5·2	+0·9	+ 6·6	+ 9·8
1957	3·2	+1·7	−1·5	− 7·3	+ 6·9	+2·1	− 0·3	+ 8·2
1958	5·9	−0·1	−2·1	−15·7	+ 1·3	+2·5	+ 5·9	+ 1·8
1959	4·4	+4·5	+2·0	+ 0·4	+ 8·7	+4·6	+24·2	+ 5·3
1960	1·9	+3·2	+2·2	+ 3·0	+ 4·6	+4·0	+21·0	+12·4
1961	2·9	+1·8	+4·1	+ 1·4	+ 6·6	+2·2	+ 8·9	+11·2
1962	4·6	+1·3	+2·9	+12·4	+ 2·4	+1·8	− 2·3	− 4·6
1963	4·7	+3·3	+2·9	+10·1	+ 6·0	+4·0	− 0·6	− 2·2
1964 (est)	2·7	+5·5	+3·0	+26·0	+15·0	+4·0	+19·0	+11·0

Monetary policies

Monetary policies are those which directly affect, not spendable incomes, as suitable fiscal policies do, but the availability or cost of borrowed money. They can be divided into two types: financial controls, which attempt to restrict the availability of loan money to particular classes of would-be borrowers; and the restriction of the quantity of money, which raises the cost of borrowing everywhere. Of the financial controls, Dow dismisses as of little practical effect the regulation requiring, until 1959, the permission of the Capital Issues Committee before borrowing or otherwise raising more than £50,000 (from 1956 to 1958 more than £10,000) in any twelve months. Restrictions on hire-purchase finance, in the form both of minimum requirements for deposits and maximum periods for repayment, were more important. Their imposition in 1952–4, 1955–8 and 1960–2 undoubtedly affected the demand for cars and other durable consumer goods. Dow puts their effect on total consumer expenditure at from £100 to £200 millions a year, or from about 0·5 to 1·0 per cent of all consumer expenditure—an effect probably greater than that of tax changes during the same periods. But this result was obtained at the cost of causing fluctuations in the demand for the relatively small quantity of goods involved of 10 or 20 per cent, and of severe dislocation in the industries concerned. It would be greatly preferable to obtain a corresponding result by much less concentrated pressure on a much wider range of products.

The third main type of financial control took the form of 'requests' to the banks to restrict their advances, either to particular classes of borrowers or in total. After 1951 these requests were reinforced by efforts to force the banks to restrict advances by starving them of liquid assets—efforts which, so long as the banks held more government securities than they needed, were largely frustrated by sales of securities, and were therefore supplemented in 1960 by the introduction of 'special deposits'. The government failed to prevent a rapid rise in advances (from a very low level) in the years before 1952 and again in 1955, but achieved considerable success in 1956–8 (as evidenced by the rapidity of the rise in advances after the withdrawal of restrictions in 1958) and again in 1961–2. Since, even without special directions, the types of advances which suffered most in periods of restriction were personal and financial, the impact effect was probably felt most strongly on the demand for durable consumption goods.

In addition to the financial controls on particular types of loans or sectors of demand, the restrictions on bank advances, the limitation of government short-term borrowing and the institution of special deposits slowed down the rate of rise of bank deposits and so reduced the ratio of bank deposits to national income. As Table 6 shows, between 1946 and 1964 net clearing bank deposits rose by about 60 per cent, while the national money income rose by 220 per cent and the ratio of deposits to income fell by nearly half. At the same time (and, in my view, consequently), the long-term rate of interest more than doubled. From 1947 to 1952 the long-term rate of interest rose at an average rate of about 9 per cent a year, from 1954 to 1957 by 10 per cent a year, and in 1959–61 by over 13 per cent a year. Only in 1952–4, 1957–9 and 1961–2 was the rise interrupted by short periods of stable or declining rates. It can thus be said that, whereas fiscal policy shows short periods of rapid tax reduction interspersed by long periods of little change, interest-rate policy shows long periods of rapid increase interspersed by only short

periods of little change. Since 1961, the fall in the bank-deposits/
national-income ratio has virtually ceased and, with the introduction of the fiscal 'regulator' of a 10 per cent increase or decrease in
rates of indirect taxation, government policy seems to have relied
less on monetary and more on fiscal measures of restraint.

The multiplicity of measures taken and the long time-lags
involved make it difficult to trace the connection between government measures and fluctuations in private-sector investment. Dow
thinks it likely that monetary measures had nearly as much effect
on private-sector industrial and commercial investment as tax
changes. My own view is that more important than either were the
lagged effects of changes in consumption expenditure, probably
operating through the much wider changes in the level of business
profits (see Table 3), and that, so long as consumption and the
profits of consumption goods industries remain high, neither changes
in company taxation nor monetary measures are likely to have
decisive effects. The one place where changes in interest rates do
seem to have had a direct effect is in private-sector house-building
(which accounts for perhaps 2 per cent of total expenditure). This
effect is probably due less to the actual rise in interest rates than to
the restrictions which building societies impose on the volume of
their loans in their efforts to avoid, or limit, increases in the rates of
interest which they pay and charge.

Dow makes two general criticisms of government contra-cyclical
policies in the post-war period. The first is of the general tendency
towards over-expansion whenever an increase in the margin of
productive potential has reduced the rate of rise of money incomes to
a non-inflationary level. He even goes to the extent of suggesting
that government contra-cyclical policies, so far from moderating the
extent of cyclical fluctuations, have actually intensified them. This
charge must, however, be regarded as not proven. The fact that
corrective action has, in general, been over-expansionary and
insufficiently restrictive, as well as usually taken too late, does not
prove that fluctuations would have been less without any action at
all.

His other criticism is that too much reliance has been placed on
monetary policy for restraining demand, and that long-term interest
rates have therefore been forced higher, perhaps much higher, than
was either necessary or desirable. While there is much to be said
for this view, before accepting it we must look at the other implications of maintaining a lower level of interest rates and of a greater

reliance on fiscal policies for restraining demand. These include a slower rise in personal consumption, a higher level of total saving and a more favourable balance of payments on current account; but they also include a higher level of net long-term foreign investment. In other words, our balance-of-payments troubles might have come to resemble those of the United States. Only if consumption demand had been so restrained as to provide a level of saving sufficient not only for investment at home but also for a high level of foreign investment, while at the same time leaving a margin of potential sufficient to prevent the emergence of excess demand, would a policy of lower interest rates have proved practicable.

11 Instability and Growth: An International Comparison, 1950–65

by T. WILSON

FOR some years international differences in rates of growth have been a central topic of economic discussion, and various explanations have, of necessity, been offered for Britain's relatively poor performance.

One on which great emphasis has been placed is the instability of the British economy and this instability has been attributed in turn to official action designed to safeguard the balance of payments. In some learned dissertations as well as in countless speeches and articles, 'stop–go' has been held responsible for much of our failure. It can, perhaps, be understood why this view has come to be held. From time to time a respectable rate of growth has been achieved—as for example in 1963–4—but progress at these higher rates has quickly been checked by balance of payments crises followed by official restraints. If such official action had not been taken, might we not have continued to enjoy the faster rate of progress? The answer is that unfortunately we could not have expected to do so. The high rates of growth temporarily achieved during recoveries have been possible partly because there had previously been recessions. Some drop from a recovery rate of growth towards a trend rate of growth was only to be expected when something like full capacity had been reached. It is true that the rate has usually dropped below trend for a time. This has, however, provided scope for subsequent expansion at more than the trend rate of growth. The real question is what effect this instability has had on the trend itself. One cannot simply take it for granted that the average rate of growth would be higher if there were no very bad years and also no very good ones. This *may* be so, but further investigation is required.

Moreover the great improvement in stability during the post-war period, as compared with the inter-war years, suggests the question whether the modest fluctuations in rates of growth that have nevertheless occurred can have been sufficiently important to carry the heavy weight of explanation they have been made to bear in

Britain. Although the news is so often full of accounts of economic crises as to suggest that we live in an age of violent instability, the truth is rather that the avoidance in this country, as elsewhere, of cyclical fluctuations on the inter-war scale may be regarded as one of the more notable achievements since the war. Indeed in most countries the statistics rarely record any absolute decline in output. In the United States there were absolute drops in 1953–4 and 1957–8, but in each year the decline was small. The Netherlands, Norway, Sweden, Canada and Denmark had absolute falls in a single year and in Britain there was a very modest decline at the beginning of the 1950s. When, however, we talk about instability nowadays, what we usually have in mind are variations in the positive rates of growth of gross domestic product. It is true, of course, that these positive rates have in fact varied a good deal—very much so in some countries. It is also true that even if output does not decline absolutely in a relatively bad year, unemployment may nevertheless rise temporarily with the usual unfortunate social consequences. One would not wish to claim that the situation is satisfactory but without doubt it has been greatly improved.

The United Kingdom, like most of the rest of the world, has enjoyed much more stable conditions than between the wars, although not necessarily more stable conditions than prevailed before the First World War. This fact need not really be regarded as inconsistent with the proposition that instability tends to hamper growth. For the decline in instability in Britain has been accompanied by a rate of growth that is high by our own historical standards—even if it is modest compared with the achievements of some other countries. It may then be suggested that if still greater stability had somehow been achieved, still faster growth would also have been attained. Is this suspicion supported by the experience of other countries? Was instability less serious elsewhere?

Some time ago a simple statistical investigation was carried out in order to see whether the United Kingdom had in fact been suffering to a quite peculiar extent from instability.[1] It became apparent that this was not so; on the contrary, Britain has had a relatively stable economy. More generally, the statistics for seven countries showed little sign of any positive correlation between stability and their rates of growth. The conclusion was not perhaps altogether surprising because one knew in a general way that some countries, such as Japan, had combined fast growth with much instability. Yet the verdict was on the whole unwelcome. For it would have been helpful

[1] Thomas Wilson, 'Instability and the Rate of Growth', *Lloyds Bank Review* (July 1966).

to have been able to identify a peculiar susceptibility to fluctuations as the outstanding cause of our slowness of growth; if the evil could thus have been confidently identified, we should have known more clearly the direction in which to concentrate efforts at reform. That reform would have been difficult goes without saying. But it would have been a help to be able to direct our efforts to one outstanding evil instead of pursuing somewhat diffused programmes for improvement. As it was, the statistical analysis, while it certainly did not exclude the possibility that harm had been caused by instability, illustrated clearly enough that rapid progress can be made notwithstanding severe fluctuations, provided the other conditions are favourable to expansion.

More recently a new investigation has been carried out which includes a larger number of countries and extends to more of the constituent series of G.N.P. and of industrial production.[1] The statistics have been taken as a rule from the O.E.C.D. publications on National Accounts complemented with some revised figures obtained from O.E.C.D., in particular for Japan and Italy. In most cases the period covered is 1950–65. The rate of growth has been estimated by fitting least-squares lines, a procedure that is clearly preferable to measuring rates of growth between terminal years but, for obvious reasons, is not wholly satisfactory. Some of the estimates are dubious, but, for the limited purpose of this paper, approximate comparisons should suffice.

The index of stability used for each series is the standard deviation of the annual percentage rates of change from the trend rate of growth. Again a word of warning is appropriate. One or two years of high instability caused by some special factors can raise significantly the standard deviation of an otherwise fairly stable series. This is something one must look out for and one must then make whatever reservations or modifications may seem appropriate. Fortunately the difficulty arises mainly in some of the constituent series for industrial production which are excluded from this paper.

The figures for gross national product are given in Table 1. It will be seen that the country with the fastest rate of growth was, of course, Japan where output was growing at nearly 10 per cent. It will also be seen that Japan had the worst record for instability. Admittedly some qualification is necessary here. The Japanese rate of growth may be somewhat exaggerated by the price indices, although a roughly plausible adjustment would still leave her at the top of the table. It is also true that growth in Japan was on the whole

[1] This work has been done with the collaboration of my colleague Dr R. P. Sinha to whom I am much indebted.

TABLE I

Rates of Growth and Instability, 1950–65

Gross National Product		Gross Domestic Capital Formation		Total Industrial Production	
Rate of Growth	Instability	Rate of Growth	Instability	Rate of Growth	Instability
Japan* 9·7	Japan 3·7	Japan* 15·3	Austria 10·8‖	Japan 14·7	Japan 8·7
Germany 6·5	Canada 3·2	Germany 9·3	Japan 10·0	Italy 8·6	U.S.A. 5·6
Italy† 5·6	U.S.A. 2·8	Italy† 8·3	Netherlands 9·0	Germany 7·9	Belgium 5·3
Austria 5·3	Netherlands 2·7	Austria 7·7	Denmark 7·2	France 6·7	Sweden 5·1
France 4·9	Austria 2·7	Denmark 7·3	Belgium 7·1	Austria 6·7	Austria 4·9
Netherlands 4·8	Denmark 2·5	France 7·2	Canada 7·0	Netherlands 5·9	Denmark 4·3
Denmark 4·1	Germany 2·3	Netherlands 6·5	Italy 6·8§	Norway 5·7	France 4·2
Sweden 4·0	Sweden 1·9	Sweden 5·8	Germany 4·8	Canada 4·8	Germany 4·0
Canada 4·0	Norway 1·8	U.K. 5·7	Norway 4·7	Sweden 4·6	Italy 3·9
Norway 3·9	Belgium 1·8	Norway 4·5	U.S.A. 4·6	Denmark‡ 4·6	Canada 3·9
Belgium 3·4	U.K. 1·6	Belgium 4·1	U.K. 4·6	U.S.A. 3·8	Norway 3·9
U.S.A. 3·2	Italy 1·5	Canada 3·8	France 4·3	Belgium 3·7	U.K. 3·8
U.K. 3·0	France 1·4	U.S.A. 2·8	Sweden 4·2	U.K. 3·1	Netherlands 3·5

* 1952–64.
† 1951–65.
‡ 1950–61.
§ Index appreciably raised by fluctuations at end of period.
‖ Great instability in period 1950–6.

accelerating and the use of a log-linear trend line tends to exaggerate the fluctuations. The fact remains that even in the sixties the annual rates of change in Japan's G.N.P. were fluctuating between 6 per cent and over 15 per cent. Western Germany wins second place for growth but only middling marks for stability. Austrian production grew rapidly but fluctuated a good deal. Both France and Italy had respectable rates of growth combined with the best records for stability. In the United States, on the other hand, slow growth was accompanied by a good deal of instability. (The United States record would, of course, be better under both headings if more recent years were included.) The United Kingdom occupies the bottom position for growth; but it is by no means the case that Britain was afflicted by relatively great fluctuations in the rate of growth. On the contrary, Britain had a relatively stable economy. Indeed the standard deviation, at 1·6, is not much above that for Italy (1·5) or for France (1·4).

The relative positions of the different countries changes somewhat when the service industries and agriculture are left out. If we now turn to the figures for industrial production we see that Belgium and Sweden look less stable, France is in a middle position for stability instead of second place, and Canada has improved her position under this heading. The United States occupies a still higher place for instability and slightly improves her position for growth. Britain, for her part, gets almost top marks for stability and bottom marks for growth!

It may be suggested that we should really turn our attention to fixed investment if we wish to see more clearly how instability may hamper progress. For the uncertainty engendered by fluctuating rates of progress may have three adverse effects: first, there may be a greater reluctance to engage in long-term commitments and, secondly, new investment projects may be less effective because it is more difficult, in face of repeated fluctuations, to implement sensible plans for investment and production; thirdly, the loss of potential output during slack years has adverse consequences for the future in so far as the lost output might have consisted of capital goods. On general grounds there may appear to be some substance in these suggestions but unfortunately the comparative figures do not, on the face of it, help us to explain the slow growth of Britain's G.N.P. in these terms. We find once more that rapid growth may be accompanied by high instability, as in the case of Japan; or a country may have slow growth and marked fluctuations as did Canada; or respectable growth and marked stability like France. Britain again gets good marks for stability and the rate of her fixed investment was a quite respectable $5\frac{3}{4}$ per cent a year. Admittedly this was far below the Japanese figure of 15 per cent or the German figure of about 9 per cent, but at least Britain no longer appears at the bottom of the list. One of the most disappointing features of British experience has rather been the relatively poor return on investment in the form of a faster growth of output. In Britain the rate of growth of G.N.P. was little more than half the rate of growth of fixed investment. The United States was at the opposite extreme with output growing rather more quickly than fixed investment. In all European countries output grew less quickly than investment but in none was the ratio as low as in Britain. If, for example, we had achieved the same ratio as Sweden, our rate of growth of G.N.P. would have been about 1 per cent faster. Of course one must allow for lags but the comparison, rough though it is, is suggestive.

A good deal of attention has been rightly devoted in the past to the relatively small proportion of Britain's national output devoted to investment, and it is encouraging that this proportion has risen markedly over the years. But we should also welcome the increasing attention now being paid to the forms investment has taken and to the ways in which new capital has been used. The shipbuilding industry affords the classic case of misapplied resources. There, and no doubt in some other industries, the explanation may be sought partly in management and industrial structure and also in the nature of the labour market and the slow natural growth of the labour force to man the new capital. Whatever the causes, the difference in the marginal capital/output ratios might be expected to make for stronger inflationary pressure in the United Kingdom than, for example, in the United States.

These figures refer to total fixed investment, public and private, and it is natural to ask whether figures relating to this large aggregate may not be misleading. But the statistics for investment in machinery and equipment do not support this view. In this case Britain, surprisingly, receives second prize for stability. Her rate of growth, though not in the top half, was a respectable 5 per cent. Canada had little more than half this rate of growth and a standard deviation about twice as high. Japan, as usual, gets top marks for growth and almost bottom marks for stability (see Table 2).

As one would expect, the growth of total consumers' expenditure has been relatively stable in all countries; but this is not, of course, true of expenditure on consumers' durables. In this case the U.K.'s record is one of great instability. Of the various constituents of British expenditure that have been analysed, this is much the most unstable and an international comparison shows that our relatively

TABLE 2

Rates of Growth and Instability, 1950–65

Consumer Durables		Gross investment in machinery & equipment		Exports		Imports	
Rate of Growth	Instability	Rate of Growth	Instability	Rate of Growth	Instability	Rate of Growth	Instability
Italy 1951–65 14·7	U.S.A. 10·7	Japan 1952–64 15·6	Austria 13·0	Italy 1951–65 14·9	Germany 8·4	Japan 1952–64 14·7	Japan 1952–64 15·3
Japan 1952–64 12·0	U.K. 10·0	Germany 9·9	Netherlands 12·4	Japan 1952–64 12·1	U.S.A. 8·1	Germany 13·79	Austria 12·3
France 11·69*	Italy 1951–65 10·0	Denmark 9·14	Japan 1952–64 11·4	Germany 11·22	Austria 7·8	Italy 1951–65 12·9	Italy 1951–65 9·8
Netherlands 10·61*	Denmark 9·0	Austria 8·70	Italy 1951–65 10·7	Austria 10·44	France 6·8	Austria 10·70	Netherlands 9·1
Germany 8·13*	Canada 8·5*	Netherlands 7·93	Canada 10·4	Netherlands 8·62	Italy 1951–65 6·4	Netherlands 8·84	Denmark 8·2
U.K. 8·06	Austria 8·2*	Italy 1951–65 7·2	U.S.A. 8·0	Belgium 7·38	Japan 1952–64 6·0	Denmark 8·13	Sweden 7·2
Norway 7·93*	Netherlands 8·2*	France 6·93	Denmark 7·6	Norway 7·20	Sweden 4·8	Belgium 7·03	Canada 7·0
Sweden 7·37*	Norway 7·5*	Norway 5·28	Norway 7·3	Denmark 7·13	Canada 4·6	Norway 6·49	France 6·7
Denmark 6·48*	Sweden 6·4*	U.K. 5·07	Belgium 6·1	France 6·14	Belgium 4·2	France 6·09	Belgium 6·5
Belgium 5·70*	Belgium 6·3*	Sweden 4·65	Sweden 5·5	Sweden 5·95	Denmark 3·6	U.S.A. 5·3	Germany 6·4
Canada 5·49*	France 4·7*	Belgium 3·54	Germany 5·5	U.S.A. 5·40	Norway 3·5	Sweden 4·72	U.S.A. 4·9
Austria 4·76*	Japan 1952–64 3·1	U.S.A. 3·0	France 5·4	Canada 4·34	Netherlands 3·2	Canada 4·20	U.K. 4·7
U.S.A. 4·0	Germany 1952–64	Canada 2·60	U.K. 5·2	U.K. 3·22	U.K. 3·0	U.K. 3·82	Norway 3·5

* 1950–64.

low index for instability in the growth of gross national product is matched by a relatively very high index for instability in expenditure on durables. These violent fluctuations are not confined to the earlier years of our period. For example, expenditure fell absolutely by $2\frac{1}{2}$ per cent between 1960 and 1961, rose by $4\frac{1}{2}$ per cent between 1961 and 1962, by over 19 per cent in the following year and by $9\frac{1}{2}$ per cent from 1963 to 1964. This is not surprising. First, the fact that these are durable goods means that each can have its own accelerator. Secondly, the changes in public policy have borne with particular severity on this group. These changes in taxation and in hire-purchase regulations have naturally provoked indignation among those in the industries concerned but there are also some considerations to be urged in favour of the policies followed. The periodic restrictions on these goods may fall with rather less severity on those who are really poor and, more generally, the fact that there is already a stock of such goods in existence means that a marginal decline in sales will not cause great hardship. Moreover any resources thus released can often be quickly transferred within the same firms to production for export. It can also be held that such changes in policy—for example with regard to hire-purchase—can be carried out fairly quickly and effectively. The most valid complaint is that the consequent instability makes it more difficult for the industries concerned to plan production and investment. The fact remains that the rate of growth of expenditure on consumers' durables in Britain has been high—about 8 per cent a year. For these goods we are in the upper part of the international league table, not at the bottom as with total gross national product. Unfortunately durables constitute only about $6\frac{1}{2}$ per cent of total G.N.P. and their rapid growth can, therefore, give only a limited impetus to the rate of growth of the total. In conclusion two inferences may be drawn: that the effects of stop–go on these industries cannot have been so bad in view of the high rate of growth that was nevertheless achieved; secondly, that it is a mistake to subject such a rapidly growing sector to the alleged vagaries of public policy. We shall not try to assess the respective merits of these two views.

After the war, when one was trying to think about problems of stabilisation policy, one was inclined to suppose that fluctuations in exports would be one of the main sources of trouble. In retrospect it is clear that this danger was exaggerated. It is true that British exports have fluctuated about twice as much as G.N.P.: the standard deviation is roughly 3. But exports have fluctuated less than fixed investment or investment in plant and machinery and much less than expenditure on consumers' durables. Exports have fluctuated less than imports not only in the British case but in the case of most of the countries covered by this inquiry. Perhaps the explanation lies along these lines. It is true that each country's exports are affected by what is happening within each country. For example the measures of July 1966 produced a rapid increase in exports for a time. But exports will also move in considerable harmony with the course of world trade, especially in the case of a large trading nation. The imports of a single nation may reflect changes in its own domestic situation more fully than do changes in its exports, especially if it is subject at times to strong inflationary pressures. It may not be surprising, therefore, that a country's imports usually fluctuate more than its exports. But there have been exceptions. French imports and French exports have fluctuated to much the same extent, and German imports have fluctuated rather less than German exports. These, of course, are very summary statements. Statistics of this kind can do little more than produce hints that suggest the need for further research.

It is interesting to observe in passing how quickly some countries can achieve a very large rise in exports. Japan is, of course, the outstanding example with exports sometimes rising by about a fifth from one year to the next. Of course it is a great deal easier to do this when total output is also capable of rising rapidly. Restrictive measures at home can then help to direct a really large flow of supplies to export markets.

Finally, reference may be made to a calculation for the U.S.S.R. along the same lines as those described above. The official figures for national income and for fixed investment have been used. It is scarcely necessary to say that these figures have been criticised from time to time on the ground that they exaggerate the rate of growth actually achieved. Whether any statistical defects also exaggerate or minimise the degree of instability is a more difficult point but it may at least be amusing to see what the official figures show. The rate of growth of national income works out at about 9 per cent or nearly as high as the rate of $9\frac{1}{2}$ per cent for G.N.P. in Japan, or about $2\frac{1}{2}$ per cent above the rate of growth in Western Germany. Gross investment grew at 11 per cent, well below the Japanese figure of 15 per cent but above those for all the other countries considered. (The West German figure was over 9 per cent.) Thus fast rates of growth are shown by these official figures, but the figures do not suggest that progress was steady. On the contrary the standard deviations for national income and fixed investment respectively are almost the same as those for G.N.P. and fixed investment in the

United States—a fact that is unlikely to cause satisfaction in either country.

Standard deviation has been used as the index of dispersion and it may be asked whether this may be not merely inadequate but actually misleading. Is it not simply a fact that a series with a slow rate of growth is bound to have a narrower range of instability than a series that is growing faster? In answering this question some different points need to be separated. First, there may be a pseudo-arithmetical point to the effect that slow average growth gives less scope for scatter. This is obviously wrong for the possibility of having years of negative growth provides any amount of scope for a high index of instability. One need only think of the combination of very slow growth with great instability in the United States between 1929 and 1937, and post-war examples can be found especially among some of the constituent groups of industrial production. Even if we take the figures for G.N.P. since the war when negative items have been rare, we find that the United States and, to a lesser extent, Canada have combined slow growth with a good deal of instability.

A valid and important point is that the use of standard deviations will conceal the possibility that any given degree of instability may do more harm in a country which, *for other reasons*, is growing slowly than in a country which, for other reasons, is growing more quickly. It is tempting therefore to use the coefficient of variation as an index that might bring out this fact because the standard deviation would then be deflated in each case by the average rate of growth.[1] The coefficient of variation is, of course, relatively high for the United States and the United Kingdom and low for such countries as Italy, Western Germany and France. But this index is liable to be misused. There is a danger that it will be described as an appropriately adjusted index of instability, and high coefficients of variation for slowly growing countries will be taken as proof of the fact that instability is one of the main causes of slow growth. This, of course, will not do. The denominator in the coefficient of variation is the rate of growth itself and it would be circular reasoning to infer that the coefficient can adequately explain the rate of growth.

Another word about the natural forces making for instability. We are all aware that the textbook theories of multiplier and accelerator grossly over-explain the cycle, especially when the model operates very mechanically with difference equations. It has long been apparent that this would not do even as an explanation of stability and

---

[1] This is what I called the 'discomfort' index in the article published in *Lloyds Bank Review*. What I had in mind was the climatic discomfort index which combines humidity and heat.

instability in the United States between the wars, and it will clearly
not suffice as a post-war explanatory mechanism. We need a much
less simplified theory of investment decisions and we need a great
deal of disaggregation. Nevertheless there is more than an element
of truth in the old model. Thus we should expect some difficulties to be encountered, apart altogether from official action,
when output has been expanding rapidly after a recession and its
growth is then brought down to the slower trend rate permitted
by the growth of capacity—from, say, $5\frac{1}{2}$ per cent to 3 per cent.
It is true that the strongest impact may be felt initially on the balance
of payments rather than domestic fixed investment and it is this,
of course, that will bring the government into action. It is also true
that in the post-war years investment in manufacturing, instead of
leading at the upper turning points, has lagged in Britain by a year
or more behind the fall in the rate of growth of total output. Nevertheless the slowing down as the reserves of manpower are exhausted
clearly creates problems for industry.

Let me emphasise once more that it is only instability with which
we have been concerned. We have *not* been testing the proposition
that growth has been hampered by inflation or that, alternatively,
industry has been held back by low levels of expenditure relatively
to capacity. For example, a country might have a good record for
stability over a number of years but might have been suffering
throughout from an excessive deflationary gap. A different approach
would be needed in order to try to assess the possible loss from
deflation—and this would not be easy. One might be tempted to
do so by working out estimates for the growth in a nation's capacity-
output year by year and by subtracting actual output from this
capacity-output. But this procedure would not really meet the bill.
It is true that in this way one would obtain estimates of the potential
output sacrificed each year but only on the assumption that capacity-
output is itself unaffected either way by the amount of inflation or
deflation in the economy. If we are interested in rates of growth,
then we cannot take capacity-output for granted.

Our concern has been only with instability and it may be objected
that this is not quite the same as 'stop–go'. For 'stop–go' means that
the government causes the economy to lurch forward unsteadily by
sometimes releasing the brake and sometimes applying it, according
to changes in the basic balance of payments. Such unsteadiness of
progress will indeed be reflected in our indices of instability, but the
latter are more comprehensive and may reflect the effect of other
types of instability as well. This objection has not much force. It is
not apparent that fluctuations created by government action would

be more harmful than those that have their origin in a variety of non-government factors. Moreover official 'stop–go' is not a peculiarly British phenomenon. There have been plenty of instances elsewhere—in Japan, in France, in Italy, in Canada and so on. At the same time it is useful to be reminded that there are other factors making for instability as well as the actions of government. The wheel has indeed come full circle. At one time it was the natural forces that were supposed to cause fluctuations in output and employment and government was to provide the stabilising policies. Today, in popular debate, it is official 'stop–go' that *creates* the instability. Of course this may be part of the truth but it is hard to believe that it is all of it.[1]

A comparison of the statistics for different countries such as that attempted here permits only a *relative* judgement and does not in itself dispose of the possibility that harm may have been caused by instability. Perhaps Britain would have done a little better[2] if her economy had been still more stable, and the same may be true of the other countries. It may not be inappropriate to confess to having a personal bias in favour of steady growth; but, admittedly, this may be because the high instability of the old trade cycle and the unemployment to which it gave rise have been, for my generation, the traditional evils. Some economists have taken a different view. Schumpeter regarded the old trade cycle as largely the price of progress but the evidence is decisively against him. Sir Dennis Robertson, for his part, advanced in more cautious terms the opinion that some degree of instability must be regarded as the price of progress. Perhaps it is true that Japanese experience lends some support to this view, for it might be too much to expect that such a headlong pace could be steadily maintained. It is a somewhat different matter when we turn to Britain. Whatever the cause of our instability, it would not be very plausible to attribute it to the sheer speed of our advance.

[1] What has been described above as the 'popular' view received weighty academic support from Professor J. C. R. Dow in *The Management of the British Economy 1945–60* (Cambridge, 1964). On p. 211 the author asks whether 'the major variations in fiscal policy were in fact not stabilizing but rather themselves the main causes of instability'. See also his conclusions in ch. xv, sect. 5.

In his new book, *Instability and Growth* (Yale, 1968), Professor Erik Lundberg also reaches some pessimistic conclusions about the effects of the policies followed in a number of countries even including Sweden and the Netherlands. This admirable survey appeared after the present paper had gone to press. It covers some of the same ground as that covered above and the methods used, though not identical, are similar. See, in particular, ch. 3.

[2] The reference on p. 193 above to the coefficients of variation is relevant at this point.

12 Economic Growth and the British Balance of Payments*

by W. A. ELTIS

THERE are two conflicting views about the effect of economic growth on the balance of payments, and this conflict is illustrated by the contrast between the words and actions of United Kingdom governments in recent years. On the one hand ministers have frequently stated that higher productivity, harder work, and all the factors which could lead to faster economic growth would lead to a greatly improved British balance of payments and to a solution to Britain's economic problems. On the other hand, by their actions, British governments have clearly taken the view that the reduction of the growth rate of the British economy to 1 per cent of zero would lead to a substantially improved balance of payments.

The statistics in Tables 1 and 2 also illustrate this conflict.

TABLE 1

	Annual growth in industrial production 1954–64	Annual growth in exports of manufacturers 1954–64 (volume)
United Kingdom	3·1%	3·3%
U.S.A.	4·5%	5·1%
France	7·2%	8·7%
West Germany	7·3%	11·1%
Italy	8·4%	18·6%
Japan	15·0%	17·0%

This table is derived from information published in the
National Institute Economic Review.

Table 1 shows the annual rate of growth in the exports of manufactured goods by the major Western developed economies set against their growth rates of industrial production in the period 1954–64. It will be seen that the countries with high growth rates of output have also had high growth rates of exports while the United Kingdom, with the lowest growth rate of output, 3·1 per cent per annum, has also had the slowest growth rate of exports, 3·3 per cent per annum. Table 1 appears to support the view that fast growth is favourable to the balance of payments.

* First published 1967.

TABLE 2

	Annual growth in U.K. industrial production	U.K. Balance of Payments current account	U.K. Current account (excluding govt. invisibles)
1953–55 expansion	5·6%	+£145m to −£155m	+£211m to −£17m
1955–58 stagnation	0·4%	−£155m to +£336m	−£17m to +£555m
1958–60 expansion	6·2%	+£336m to −£275m	+£555m to +£8m
1960–62 stagnation	1·1%	−£275m to +£101m	+£8m to +£462m
1962–64 expansion	5·6%	+£101m to −£393m	+£462m to +£40m
1964–66 stagnation	1·5%	−£393m to −£61m	+£40m to + 411m

Source: *The British Economy, Key Statistics 1900–66* published by *The Times* for the London and Cambridge Economic Service.

Table 2 shows changes in the current account of the United Kingdom's balance of payments between 1953 and 1966 set against the United Kingdom's growth rate of industrial production in that period. Several things emerge from this table. First, the years of expansion where industrial production rose 5–6½ per cent per annum were years when the United Kingdom's current account deteriorated substantially while the years of stagnation were years when the current account improved. This is true, whether government spending abroad is included or excluded from the current account. Second, the underlying United Kingdom balance of payments (where this includes government invisibles) has deteriorated steadily from 1953 to 1966. In 1955 when expansion was terminated, the United Kingdom had a deficit on current account of £155m; in 1960 when expansion was terminated, the deficit was £275m; in 1964 the deficit was £393m. In other words, with each successive cycle, the current account deficit at the peak of the boom has been larger. Moreover, each period of stagnation has resulted in a smaller surplus. In 1958, after three years of stagnation, the surplus was £336m; in 1962, after two years of stagnation, the surplus was £101m, while in 1966, after two years of stagnation, there was still a deficit of £61m. However the last column in Table 2 which shows the current account excluding net government invisible imports does not show continuous deterioration in the period, and this suggests that the underlying deterioration in the current account may be quite largely due to the fairly steady growth of net government invisible imports from £66m in 1953 to £472m in 1966. Thus, to summarise, Table 2 suggests that periods of slow growth have led to an improved balance of payments and of fast growth to a worsened balance of payments in the case of the United Kingdom. It also suggests that the underlying United Kingdom balance of payments has shown continuous deterioration in the past thirteen years, and that this may be quite largely attributable to growing government spending overseas.

In the argument below three factors which may have influenced the United Kingdom's balance of payments will be analysed. First, the relationship between economic growth and growth in imports by the United Kingdom and by foreign countries will be analysed. This line of analysis which will suggest that fast growth by the United Kingdom results in rapid import growth will emphasise the unfavourable effect of growth on the balance of payments. The second line of analysis is to investigate the relationship between a country's growth rate and changes in its price level. It will be argued that faster growth leads to a slower rise in a country's price level than would otherwise have occurred so that its export prices will rise less quickly, and its home-produced goods will be more competitive with imports. Hence, with this second line of analysis, fast growth will be favourable to a country's balance of payments. The third line of analysis will be to consider the excess-demand situation which may occur during a period of rapid expansion, and to analyse the effect of this on a country's balance of payments. This line of analysis will suggest that rapid import growth in the United Kingdom's periods of expansion may be associated with the over-working of productive capacity in those periods rather than with expansion itself.

Growth and imports

Growth in production by the United Kingdom leads to increased imports for several reasons. More raw materials are needed if more goods are produced. With growth in production, real incomes grow, and as people become richer, they spend more on food, much of which is imported, and they spend more on manufactured goods and some of these are imported. Similarly, when output is raised in the rest of the world, foreign real incomes rise, and more is spent abroad on imports, some of which come from the United Kingdom. Imports will be affected by price, quality and availability as well as by change in real incomes, and these other factors will be brought into the argument at a later stage.

In periods of growth in the United Kingdom, imports can be expected to grow quickly because real incomes and import require-ments grow quickly, while they should grow slowly (if at all) in periods of stagnation. Exports, on the other hand, grow whether there is expansion or stagnation provided there is continuous growth in output and real incomes in the rest of the world. Thus, the United Kingdom's current account should improve in periods of stagnation when there is little growth in imports, while exports grow because of growth in the rest of the world. Conversely, there could be deterioration in the current account in periods of expansion, because this would lead to substantial growth in imports, while it would only lead to a large enough growth in exports to balance this if a sufficient proportion of growing foreign incomes is spent on United Kingdom goods. This line of argument would suffice to explain the figures in Table 2 if growth in output and real incomes in the United Kingdom led to a substantial increase in imports, while growth in real incomes in the rest of the world was not particularly favourable to British goods.

There are two considerations which point to the possibility that the United Kingdom's difficulties may be of this kind. First, it is possible that some United Kingdom manufacturers of, for instance, furniture, furnishings, and radios, design their goods with United Kingdom consumers with low incomes in mind, while foreign manufacturers, for instance Scandinavian, Swiss and German, often manage to design and sell goods to the workers of their countries which also appeal to people with higher incomes. Then, as United Kingdom workers become richer they may spend a higher proportion of their incomes on foreign goods, while foreign workers in the countries mentioned might spend a higher proportion of their incomes on their own goods. A second possibility is that the United Kingdom may be particularly weak in the design of certain kinds of machinery. The *London and Cambridge Economic Bulletin* has recently mentioned the very startling statistic that in periods of expansion one-half of all the machinery which is installed in the United Kingdom is imported. There are pointers to the possibility that the United Kingdom's problem may be high capital import requirements associated with growth, and a high propensity to spend increased consumer incomes on imports, while growth in the rest of the world is less favourable than this to British exports. In consequence, the United Kingdom's balance of payments only improves when its growth rate is substantially less than foreign growth rates. With this line of analysis, the rapid growth of German, Japanese, French and Italian exports would be explained if the goods these countries exported benefited to a greater extent than United Kingdom goods from growing world incomes.

Growth and prices

The next factor to analyse is the effect of faster growth on United Kingdom prices. If an increase of 1 per cent in the United Kingdom's growth rate resulted in wage increases which were higher by 1 per cent per annum than they otherwise would have been, faster growth would leave wage costs per unit of output unaltered. Wherever the growth rate was increased, wages would rise *pari passu* and wage costs per unit of output would be independent of the growth rate. However, it is possible that an addition of 1 per cent to the growth rate would result in an addition of less than 1 per cent per annum to the annual rise in money wages, in which case growth would have a favourable effect on wage costs per unit of output and on prices. It is almost certain that faster growth will be associated with some increase in the annual rate of growth of money wages, because many workers are paid by piece-rates or at least receive part of their income on the basis of piece-rates. An increase in the growth rate will mean a faster increase in the number of pieces produced by these workers and therefore a faster rise in their wages. A faster rise in the wages of workers working on piece-rates is likely to be accompanied, through principles of comparability applied in the individual firm and through competition for workers between industries, by faster rises in the wages of workers not working on piece-rates. One pointer to the relation in the United Kingdom between the growth rate and the growth of money wages and prices is to be found in an econometric study by Dicks-Mireaux, who found that in the period 1946–59 an increase in productivity of 1 per cent was associated with prices which rose 0·5 per cent less than they otherwise would have done.[1] Taking this evidence, it could be concluded that a 1 per cent increase in the rate of growth of productivity might lower prices by perhaps 0·5 per cent per annum. A second pointer can be found from the information in Table 3.

TABLE 3

	Annual growth rate in U.K. industrial production	Annual rise in retail prices	Annual rise in prices of manufactures
Expansion periods (1953–5, 1958–60, 1962–4)	5·8%	2·1%	1·4%
Stagnation periods (1955–8, 1960–2, 1964–6)	0·9%	4·0%	2·9%

Source: *The British Economy, Key Statistics 1900–66.*

[1] L. A. Dicks-Mireaux, 'The Interrelationship between Cost and Price Changes, 1946–59', *Oxford Economic Papers* (1961).

Here the United Kingdom's performance between 1953 and 1966 is divided into expansion years and stagnation years, and it will be seen that the annual inflation of manufacturing prices averaged 1·4 per cent in expansion years and 2·9 per cent in stagnation years.[1] The annual rise in the cost of living averaged 2·1 per cent in expansion years and 4·0 per cent in stagnation years.[2] The evidence of this table suggests that the 5 per cent per annum faster growth of industrial production in the years of expansion was associated with a slowing of $1\frac{1}{2}$ per cent per annum in the rate of inflation of prices of manufactures. This suggests that each 1 per cent by which the growth rate of industrial production is increased may reduce prices by perhaps 0·3 per cent per annum. This evidence and that of Dicks-Mireaux suggests that faster growth is associated with a slower rate of inflation which must have a favourable effect on the balance of payments, and that the relationship is such that 1 per cent on the growth rate reduces the rate of inflation by perhaps 0·3 to 0·5 per cent per annum.

The relationship between the growth rate and price inflation, and the factor considered earlier, the relationship between the growth rate of incomes and growth of imports, can be brought together to show how their combined effect might affect the United Kingdom's balance of payments. With plausible assumptions it can be suggested that faster growth might have an entirely neutral effect on the balance of payments when price and income effects are combined. An increase in the rate of growth of 1 per cent per annum could be expected to raise both the growth rate of imports and the growth rate of exports by 0·6 per cent per annum.[3] It is

[1] Cf. Sir Roy Harrod, *Towards a New Economic Policy* (1967) pp. 12–14.
[2] Recent evidence suggests that the present government's prices and incomes policy, etc., has not led to a significant change in this pattern. The cost of living rose 3·7 per cent from Jan 1966 to Jan 1967.
[3] If the United Kingdom's growth rate is 1 per cent faster, its prices may become 0·4 per cent per annum lower than they otherwise would have been. The price elasticity of demand for United Kingdom exports may be about $-2\frac{1}{2}$ (see A. J. Brown, 'The Fundamental Elasticities of International Trade', in *Oxford Studies in the Price Mechanism*, ed. T. Wilson and P. W. S. Andrews (1951), in which case 0·4 per cent lower export prices would increase the quantity of exports 1 per cent, and their money value 0·6 per cent. Turning to imports, 0·4 per cent lower prices would reduce the quantity and value of imports 0·4 per cent if the price elasticity of demand for imports was -1. (M. Fg. Scott estimated that it was $-1\frac{1}{2}$ in *A Study of U.K. Imports* (1963) but he found an elasticity of -7 for manufactured imports, and the result of the recent import surcharge suggests that it cannot now be as high as this.) Then, taking price effects only into account, 1 per cent faster growth would raise the value of exports 0·6 per cent per annum, and reduce imports 0·4 per cent per annum. However, with 1 per cent faster growth, real incomes would rise 1 per cent per annum faster, and following Scott (who estimated that the income elasticity of demand for United Kingdom imports was about 1), this

then unlikely that the growth rate will affect the balance of payments to the extent needed to explain the information in Table 2, which suggested that faster growth has a highly unfavourable effect on the United Kingdom's balance of payments. It is then likely that further factors not so far brought into the analysis may be of importance in explaining the evidence of Table 2.

One further factor which may be of importance in explaining the very rapid growth of exports of countries that have achieved fast growth of output is that faster growth might lead to more rapid redesign of products, speedier introduction of new products, and more rapid adjustment of a country's pattern of production to changing patterns of home and world demand. If this is so, the extraordinary export performance of Japan, Italy, West Germany and France may be due to their high growth rates through the mechanism of speedier redesign and speedier introduction of new products and the improvements in quality which may be associated with rapid growth, as well as through price effects. In particular, rapid growth may make it more economic for a firm to launch new products because it will be able to maintain sales of its existing products to a very large extent and at the same time sell the new products through the extra incomes associated with rapid growth. With stagnant production, a new product or a redesigned product can only be launched at the expense of existing products. The high investment associated with rapid growth may also be a factor here, because more new products may be launched in a situation where many new factories are in any case being built, rather than in a situation where existing factories are being partly refurbished.

Over-capacity working and imports

The final factor which will be analysed is the association between periods of expansion in the United Kingdom and the degree of capacity working.

Figure 1 shows the relationship between the share of investment in value-added by the representative United Kingdom company producing consumer goods, and the degree of capacity working of that company. At 100 on the horizontal axis, the firm is producing what it considers to be the ideal output given its productive capacity at that time. If it produces at 95, this means that it would ideally

---

would raise imports by an extra 1 per cent per annum. Then, taking income as well as price effects into account, both imports and exports would rise an extra 0·6 per cent per annum as a result of 1 per cent faster growth, so the effect of faster growth on the balance of payments would be neutral.

wish to produce 5 per cent more if it could sell it, given its plant and machinery. If it is producing at 103, this means that its plant is being overworked and ideally it would prefer to have 3 per cent more plant to produce that particular output. There are many factors which influence the amount a firm invests and it can be assumed that the degree of capacity working is one of these. The line I – I in Figure 1 rises from left to right because it can be assumed that where a company has more plant than it needs to produce current output, investment in new plant will be a lower proportion of its value-added than it will be in a situation where it is short of plant. In the United Kingdom stop–go cycle, the degree of capacity working may move from something like 96 at the end of a recession

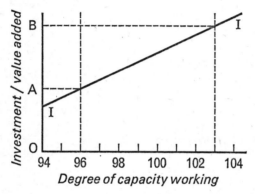

Fig. 1. Investment and the Degree of Capacity Working
The line I–I represents investment in new plant as a proportion of value-added,

to something like 103 at the peak of the boom. In other words, demand may rise something like 7 per cent in relation to productive capacity in the boom and fall 7 per cent in the subsequent recession. The effect of this is to raise investment in plant and machinery by manufacturing industry in the way illustrated by the diagram in the boom, and to reduce it during the subsequent recession. This has two important effects on the balance of payments.

First, it might be thought that if industry is working at 102 or 103 at the peak of the boom, this will not lead to a substantial growth in imports. It should be posssible for the representative firm to meet a demand which is 2 or 3 per cent higher than its capital is ideally geared to produce. However, the diagram illustrates the position of the *representative* firm. There will be many firms which, when the representative firm is working at 102 or 103, might need to work at 108, 110 or 115. This would lead to substantial pressure on the

labour market, and in addition, it would often be quite impossible
to produce at 110 or 115. Where this was the case the output which
could not be produced domestically at the height of the boom would
be imported. This factor might explain the rapid growth of imports
in periods of expansion in the United Kingdom.

There is a further factor. Figure 1 shows the position of the
representative firm in the consumer goods industries. In the industries which manufacture capital equipment, there will be more
strain, for the difference between the demand for plant and machinery at the height of the boom and in recession will be much more
than 7 per cent. During a recession where the representative firm
in the consumer goods industries is working at 96, investment is OA.
At the height of the boom where the representative firm in the
consumer goods industries is working at 103, investment is OB.
Hence, the demand for investment goods fluctuates between OA
and OB. It is possible that in purely financial terms, it would pay a
firm manufacturing investment goods, for instance a firm in the
machine tool industry, to have capacity to produce little more than
OA which could be used throughout the cycle, rather than to have
capacity to produce OB which would be under-utilised for most of
the cycle. If firms of this kind do in fact have capacity which only
slightly exceeds that needed to produce OA, machinery would need
to be imported very substantially throughout the boom, which would
be a further factor increasing imports in the course of the boom.
Thus, imports could be expected to rise in the course of the boom,
both because some firms would need to work at 110 to 115 to meet
demand at the height of the boom and would be unable to do this,
and because the machinery-producing industries and firms may
base their capacity on a demand level of OA or little more than OA
which could be maintained throughout the cycle, rather than on a
level close to OB which would avoid the need for imports in the
boom.

TABLE 4

	Annual growth rate in U.K. industrial production	Annual growth in exports (volume)	Annual growth in imports (volume)
Expansion periods	5·8%	4·9%	7·9%
Stagnation periods	0·9%	2·7%	1·3%

Source: *The British Economy, Key Statistics 1900–66.*

Table 4 shows the average growth in exports and imports during
stagnation periods and periods of expansion. It will be seen that

exports have grown faster in periods of expansion, 4·9 per cent per annum, than in periods of stagnation. Imports, however, have grown by only 1·3 per cent in periods of stagnation, against 7·9 per cent per annum in periods of expansion. Hence, the effect of expansion has been to lead to a worsening balance of payments as shown in Table 2, because, while the effect of expansion on exports was favourable, as was to be expected from the argument of the last section, it was highly unfavourable to imports. The reasons why expansion has had an unfavourable effect on imports may be the reasons just outlined, and this may be the crux of the United Kingdom's problem. In stagnation, our exports have grown 2·7 per cent per annum, our imports 1·3 per cent per annum and the balance of payments has improved. In expansion, our exports have grown 4·9 per cent per annum, our imports 7·9 per cent, and the balance of payments has worsened to an intolerable extent. Hence, expansion has had to be halted.

Future policy for growth

Policy to achieve future growth with a satisfactory balance of payments in the United Kingdom must focus on two problems. The first problem is that the propensity to spend growing real incomes on imports must be reduced. To do this the sectors of the economy where heavy importing occurs in periods of expansion must be identified and attempts made to increase the home production of these goods. This problem is being tackled through the little Neddies and it must be recognised that it will take time to achieve a substantial improvement. A further problem is whether it is indeed true, as suggested earlier, that many British designs appeal to a working-class rather than a middle-class market, and whether anything can be done to improve the situation. Here the amount that public policy can achieve is very limited.

The second factor which policy needs to work at is the line I – I in Figure 1. It is possible that Britain's competitors have much higher I – I lines, so that they invest much more at a degree of capacity working of 96 or 97 than the United Kingdom. Hence, they can achieve higher rates of investment without the need to run their economies at 100, 102 or 103. Expansion in those countries will not then be associated with the kind of shortages and resultant rapid import growth that is associated with expansion in the United Kingdom. The United Kingdom's problem is then to raise its I – I line so that there will be more investment in the United Kingdom at 96 or 97 on Figure 1, with less consequent need to run the United Kingdom economy for certain periods at 102 or 103. It was one of the objects of *The National Plan* to achieve an upward shift in the I – I line. The hope was that expectations of expansion through the plan and the atmosphere of the time would cause firms to raise their investment substantially. The failure of the plan, and statements by ministers that businessmen who had based their investment on the plan's forecasts did not know their own job, must have done much to undermine any future policy to raise investment through indicative planning.

The remaining way in which investment might be raised without over-capacity working is through the tax system and through investment incentives. Here the United Kingdom already has the most formidable incentives for investment in the western world. Cash grants of 25 per cent (and 45 per cent in development areas) are formidable instruments to make marginal investments profitable. However, they have a seriously distorting effect on investment. A firm which spends £1000 on plant and machinery which yields total gross profits of £970 over a period of four years will earn a 10 per cent net rate of return on capital, since the investment will cost the firm only £750 with a 25 per cent grant, and gross profits of £970 over the next four years will produce a 10 per cent net rate of return and the recovery of the firm's original £750.[1] However, the investment of £1000 which resulted in aggregate gross profits of only £970 will have reduced the United Kingdom's growth rate, for £1000 of plant and machinery is put into the economy and only £970 is obtained from this—less than sufficient with zero profits to replace the investment and maintain capital intact. It can be argued that 'free depreciation' which has no distorting effect on investment and cannot make an investment which yields no net profits profitable, would be a more efficient way of stimulating investment. A further possibility is that lower overall rates of company taxation would provide more finance for investment and more stimulus to invest and this might have some effect on the I – I line. These lines of policy are however again bound to act slowly. Moreover, it is improbable that a Labour government would introduce 'free depreciation' or lower rates of company taxation. Their effect on investment is bound to be uncertain and it might be

[1] Discounting at 10 per cent per annum, the first year's gross profits of £242 10s. od. (one-quarter of £970) have a 'present value' of £218; the second year's gross profits of £242 10s. od. have a 'present value' of £196, the third year's of £177, and the fourth year's of £159. Hence the 'present value' of the total gross profits of £970, discounted at 10 per cent per annum, is £(218 + 196 + 177 + 159) = £750, which equals the £1000 cost of the investment less a £250 cash grant—so 10 per cent net will be earned on the original £750.

small, so there can only be limited confidence that these measures would lead to a substantial change in the United Kingdom's basic problem that rapid growth is associated with rapid import growth.

There is moreover a further difficulty, for the worsening of the United Kingdom's underlying balance of payments from 1953 to 1966 has created a serious situation. The 1955 boom only resulted in a current account deficit of £155m and the subsequent recession produced a surplus of £336m, while the present situation is one where expansion in 1964 produced a current account deficit of £393m and recession has still failed to produce a surplus. A substantial improvement in the current account is needed, and it is to be hoped that the devaluation of the £ to $2·40 will produce this. It must be added that the old troubles will return before long if the fundamental problems are not solved, and expansion continues to lead to very rapid import growth.

13 Long-term Growth and Short-term Policy*[1]

The productive potential of the British economy, and fluctuations in the pressure of demand for labour, 1951–62

by W. A. H. GODLEY and
J. R. SHEPHERD

Introduction and summary

ONE of the main aims of short-term economic policy in Britain has been to regulate the pressure of demand for labour, and to keep the fluctuations of the unemployment percentage within fairly narrow limits. High unemployment is obviously undesirable; at the other end of the scale, if the pressure of demand for labour is too strong, this tends to lead to excessively high wage increases and to balance-of-payments difficulties. It is for the government to decide at what pressure it wishes to run the economy, and to try to keep it there.

To regulate the pressure of demand for labour is, however, a complex matter; it requires, among other things, that the government should be able to forecast the movement of the unemployment percentage for some time ahead. Government economic forecasts begin as forecasts of the trends in total demand, which lead on to forecasts of the movement of output. The problem is then to decide what this increase in output implies for the movement of employment and of unemployment. These are the relationships analysed in this article; in the course of the analysis, some conclusions emerge about the underlying rate of growth of which the economy is capable.

The first section deals with the relationship of employment to unemployment. The analysis here begins with the upward trend in the supply of labour, arising partly from demographic changes (with more people of working age), and partly from a tendency for partici-

---

* First published 1964.
[1] This article owes a great deal to some unpublished work of Mr W. A. B. Hopkin of the Treasury, which provided some of the basic ideas and indicated a method of estimating the relationships.

pation rates to rise (that is, from a higher proportion of the population of working age deciding to look for work). The calculations suggest that, over the past five years, the trend rise in participation rates has slowed down considerably—and indeed that by 1961 they had virtually stopped rising altogether. Fluctuations of employment around the trend in the labour supply are matched by opposite, but not equal, fluctuations in unemployment: because of the movement in and out of the labour force of the unregistered unemployed —married women, for example, or people near retirement age who do not bother to register as unemployed if dismissed—an increase in employment above the trend of 250 thousand, for instance, would normally be accompanied by a decrease in unemployment of only 100 thousand.

The second section deals with the relationship between output, employment, and consequently unemployment. Here, the analysis suggests the following basic picture. First, if there is no change in unemployment, then by definition output is rising in line with 'productive potential'. Changes in productive potential are made up of changes in the labour supply, and a smooth trend in productivity. (The long-term productivity trend which fits the figures best is one which shows a slow but steady acceleration over the period.) Secondly, for every 1 per cent increase in output over and above this rise in productive potential, 'equilibrium' employment will tend to rise by $\frac{1}{2}$ per cent. The term equilibrium has to be used, because actual employment appears to take time to adjust to equilibrium employment; employers, that is, take time to adjust their labour force to the desired level which fits the new level of output. It is this third element in the relationship—the lag in the adjustment of actual to 'equilibrium' employment—which explains, for example, why employment went on rising in 1961 after output had stopped increasing. Further, since there is a lag before actual employment adjusts to equilibrium employment, there will be a lag before actual unemployment adjusts to equilibrium unemployment as well. Normally when output is rising faster than the productive potential of the economy, actual employment will be lower, and actual unemployment higher than their equilibrium levels.

In the third section these relationships are applied to the analysis of the current economic situation. Perhaps the main conclusion is that whereas actual unemployment in June of this year, seasonally adjusted, was 1·6 per cent, equilibrium unemployment is a good deal lower than this—perhaps 1·3–1·4 per cent. That is, even if output from June onwards is adjusted to the long-term trend in the economy's productive potential, unemployment will fall slowly for some time.

Further, the analysis enables one to assess the recent figures of productivity, as soon as there are reasonably reliable figures for unemployment, output, and employment. It provides ways of allowing both for the short-term effect of changes in the pressure of demand and for time-lags in the reaction of employment; so it should be possible to identify any change in the underlying productivity trend. On balance, the evidence of the output and unemployment figures for 1964 suggest that there has not in fact been any recent sharp jump in this trend.

Finally, a technical appendix gives a detailed account of the equations used.

Employment, unemployment and the supply of labour

If we compare the movement of employment and the movement of unemployment over the period 1951–62 (Chart 1), two characteristics stand out. First, the short-term fluctuations in employment are much larger than those in unemployment. Secondly, whereas employment is trending upwards during the period, there is no matching downward trend in unemployment—which indeed, if anything, shows a slight upward trend as well.

The first of these two phenomena—larger fluctuations in employment than in unemployment—is explained by the 'unregistered unemployed'. These are various groups of marginal workers, such as married women and those close to retirement or who are retired, who may come into the labour force when labour is scarce, and so increase the figure of employment; but who, if dismissed in times of recession, do not register as unemployed. Unregistered unemployment of this kind may reasonably be expected to move fairly closely with registered unemployment. It could be argued that a rise in the demand for labour would affect the registered unemployed first and the unregistered unemployed afterwards; but the figures suggest that any such delay is extremely short.

The second phenomenon—the long-term upward trend in the supply of labour—must result either from an increase in the number of people who are in those age and sex groups which make up the working population—that is, from demographic changes; or it may result from an increased propensity of those people to seek employment—that is, from participation rate changes; or, of course it may be a mixture of them both. It was necessary to separate these two factors out.

We first calculated the contribution of the purely demographic change to the upward trend in employment by applying the 1960

participation rates for each sex and age group[1] to the population
figures for each year. The remaining increase in the trend of employment (given that there was no downward trend in unemployment)
must have been due to a rise in participation rates. Table 1 sets out
the figures for these two factors in the five years before, and in the
four years after, the first half of 1957.[2] Demographic factors were
contributing rather more to the increase in employment in the

TABLE I

Explanation of changes in employment between periods of
equal unemployment*

Thousands, annual averages

	Change in employment	Contribution of demographic factors	Residual: contribution of participation rate changes
1952, 1st half to 1957, 1st half	172	−22	194
1957, 1st half to 1961, 1st half	100	64	36

Source: See Appendix, page 222.

(*) Unemployment averaged 296 thousand in the first half of 1952, 292 thousand
in the first half of 1957, and 294 thousand in the first half of 1961.

second half of the period than in the first; but the opposite is true for
participation rates. There seems to have been a big increase in the
propensity to seek employment up to 1957 and only a small further
rise from then on.

There are many possible reasons for changes in the trend in
participation rates (excluding, that is, the effects of short-term
variations in demand), such as changes in the duration of full-time
education, in the age at which women have children, and in the
size of their families. We have not attempted to explain these
changes;[3] but we have assumed that they depend on influences most
of which occur fairly continuously over a period of time, so that

[1] Married women were treated separately from single.

[2] These periods were chosen because the pressure of demand for labour, as
measured by unemployment, was about the same in the first half of 1952, the first
half of 1957, and the first half 1961.

[3] For a discussion of some of the factors involved, see W. Beckerman and J.
Sutherland, 'Married Women at Work in 1972', *National Institute Economic Review*,
no. 23 (Feb 1963).

there should be a reasonable degree of continuity both in the level and the rate of change in participation rate trends. It should therefore be possible to represent the net effect of changes in these trends by some form of time trend. The evidence suggests that it is not a simple straight-line trend (which is hardly surprising, since no such trend could continue indefinitely).

To take account of all these factors, therefore, our first regression equation related employment, adjusted for demographic factors, to the current level of unemployment, and to various forms of time trend (which represent the trend change in participation rates). The calculations, which are described in the Appendix and illustrated in Chart 1, indicate that for each change upwards or downwards in registered unemployment of 100 thousand there will normally be a change in employment of about 250 thousand below or above the trend increase in the supply of labour (that is, the sum of the demographic change and the changes in participation rate trends).

We thought that the figures might show that this relationship, between the movement of employment and that of unemployment, differed according to the pressure of demand; that is, we expected that at low levels of unemployment a smaller proportion of the change in employment would come from the registered unemployed, and conversely for a high level of unemployment. Over the range of unemployment experienced in the period 1951–62 there was not much evidence of this.[1] But something of this kind seems to have happened in 1963–4 (page 222), when the pressure of demand was much lower than in 1951–62. An exceptionally large proportion of the fall and subsequent recovery in employment in 1963–4 seems to have had its counterpart in the rise and subsequent fall in registered unemployment.

The calculations also support the conclusion suggested by the comparison of the effects of participation rate changes at three points of time (Table 1) that the contribution of changes in participation rates to the labour supply seems to have altered its trend somewhere in the middle of the decade. For the first half of the period, the calculations suggest an upwards participation trend of about 200 thousand a year. Thereafter, the most plausible interpretation of the figures suggests that this upward trend started to decelerate around 1956 and gradually fell away to little more than zero in 1961.

There is one general caveat to this analysis of participation trends. We have assumed that the changes do not depend on the absolute level of the pressure of demand for labour. There is evidence that

[1] See Appendix, pages 224–5.

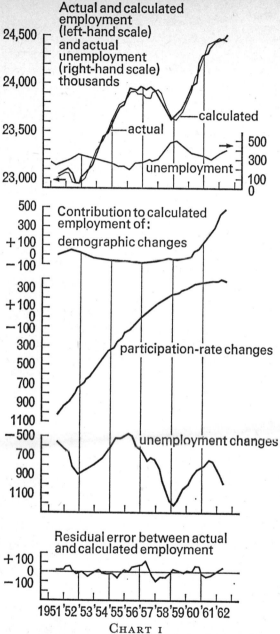

Actual and calculated employment (left-hand scale) and actual unemployment (right-hand scale) thousands

24,500
24,000
23,500
23,000

calculated
actual
unemployment

500
300
100
0

Contribution to calculated employment of:

demographic changes

500
300
+100
0
−100

participation-rate changes

300
+100
0
−100
300
500
700
900
1100

unemployment changes

−500
700
900
1100

Residual error between actual and calculated employment

+100
0
−100

1951 '52 '53 '54 '55 '56 '57 '58 '59 '60 '61 '62

CHART I

Employment and Unemployment, 1951–62

Source: See Appendix, page 224.

they do not, in that over fairly long periods (for example 1952–5), when the pressure of demand was changing a good deal, a smooth trend in participation rates still fits the figures quite well. But it is possible that participation rates do respond very slowly to the pressure of demand for labour—so slowly that in periods no longer than 1952–5 the effect is not seen. The average pressure of demand in the early part of the period, when unemployment averaged 215 thousand, was a good deal higher than in the later part, after 1956, when unemployment averaged 363 thousand; and this difference could have accounted for some of the change in participation rates. But there are not enough years for it to be possible to test for a very long lag of this kind.

Employment and output

The second part of the analysis examines the relationship between the movement of output and the movement of employment. Because of the long-term rise in productivity, of course, the output trend generally rises faster than the employment trend. In the fluctuations around this trend, the short-term changes in employment are smaller than those in output, and they lag behind the changes in output as well (Chart 2).[1]

The explanation which the analysis tested begins with the concept of the 'productive potential' of the economy. It assumes that this is set by the growth in the labour supply, and by the underlying productivity trend. This underlying productivity trend need not be constant—indeed, the calculations suggest that it has been accelerating slightly; but it is assumed to be smooth.

So long as output rises in line with productive potential, defined in this way, then employment will rise in line with the labour supply, unemployment will not change, and there will be no change in the pressure of demand for labour.

When output fluctuates above or below this trend in productive potential, the adjustment of employment to output can be described in two stages. First, 'equilibrium' employment—defined as the level of employment which employers would eventually like to reach to match any given level of output—fluctuates less than

[1] This cyclical behaviour of employment in manufacturing industries was one of a number of subjects recently explored by Mr R. R. Neild, assisted by Mr J. R. Shepherd, in *Prices and Employment in the Trade Cycle* (1963). In this study it was convincingly established that short-term changes in employment were proportionately smaller than those of output and that they responded with a time lag.

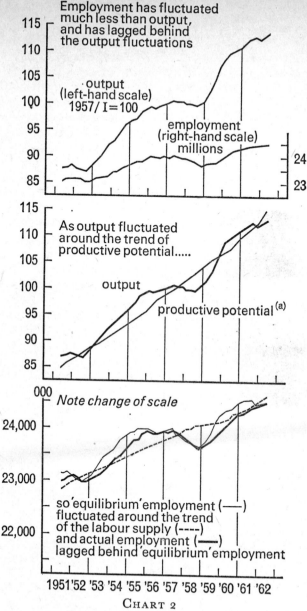

Employment has fluctuated much less than output, and has lagged behind the output fluctuations

output (left-hand scale) 1957/ I = 100

employment (right-hand scale) millions

As output fluctuated around the trend of productive potential.....

output

productive potential [a]

Note change of scale

so 'equilibrium' employment (——) fluctuated around the trend of the labour supply (----) and actual employment (——) lagged behind 'equilibrium' employment

1951 '52 '53 '54 '55 '56 '57 '58 '59 '60 '61 '62

CHART 2

Output and Employment, 1951–62

Source: See Appendix 1.

(a) The *level* of the trend of productive potential is arbitrary; it corresponds to an unemployment rate of 1½ per cent. The *slope* of the trend, however, would have been the same whatever unemployment trend had been chosen.

output. This is mainly because some employees, both in administration and in production, are regarded as an overhead; their number is not increased when there is a short-term rise in output, nor is it reduced when there is a short-term fall. But, secondly, actual employment will not adjust to 'equilibrium' employment straight away; firms take time to adjust their labour force to changes in output. It takes time to hire additional workers; and firms also delay dismissals when demand falls off.

This is the basic structure of the hypothesis (illustrated in Chart 2) which our analysis tested; but it also allowed for various other factors. When the labour supply deviated from its steady upward trend—that is, when there was either an exceptionally large addition to the labour force, or an exceptionally large withdrawal from it—it was assumed that this would affect the productivity trend. For instance, when 100 thousand or more extra elderly workers suddenly left the labour force in 1958 (having qualified for pensions under the ten-year rule) it is unlikely that output was affected proportionately, or that there was a compensating increase in employment of other people. Similarly the unusually large number of young people who reached the age of 15 in 1961 and 1962, most of whom joined the labour force, will initially have contributed less output per head than an average worker. So the productive potential of the economy will not have been increased to the full extent of the addition to the labour force.

Secondly, a special adjustment is needed to take account of negotiated reductions in the normal working week. Thirdly, the reaction of employment to a downswing in output may well differ from its reaction to an upswing; the two must be considered separately.

The results

These hypotheses of the way in which employment reacts to the movement of output did in fact provide a good explanation of the quarterly movement of employment between 1951 and 1962, on the following set of assumptions.

First, that the long-term trend of productivity accelerated steadily over the eleven-year period. In 1951–3, the underlying growth of productivity was about 1·8 per cent a year, and by 1960–2 almost 2·5 per cent. To turn these figures into a series for productive potential, the change in the labour force must be added, and also the necessary allowances must be made for the effect on productivity of any unusual changes in the labour supply, and of cuts in the standard working week. We assumed[1] that, for every deviation from trend in the supply of labour of 1 per cent, only ¾ per cent is eventually added to the productive capacity of the economy—and that there is a once-and-for-all reduction in the trend of productivity of ¼ per cent. We also assumed[1] that each cut of 1 per cent in the standard working week reduced productive potential by 0·2 per cent. Table 2 shows how these various factors add together to a productive potential series.

TABLE 2

Analysis of changes in productive potential

Changes during year ending in second quarter of	Change in productive potential*	Underlying growth of productivity†	Average growth of labour supply	Contributions to growth of productive potential of Deviations from average in growth of labour supply	Changes in normal hours
1952	2·66	1·77	0·69	0·17	–
1953	2·62	1·85	0·69	0·06	–
1954	2·60	1·93	0·69	−0·01	−0·02
1955	2·75	2·01	0·69	0·03	–
1956	2·75	2·08	0·69	−0·03	–
1957	2·75	2·16	0·69	−0·08	−0·02
1958	2·89	2·24	0·69	−0·01	−0·05
1959	2·85	2·32	0·69	−0·15	−0·02
1960	2·64	2·39	0·69	−0·17	−0·28
1961	2·74	2·47	0·69	0·01	−0·44
1962	3·30	2·55	0·69	0·24	−0·18

Source: See Appendix, page 232.

* This is not exactly the sum of the remaining columns in the table, because of the form of the regression equation, which is linear in logarithms.

† Assuming average growth of labour supply.

Secondly, each 1 per cent fluctuation in output above or below the productive potential trend will raise or lower equilibrium employment by just over ½ per cent, or 130 thousand workers.

Thirdly, actual employment adjusts to equilibrium employment according to the pattern shown in Table 3. If equilibrium employment is falling, or shows only a small rise, then the movement of actual employment covers some 70 per cent of the change in equilibrium employment; that is, employers will make most of the adjustment straight away. But as the rise in equilibrium employment increases above 30 thousand, then employers tend to make only 25–30 per cent of the adjustment in the first quarter.

[1] As explained in the Appendix, it was not possible to determine with any precision what were the effects on capacity of changes in the labour supply or in normal hours. We have, therefore, imposed values for these relationships, the bases of which are given in the Appendix, page 227.

TABLE 3

Rule for the adjustment process of actual to equilibrium employment

Thousands

Gap between equilibrium employment and actual employment the previous quarter	Change in actual employment compared with previous quarter
—200	—140
—160	—112
—120	— 84
— 80	— 56
— 40	— 28
0	0
+ 40	+ 24
+ 80	+ 34
+120	+ 43
+160	+ 53
+200	+ 62
+240	+ 72

Source: See Appendix, page 228.

The explanation which these assumptions give of the actual movement of employment over the period 1951–62 seems to be satisfactory. The mean error[1] was 23 thousand (under 0·1 per cent).

Developments since 1962

The analysis we have been describing was based on the period up to mid-1962. During the next year, up to mid-1963, the exceptionally severe winter probably distorted the relationships; and for the year up to mid-1964, the figures both for employment and for output are subject to revision. Nonetheless, it seemed important to try to form some provisional judgement of what has happened in the last two years, in terms of this analysis.

The assumptions made about the movement of output and of productive capacity for the two most recent years are set out in Table 4. We assumed that the underlying productivity trend continued to accelerate at the same rate as in the period 1951–62.

[1] That is, the arithmetic mean of the absolute error, irrespective of sign. The values of employment calculated from these relationships were obtained by taking an initial value for actual employment, and then by applying the adjustment rule to equilibrium employment and the calculated value of employment in the previous quarter. This mean error compares favourably with the mean error of 0·4 per cent for changes over four quarters obtained from the best equation in Mr Neild's study. But fluctuations in manufacturing employment tended to be proportionately bigger than in total employment.

TABLE 4

Mid-1962 to mid-1964: assumptions about output, labour and
productive potential

		Gross domestic product*	Change in productive potential	Underlying growth of productivity	Average growth of labour supply	Contributions to growth of productive potential of Deviations from average in growth of labour supply	Changes in normal hours
		1958 = 100		Per cent changes during year ending in second quarter			
1962	I	111·2					
	II	113·5					
	III	114·2					
	IV	114·0					
1963	I	112·7					
	II	116·3	3·45	2·63	0·69†	0·13†	−0·02
	III	117·9					
	IV	120·5					
1964	I	122·2					
	II	123·1	3·22	2·71	0·69†	−0·03†	−0·08

Source: See Appendix.

* These estimates, in real terms, are derived from official estimates of gross domestic product up to the end of 1963, and on the movement of industrial production and various demand indicators in the first half of 1964.

† The change in the labour supply in the year ending mid-1963 is assumed to be made up of a demographic contribution of + 210 thousand, and a participation rate contribution of + 10 thousand; the change in the year ending mid-1964 is assumed to be made up of a demographic contribution of + 140 thousand, and a participation rate contribution of + 10 thousand.

The demographic contribution to the labour supply was probably about 210 thousand in 1962–3, and we have tentatively assumed that it was of the order of 140 thousand in 1963–4. For participation rates, extrapolation of the 1951–62 relationships would suggest a negative contribution; but assuming that the employment figure is revised upwards (see below), this could hardly be right, and we have allowed for a small positive item. The reduction in normal working hours was rather more marked in the year ending mid-1964 than in the year ending mid-1963.

The forecasts of employment derived from these assumptions were fairly good up to the middle of 1963, the last date for which a reliable employment figure is available (Table 5).[1] From the third quarter of 1963, however, recorded employment falls well behind the forecast. The provisional estimate of employment for the second quarter is 24,640 thousand, some 200 thousand lower than the forecast.

However, it is probable that the employment figures for the period since June 1963 will be revised upwards substantially; this has often happened before. If so, the accumulated error between the mid-year benchmark figures will be spread evenly over the provisional

[1] The mean discrepancy between 'forecast' and actual employment between 1962, first quarter, and 1963, second quarter, was 25 thousand or 0·10 per cent.

monthly figures. To produce an upward revision of 200 thousand, therefore, in the figure for the second quarter of 1964, the June 1964 figure would have eventually to be revised by 220 thousand; this is rather larger than the revision to the June 1963 figure. If a revision of this order is made, then the employment figures will fit the forecast quite well (Table 5).[1]

The unemployment forecasts, however, derived from the actual employment figures up to mid-1963 and the revised employment figures from then on, do not fit the actual figures well during the rise to the peak of unemployment at the beginning of 1963 and the fall to the end of that year. Actual unemployment went up much faster and came down much faster than the forecast figures (Table 5).

It is not surprising that this should have happened. The pressure of demand for labour in 1963 fell to a level which was quite outside the experience of the years 1951–62, on which the calculations were based. It is plausible to assume that, when the pressure of demand falls below a certain point, a larger proportion than usual of those leaving the labour force will register as unemployed, and that when the pressure of demand recovers again from that low point, an unusually large proportion of the increase in employment would also come from the registered unemployed. This is what seems to have happened in 1962–3. By the beginning of 1964 the unemployment figures were back in line with output and the revised employment figures.

These assumptions, then, give a plausible, if tentative, interpretation of recent events. It is an interpretation which hangs on the eventual upward revision of the employment figure, when the June National Insurance card count is made.[2] It may be that the figures will not be revised upwards. If they are not, then it would imply a remarkable jump in productivity, coming either from a much bigger cyclical response than usual to the upturn in demand, or from a sudden discontinuity in the long-term trend. This would have had to happen entirely since the middle of 1963, as recorded employment was, if anything, higher than the forecast until then. Secondly, it would imply a sharp fall in the trend of participation rates over the last two years. Comparing the second quarter of 1964 with that of 1962, unemployment was about the same, and recorded employment has risen only by about 150 thousand. But the demographic contribution to the labour supply in these two years was

[1] The mean discrepancy between these revised figures and the forecast is 23 thousand, or 0·09 per cent.

[2] The revision to the June 1963 figure was first announced in October of that year.

TABLE 5

Forecast and Actual Employment and Unemployment,* 1962–4

Thousands, seasonally adjusted

	Recorded employment	Suggested revision	Revised employment	Forecast employment	Error (3)–(4)	'Actual' unemployment†	Unemployment forecast from (3)	Error (6)–(7)	Equilibrium employment	Equilibrium unemployment
	(1)	(2)	(3)	(4)	(5)	(6)	(7)	(8)	(9)	(10)
1962 I	24,475		24,475	24,475	1	350	349	1	24,479	348
II	24,503		24,503	24,490	13	384	364	20	24,496	368
III	24,561		24,561	24,510	51	421	367	54	24,522	381
IV	24,516		24,516	24,454	62	464	403	61	24,430	435
1963 I	24,457		24,457	24,445	12	518	440	78	24,441	447
II	24,492		24,492	24,480	12	521	443	78	24,531	429
III	24,557	+35	24,592	24,558	34	486	423	63	24,743	364
IV	24,566	+90	24,656	24,653	3	453	418	35	24,895	322
1964 I	24,565	+146	24,711	24,755	−44	413	413	0	25,018	291
II	24,640	+200	24,840	24,849	−9	375	368	7	25,086	280

Source: See Appendix, page 224.

* Wholly unemployed excluding school-leavers, seasonally adjusted.
† This is a lagged series (see Appendix, page 224 equation 7), and is equal to two-thirds of unemployment in the current quarter plus one-third of unemployment in the previous quarter.

probably around 350 thousand; so, if the employment figure is right, there must have been a substantial reduction in participation rates over this period. This also seems unlikely.

On balance, therefore, the evidence seems to be against either any sharp change in the underlying productivity trend or any different order of response of productivity to the cyclical rise in demand. What recent figures have been showing is the normal short-term acceleration in an economic upswing. This judgement is based on the unemployment and output figures, and it assumes that the employment figures will be revised to fit them.

Actual and equilibrium unemployment

If we accept, then, that the 1951–62 relationships between output, employment and unemployment can reasonably be made to fit the experience of 1963 and 1964 so far, then there is an important conclusion to be drawn about equilibrium employment and unemployment. Since output has been rising faster than productive potential for rather over a year, equilibrium employment in the second quarter of 1964 was substantially higher than the suggested level of actual employment—by some 245 thousand. This in turn implies that equilibrium unemployment was 70 thousand less than actual unemployment.[1] In other words, if from now on output rises only in line with productive capacity, unemployment is still likely to fall by a further 70 thousand—that is, to a level where the seasonally adjusted unemployment percentage, in the form in which it is normally quoted (including the temporarily stopped), will be about 1·3–1·4 per cent.[2]

APPENDIX[3]

I. *The relationship of employment and unemployment*

The following symbols have been used:

E = Total employment, including the armed forces, quarterly,

---

[1] Actual unemployment here refers to the recorded level in the second quarter, and so differs from the lagged series in Table 5.

[2] See author's note, p. 232.

[3] Updated estimates of some of the key equations in this article can be found in a short paper by J. R. Shepherd, 'Productive potential and the demand for labour', *Economic Trends*, CLXXVIII (Aug. 1968).

seasonally adjusted. Since employment in building and agriculture is sometimes affected by unusually cold or warm winter months, the ratio of employment in these two industries (each after adjustment for normal seasonal variations) to other employment was assumed to move smoothly between the third quarter of each year and the second quarter of the following year.

To obtain the demographic contribution to the labour supply the population at each mid-year was divided into males, single women and married women, with each classification further divided up into five-year age groups. In 1961 and 1962, the 15–19 age group was further divided up into one-year groups because of the unusually large number of people who suddenly entered. Each group was multiplied by mid-1960 participation rates and the total summed. The initial value (June 1951) was then subtracted throughout to obtain D, the variable used in the regressions.[1]

U = The number wholly unemployed excluding school-leavers, seasonally adjusted. To take account of abnormal winter weather, it has been assumed that unemployment in construction and agriculture moved smoothly between mid-year points. To allow for the possibility that there will be some lag between a change in registered unemployment, and the full extent of the associated change in employment, a lagged variable for unemployment was introduced:

$$\bar{U} = \tfrac{2}{3}U + \tfrac{1}{3}U_{-1}$$

To test the possibility that an increasingly large proportion of those losing their jobs register as unemployed when unemployment is high, and conversely, two other symbols were employed:

$$U' = 0, \text{ when } U \geqslant 300$$
$$= 300 - U, \text{ when } U < 300$$
$$\bar{U}' = 0, \text{ when } \bar{U} \geqslant 300$$
$$= 300 - \bar{U}, \text{ when } \bar{U} < 300$$

---

[1] One further consideration was introduced; the late age entrants to the National Insurance scheme became eligible for pensions in 1958 provided they had continued their contributions. The number who left employment as a result of their eligibility was less than the number who started receiving pensions, since some people continued at work with their pensions and others, having already retired, had continued their contributions. The change in 1958 in the participation rates of elderly people suggests that about 130 thousand left the labour force from this cause, and this number we have deducted from D in 1958 and 1959. But for the scheme, however, these people would probably have retired before 1958. We therefore assumed that the scheme added 130 thousand to D in the four years prior to 1958, as follows, in thousands: 1953/54 + 5, 1954/55 + 10, 1955/56 + 25, 1956/57 + 35, 1957/58 + 45, 1958/59 − 100, 1959/60 − 30.

U_n = the number of 'unregistered unemployed', that is those people not in jobs who would, under suitable demand conditions, be willing and able to work, but who are not registered as unemployed. Thus the total labour force $F = E + U + U_n$

t is a time trend having 1956 IV = 0.

t′ is a special trend equal to 0 for all periods up to and including 1957 I and rising one per quarter thereafter.

t″ = 0 up to and including 1955 II and rising one per quarter thereafter.

Our hypotheses are, first, that the total labour force is determined by the number of people in the various age groups and by some kind of time trend; second, that changes in the number registered as unemployed are related to changes in the unregistered unemployed. Thus we can write:

(1) $F = D + f(t)$

(2) $U_n = g(U)$

which give, by substitution

(3) $E - D = U + g(U) + f(t)$

A number of experiments were carried out to discover the most appropriate forms for $g(U)$ and the time trend. The main results are shown in the following table:

(4) $E - D = 24,260 -$
$\qquad 2 \cdot 06\bar{U} + 2 \cdot 26\bar{U}' + 34 \cdot 5t$ $R^2 = \cdot 936$
$\qquad (0 \cdot 41) \quad (0 \cdot 81) \quad (1 \cdot 43)$ S.E. $= 106 \cdot 2$

(5) $E - D = 24,239 -$
$\qquad 2 \cdot 03\bar{U} + 2 \cdot 39\bar{U}' + 34 \cdot 5t - 0 \cdot 05t^2$ $R^2 = \cdot 937$
$\qquad (0 \cdot 42) \quad (0 \cdot 87) \quad (1 \cdot 44) \quad (0 \cdot 12)$ S.E. $= 107 \cdot 3$

(6) $E - D = 24,546 -$
$\qquad 2 \cdot 34\bar{U} + 0 \cdot 56\bar{U}' + 48 \cdot 9t - 32 \cdot 1t'$ $R^2 = \cdot 991$
$\qquad (0 \cdot 16) \quad (0 \cdot 33) \quad (1 \cdot 10) \quad (2 \cdot 12)$ S.E. $= 41 \cdot 0$

(7) $E - D = 24,637 -$
$\qquad 2 \cdot 66\bar{U} + 0 \cdot 35\bar{U}' + 48 \cdot 5t - 0 \cdot 90t''^2$ $R^2 = \cdot 990$
$\qquad (0 \cdot 17) \quad (0 \cdot 36) \quad (1 \cdot 15) \quad 0 \cdot 063)$ S.E. $= 43 \cdot 4$

(8) $E - D = 24,646 -$
$\qquad 2 \cdot 66U + 0 \cdot 17U' + 48 \cdot 3t - 0 \cdot 90t''^2$ $R^2 = \cdot 987$
$\qquad (0 \cdot 19) \quad (0 \cdot 40) \quad (1 \cdot 29) \quad (0 \cdot 071)$ S.E. $= 49 \cdot 0$

(9) $E - D = 24,812 -$
$\qquad 3 \cdot 61\bar{U} + 1 \cdot 27\bar{U}^2 + 48 \cdot 4t - 0 \cdot 89t''^2$ $R^2 = \cdot 989$
$\qquad (0 \cdot 90) \quad (1 \cdot 37) \quad (1 \cdot 19) \quad (0 \cdot 066)$ S.E. $= 43 \cdot 9$

Equations 4 and 5 each contain a single trend throughout the period, one being linear, the other quadratic. The results were, however, very much inferior to those of equations 6 and 7, in each of which the trend is broken, confirming that an important change of trend of participation took place around the middle of the decade.

Equation 6, with two linear trends, gave the best 'explanation' of employment (by the criterion of goodness of fit), but the implications were not very acceptable, since they indicated a contribution to the labour force from the participation trend of about 200 thousand a year in the first period changing abruptly to 70 thousand a year after 1957. Equation 7 gave nearly as good a fit and seems theoretically preferable since it implies no sudden change in the participation trend; it suggests that the participation contribution was 200 thousand in the first half of the period but gradually fell away and was little more than zero at the beginning of 1962. The trend was permitted to alter earlier in the case of equation 7 than in that of 6 since it is some time before the quadratic term makes much difference. Equation 8 is identical with 7 but for the inclusion of unemployment in the current quarter only, with no time lag. This produces a significant increase in the standard error. This implies that there is a slightly more immediate reaction of registered unemployed than of unregistered to a rise in employment.

The purpose of including either $\bar{U}'$, or U' or $\bar{U}^2$ in each equation was to see whether, as unemployment rises, an increasingly large proportion of those losing their jobs register as unemployed. Over the range of fluctuations experienced,[1] however, the relationship appears to be linear, since the coefficients of U' $\bar{U}'$ and U^2 were small and poorly determined.

Using the criteria both of goodness of fit and of the plausibility of the coefficients, equation 7 appears to be the best. The standard error of estimate (S.E.) is fairly low (under 0·2 per cent), but there is one rather bad period of discrepancy in 1957, when a fairly large rise in unemployment (which was confirmed by a fall in unfilled vacancies) apparently had no counterpart in employment. There is also some positive serial correlation in the residuals. But one reason for this may be that provisional figures are revised by spreading the error accumulated between annual benchmarks (obtained from a count of insurance cards) evenly between the monthly changes. This would tend to produce serial correlation in the statistical error.

---

[1] The experience of 1947, when registered unemployment rose above a million, is unfortunately no guide to the behaviour of the relationship when the pressure of demand is very low, since the greater part of the increase was in the temporarily stopped.

There is no serial correlation of residuals of the mid-year observations, the only points at which thoroughly reliable figures for employment are available.

II. *Employment and output*

The additional symbols adopted were as follows:

P = A three-quarter moving average of gross domestic product,[1] seasonally adjusted.

L, the 'labour force' is the calculated level of employment for a fixed pressure of demand. The level of demand selected (arbitrarily) for the calculation was that corresponding to unemployment (excluding the temporarily stopped) equal to $1\frac{1}{4}$ per cent[2] of the labour supply. Thus, using equation 7,

$$L = D + 24{,}637 - 2{\cdot}66\,(0{\cdot}0125L) + 48{\cdot}5t - 0{\cdot}90t''^2$$
$$= 0{\cdot}9678D + 23{,}844 + 46{\cdot}9t - 0{\cdot}87t''^2$$

H = Quarterly index of normal hours.

t = A time trend with 1957 I = 0.

E* = The level of employment with which employers would be satisfied given P, H and L.

K = An arbitrary constant.

The two basic assumptions were.

(10) $E^* = f(PLHt)$

(11) $E - E_{-1} = f(E^* - E_{-1})$

It was argued (page 216) that equilibrium employment does not fully reflect deviations from trend in output, because it is likely to be affected by the pressure of demand. The first relationship can therefore best be formulated by bringing in the pressure of demand specifically; this is done here by using the ratio of equilibrium employment to the labour supply.

The relationship will therefore be of the form:

---

[1] This is a 'compromise' estimate of gross domestic product at constant prices, which makes use of the official estimates of income, expenditure and real output. The way in which they were prepared is described in 'Measuring National Product' by W. A. H. Godley and C. Gillion, *National Institute Economic Review*, no. 27 (Feb 1964).

[2] This is roughly comparable with $1\frac{1}{2}$ per cent for the unemployment percentage as usually expressed—that is, the unemployed, including the temporarily stopped, as a percentage of the total number of employees.

$$(12)\ E^* = \frac{P}{f_1(L, H, t) \cdot f_2\left(\frac{E^*}{L}\right)}$$

The function, $f_1(L,H,t)$ represents the underlying productivity trend; that is, the productivity obtainable at a given pressure of demand.

It would be possible, in principle, to make direct estimates of the effects of the labour supply and of changes in the working week. In practice the data are too limited for the coefficients to be other than very poorly determined. The only significant changes in the working week occurred in one short period in 1960 and 1961, coinciding with a spurt in the demographic contribution to the labour supply. Accordingly it seems preferable to impose the values which appear most plausible.

In accordance with the discussion on page 216 it has been assumed that changes in the supply of labour do not produce proportionate changes in capacity. The assumption made was that a change in the labour supply brings about an immediate increase in capacity proportional to half the change in the labour supply, and a further increase in capacity a year later proportional to one-quarter of the change in the labour supply. Strictly a distributed lag should be imposed but in the present context the quantitative differences from the simpler procedure used would be trivial.

It has been assumed that quarterly productivity (in terms of gross domestic product per employed person) is reduced by one-fifth of the reduction in the normal working week. The basis of this assumption was that (a) reductions in the normal working week covered no more than 60 per cent of all employees, (b) one-half of the reductions in 'normal hours' were compensated for by increased overtime and (c) each one per cent cut in the number of hours actually worked produced an increase in hourly productivity such that quarterly output per man fell only $\frac{2}{3}$ per cent. Of these assumptions (b) is based on inspection of changes in hours worked over the period when 'normal hours' were falling, taking into account the movement of output and unemployment at that time. Assumption (c) is no more than a guess.

The productivity trend includes a quadratic as well as linear term in logarithms in order to measure any acceleration or deceleration. Inserting this form of productivity trend the full relationship may be written as follows:

$$(13)\ E^* = \frac{K \cdot P}{10^{(\alpha, t + \alpha_2 t^2)} L^{-\frac{1}{2}} L_{-\frac{1}{4}} H^\delta \left(\frac{E^*}{L}\right)^\beta}$$

Writing logarithms (to base 10) as lower-case letters this may be simplified to give:

$$(14)\ e^* - l = \frac{1}{1 + \beta}\ (a + p - \tfrac{1}{2}l - \tfrac{1}{4}l_{-4} - \tfrac{1}{5}h - \alpha_1 t - \alpha_2 t^2)$$

It did not seem possible to specify *a priori* any conveniently simple form for equation 11, since it seemed highly probable that the relationship was not linear. Consequently a simultaneous solution of equations 10 and 11 was ruled out on the grounds of being computationally unmanageable and also unduly restrictive. We therefore resorted to an iterative procedure, from which a solution of equation 11 emerged which was both inherently plausible and simple graphically.

The iterative procedure started with a rough estimate of the long-term growth of capacity, and of the cyclical factor relating changes in output to changes in employment (derived from the amplitude of cyclical fluctuations in employment in the past in relation to those of output) from which provisional values of E^* were calculated. The values of $E^* - E_{-1}$ were then plotted against

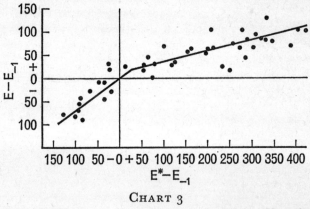

CHART 3

Rules for the Adjustment Process of Actual to Equilibrium Unemployment

The scatter diagram shows, for each quarter from 1951 to 1962 II, the change in actual employment, and the difference between equilibrium employment in one quarter and actual employment in the previous quarter.

those of $E - E_{-1}$ on a chart similar to Chart 3, which made it possible to infer a simple rule governing the adjustment process. This rule was applied to obtain 'predicted' values of E throughout the period using only E^* and one initial value for E. A comparison of these 'predictions' with recorded values of E led to modifications of the adjustment rule.

If our main concern had been to provide a way of forecasting employment one quarter ahead from the latest recorded level (as is provided by those regression equations which include among the independent variables the dependent variable lagged one quarter) then our adjustment rule would probably have been the one which gave the best fit to the points on the chart. Since, however, our object is to provide the best way of forecasting over much longer periods than one quarter ahead, we attempted at each stage of the iterative process to obtain the best explanation of the movement of employment over the whole period in terms of output alone, without reference to the actual levels of employment in earlier quarters. The adjustment rule selected was one which performed this function well, and is not necessarily that which gives the best fit to the points on the chart.

Having inferred a provisional adjustment rule, new values for E^* were calculated from recorded employment, and these were used to recalculate equation 14. The whole process was then repeated until a satisfactory convergence was obtained. The final result is believed to be independent of the initial assumptions.

The following results were obtained from the final version of equation 14, using estimates of E^* obtained from the adjustment rule shown in Chart 3.

$$(15) \quad e^* - l = \cdot87668 + 0 \cdot 519 \, (p - \tfrac{1}{2}l - \tfrac{1}{4}l_{-4} - \tfrac{1}{5}h)$$
$$(0 \cdot 0299)$$
$$- \, 0 \cdot 001315t - 0 \cdot 00000536t^2$$
$$(0 \cdot 000071) \quad (0 \cdot 00000144)$$
$$R^2 = 0 \cdot 895 \qquad \text{S.E.} = 0 \cdot 0014 \qquad d = 1 \cdot 93$$

The 'actual' and calculated values of E^* from this equation are plotted in Chart 4.

The 'predicted' values for employment derived from the adjustment rule shown in Chart 2 and equation 15 seem satisfactory, the mean error being 23 thousand[1] or under 0·1 per cent. The predicted change in each quarter compared with the recorded level in the previous quarter was also calculated by applying the adjustment rule to successive values of $E^* - E_{-1}$, and the mean error here was only 17 thousand. This second procedure is equivalent to the technique of including a lagged dependent variable among the independent variables for the regression.

'Predicted' values for employment were used to calculate 'predictions' of unemployment using a rearrangement of equation 7. The results for the period up to mid-1962 were quite satisfactory

---

[1] The arithmetic mean of the absolute errors regardless of sign.

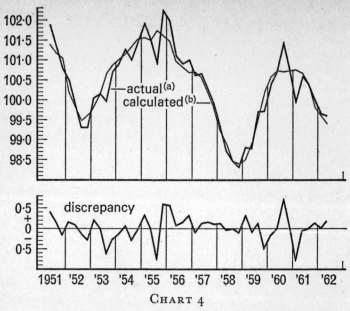

CHART 4

'Actual' and Calculated Values of Equilibrium Employment

(a) 'Actual' values of equilibrium employment are those derived, by the adjustment process illustrated in Chart 3 and in Table 3 from the actual values of employment.
(b) 'Calculated' values of equilibrium employment are those calculated from output with equation (15).

(giving a mean error of 10 thousand but, as indicated on page 220, the predictions of unemployment were poor for 1963).

While the nature of the adjustment process did not emerge very clearly from the data, it is clear at least that the slope of a line fitted to the points in the left-hand half of Chart 2 would be steeper than that fitted to the points in the right-hand half, indicating a more rapid adjustment process when employment is falling than when it is rising. The data also suggested that while the absolute size of an upward movement is positively related to the size of the adjustment to be made, a smaller proportion of the whole adjustment is made when this is large than when it is small.

III. *Unemployment and output*

Relationships have been produced between employment and unemployment, and between employment and output, and a relationship between unemployment and output has been deduced from these.

However, there are advantages in estimating this last relationship directly. The quarterly unemployment statistics are undoubtedly accurate which is probably not true of employment; moreover in the analysis of a current situation unemployment statistics are available promptly while acceptable employment figures may be delayed a year or more. For some purposes, therefore, the most satisfactory way of measuring employment may be to use estimates of employment calculated from the general relationship between employment and unemployment, and from the quarterly unemployment figures.

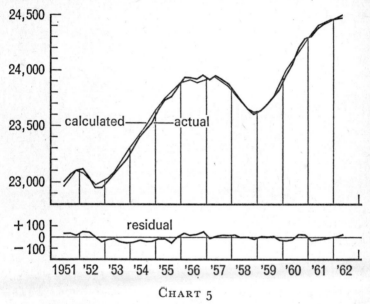

CHART 5

Actual Employment, and Employment Calculated from Output

A relationship using calculated employment figures $(E_{(u)})$ obtained in this way was fitted to output in exactly the same way as that used for the actual employment figures. The same adjustment rule was used but slightly different coefficients were obtained.

$$(16) \quad e^*_{(u)} - l = 0.88295 + 0.5232 \left(p - \tfrac{1}{2}l - \tfrac{1}{4}l_{-4} - \tfrac{1}{5}h\right)$$
$$(0.0299)$$
$$- 0.001328t - 0.000004496t^2$$
$$(0.000071) \qquad (0.000001439)$$
$$= .897 \quad \text{S.E.} = 0.0014 \quad d = 1.08$$

In contrast to the calculations using actual employment figures there was some correlation of the residuals. The unemployment figures implied by the relationship were calculated and compared with the actual unemployment. Once again, they follow the actual movement of unemployment quite well, the mean error being 12 thousand.

IV. *The capacity trend*

Equation 15 can be rearranged to provide an estimate of the movement of productive potential. This is defined here as the level of output, at any one point of time which would make equilibrium employment equal to the labour supply (that is $e^* - l = 0$), and therefore equilibrium unemployment (excluding the temporarily stopped) $1\frac{1}{4}$ per cent of the labour supply. Thus from equation 15 we obtain:

$$(17)\quad c = -\,1 \cdot 68900 + 0 \cdot 002534t + 0 \cdot 000010327t^2 + \\ (\tfrac{1}{2}l + \tfrac{1}{4}l_{-4} + \tfrac{1}{5}h),$$

where c = log capacity.

The coefficients are ratios of estimated least squares coefficients and the usual significance test does not apply. But the estimated standard error for the time-trend coefficient was about ($\cdot 0000345$) and for the acceleration (t^2) coefficient was about ($0 \cdot 000003$).[1] The pattern of residuals in equation 15 and the absence of serial correlation indicates that there was not, as has sometimes been suggested, any sudden jump in the rate of growth of capacity some time in the middle of the period.

Authors' note (July 1969)
Subsequent experience broadly confirms the assessment published in August 1964. The upward revision to the growth in employment turned out to be 140 thousand whereas a revision of 220 thousand was put forward as needed to obtain broad consistency with the relationships. The estimate of output movements in the first half of 1964 appears to have been about right.

The build-up of an excess of equilibrium over actual employment is confirmed by the substantial continued rise in employment and fall in unemployment after mid-1964 when output was rising at below the growth rate of productive potential. For example, between mid-1964 and mid-1965 employment rose (in the latest estimates) by 242 thousand (1 per cent) and unemployment (wholly unemployed) fell by 51 thousand. Even if a small time-lag is allowed for by comparing G.D.P. in the first halves of 1964 and 1965 the rise in output was only about 3 per cent—no greater than the estimated rise in productive potential.

[1] Estimated from the variances and covariances of the regression coefficients.

Bibliographical Guide

THE following bibliography does not provide an exhaustive list of all the literature on the British economy in the twentieth century. Rather it is designed to draw attention to some of the most important works which will be useful to the reader in further study.

One of the most important source books for British economic statistics is B. R. Mitchell and Phyllis Deane, *Abstract of British Historical Statistics* (1962). Unfortunately many of the series in this volume end in 1938 so for the later period readers should consult The London and Cambridge Economic Service, *Key Statistics of the British Economy 1900–66* (1967). This volume contains continuous series of all the most important economic indicators for the twentieth century. An excellent introduction to the problems involved in using statistical data and measuring economic performance can be found in Michael Lipton, *Assessing Economic Performance* (1968). Similarly, a very important work by Edward F. Denison, *Why Growth Rates Differ* (1968) devotes some space in the earlier part of his volume to these difficulties, including the problem of international comparisons of economic data. All statistics, of course, have limitations and should therefore be used carefully, though the reader should not take too seriously Oscar Morgenstern's vigorous attack on quantitative assessment in his *On the Accuracy of Economic Observations* (2nd ed. 1963).

There are a number of textbooks covering the period up to the Second World War and beyond. Among the most readable are A. J. Youngson, *Britain's Economic Growth 1920–1966* (1967) and R. S. Sayers, *A History of Economic Change in England 1880–1939* (1967), while W. Ashworth, *An Economic History of England 1870–1939* (1960) and S. Pollard, *The Development of the British Economy 1914–1950* (1962) contain extensive bibliographical notes. Although published over twenty years ago Alfred Kahn's *Great Britain in the World Economy* (1946) is still one of the best accounts of Britain's inter-war economy in an international setting.

A more specialised study of the 1930s is H. W. Richardson, *Economic Recovery in Britain 1932–39* (1967). This is essential reading for every student of the inter-war years since it not only places the 1929–32 depression in perspective but also revises popular notions about the dimensions and causes of the British recovery.

There are many books and articles dealing with various aspects of the British economy before 1939. However, since all the most important works including the main statistical sources have been reviewed at some length in D. H. Aldcroft and H. W. Richardson, *The British Economy 1870–1939* (1969) the reader is referred to this source for further information on the earlier period.

For the post-1945 period there are now available a number of good general studies of Britain's economy. The following works provide the best introductions for the reader new to the subject: Samuel Brittan, *The Treasury under the Tories 1951–1964* (1965); J. and A. M. Hackett, *The British Economy, Problems and Prospects* (1967); R. F. Harrod, *The British Economy* (1963) and Andrew Shonfield, *British Economic Policy since the War* (2nd ed. 1959). More advanced texts which examine in depth some of the key issues relating to the growth and management of the British economy are: R. Caves, *Britain's Economic Prospects* (1968); J. C. R. Dow, *The Management of the British Economy 1945–1960* (1964); P. D. Henderson (ed.), *Economic Growth in Britain* (1966); A. R. Prest (ed.), *A Manual of Applied Economics* (1966); and the two volumes edited by G. D. N. Worswick and P. H. Ady, *The British Economy, 1945–50* (1952) and *The British Economy of the 1950s* (1962). The book by Caves is especially important since it is an independent assessment by American observers.

In addition, the following empirical studies of the growth experience of a number of countries including Britain should be consulted: Edward F. Denison, *Why Growth Rates Differ* (1968); Angus Maddison, *Economic Growth in the West* (1964); and M. M. Postan, *An Economic History of Western Europe 1945–1964* (1967). Denison's study is by far the most important since it is the first major attempt to analyse in any detail the contribution made by different variables to growth in a number of countries.

Those attracted by the more theoretical aspects of economic growth will find an excellent introduction in W. A. Eltis, *Economic Growth* (1966).

The studies listed above will provide the reader with a comprehensive survey of the developments in, and the problems of, the British economy since the war. Some of them contain useful bibliographies. However, there are a number of more specialised works dealing with aspects such as investment, management, the balance of payments, etc. A selection of some of the more important items is given below under the headings of books, articles, and official publications.

Books and Pamphlets

TIBOR BARNA, *Investment and Growth Policies in British Industrial Firms* (1962).

SAMUEL BRITTAN, *Inquest on Planning in Britain* (Political and Economic Planning Series No. 499, January 1967).

C. CLARK, *Growthmanship* (Hobart Paper, 2nd ed. 1962).

A. R. CONAN, *The Problem of Sterling* (1966).

J. COOPER, *A Suitable Case for Treatment: What to do about the balance of payments* (1968).

G. DENTON, M. FORSYTH, and M. MACLENNAN, *Economic Planning and Policies in Britain, France and Germany* (1968).

P. DONALDSON, *Guide to the British Economy* (1965).

J. H. DUNNING and C. J. THOMAS, *British Industry: Change and Development in the Twentieth Century* (1963).

FRED HIRSCH, *The Pound Sterling: a Polemic* (1965).

N. KALDOR, *Causes of the Slow Rate of Economic Growth in the United Kingdom* (1966).

PETER B. KENEN, *British Monetary Policy and the Balance of Payments 1951–1957* (1960).

C. P. KINDLEBERGER, *The Terms of Trade: A European Case Study* (1956).

C. P. KINDLEBERGER, *Europe's Postwar Growth: The Role of Labour Supply* (1967).

ALFRED MAIZELS, *Industrial Growth and World Trade* (1963).

E. J. MISHAN, *The Costs of Economic Growth* (1968).

F. W. PAISH, *Studies in an Inflationary Economy* (1962).

A. T. PEACOCK and J. WISEMAN, *The Growth of Public Expenditure in the United Kingdom* (2nd ed. 1967).

G. POLANYI, *Planning in Britain: The Experience of the 1960s* (Institute of Economic Affairs, Research Monograph).

POLITICAL AND ECONOMIC PLANNING, *Growth in the British Economy* (1960).

B. C. ROBERTS, *National Wages Policy in War and Peace* (1958).

W. E. G. SALTER, *Productivity and Technical Change* (1960).

J. R. SARGENT, *Out of Stagnation: A Policy for Growth* (Fabian Tract, 1963).

T. W. SCHULTZ, *The Economic Value of Education* (1964).

MICHAEL SHANKS, *The Stagnant Society* (1961).

ANDREW SHONFIELD, *Modern Capitalism* (1965).

I. SVENNILSON, *Growth and Stagnation in the European Economy* (1954).

R. TRIFFIN, *The Evolution of the International Monetary System* (1964).

S. J. WELLS, *British Export Performance: A Comparative Study* (1964).

B. R. WILLIAMS, *Technology, Investment and Growth* (1967).

T. WILSON, *Planning and Growth* (1964).

Articles

FRANK BLACKABY and MICHAEL ARTIS, 'On Incomes Policy', *District Bank Review* (Mar 1968).

FRANK BRECHLING and J. N. WOLFE, 'The End of Stop-Go', *Lloyds Bank Review* (Jan 1965).

H. A. CLEGG, 'A Policy for Incomes?', *Lloyds Bank Review* (Apr 1962).

D. J. COPPOCK, 'The Causes of Business Fluctuations', *Transactions of the Manchester Statistical Society* (1959).

B. M. DEAKIN and K. D. GEORGE, 'Productivity Trends in Service Industries', *London and Cambridge Economic Bulletin*, LIII (1965).

ELY DEVONS, 'The Case for Investment and Productivity', *Lloyds Bank Review* (Oct 1955).

T. P. HILL, 'Growth and Investment According to International Comparisons', *Economic Journal*, LXXIV (1964).

C. P. KINDLEBERGER, 'Foreign Trade and Growth: Lessons from British Experience since 1913', *Lloyds Bank Review* (July 1962).

ANGUS MADDISON, 'Economic Growth in Western Europe 1870–1957', *Banca Nazionale Del Lavoro Quarterly Review*, XII (1959).

ANGUS MADDISON, 'The Post-War Business Cycle in Western Europe and the Role of Government Policy', *Banca Nazionale Del Lavoro Quarterly Review*, XIII (1960).

ANGUS MADDISON, 'Growth and Fluctuation in the World Economy 1870–1960', *Banca Nazionale Del Lavoro Quarterly Review*, XV (1962).

ANGUS MADDISON, 'How Fast can Britain Grow?', *Lloyds Bank Review*, (Jan 1966).

P. M. OPPENHEIMER, 'Is Britain's Worsening Trade Gap Due to Bad Management of the Business Cycle?', *Bulletin of Oxford University Institute of Statistics*, XX (1958).

D. C. PAIGE, F. T. BLACKABY, S. FREUND, 'Economic Growth: The Last Hundred Years' *National Institute Economic Review* (July 1961).

M. PANIC and T. SEWARD, 'The Problem of U.K. Exports', *Bulletin of Oxford University Institute of Statistics*, XXVIII (1966).

F. PAUKERT, 'Technological Change and the level of Employment in Western Europe', *British Journal of Industrial Relations*, VI (1968).

D. W. PEARCE and J. TAYLOR, 'Spare Capacity: What Margin is Needed', *Lloyds Bank Review* (July 1968).

H. TYSZYNSKI, 'World Trade in Manufactured Commodities 1899–1950', *Manchester School*, XIX (1951).

T. WILSON, 'Instability and the Rate of Growth', *Lloyds Bank Review* (July 1966).

Official Publications

Economic Commission for Europe, 'Some Factors in Economic Growth in Europe during the 1950s', Part 2 of *Economic Survey of Europe in 1961* (1964).

National Economic Development Council, *The Growth of the United Kingdom Economy* (H.M.S.O. 1963).

National Economic Development Council, *Conditions Favourable to Faster Growth* (H.M.S.O. 1963).

National Economic Development Council, *Management Recruiting and Development* (H.M.S.O. 1965).

Organisation for Economic Co-operation and Development, *The Residual Factor in Economic Growth* (1964).

Organisation for European Economic Co-operation, *The Problem of Rising Prices* (1961).

Report of the Committee on the Working of the Monetary System, Cmnd 827 (1959).

Index